Descriptosaurus: Fantasy

Descriptosaurus: Fantasy builds on the vocabulary and descriptive phrases introduced in the original bestselling *Descriptosaurus* and, within the context of fantasy, develops the structure and use of the words and phrases to promote colourful cinematic writing. This essential guide will enable children to take their writing to the next level. It incorporates the essential skills and creative devices that are used in other genres while extending them to themes of battles, sieges, magic and mystery to unleash children's imaginations.

This new system also provides a contextualised alternative to grammar textbooks and will assist children in acquiring, understanding and applying the grammar they will need to improve their writing, both creative and technical.

Alison Wilcox has extensive teaching experience in schools in England and Scotland. Colleagues describe her methods as 'innovative and inspirational to even the most reluctant of writers'.

Descriptosaurus

Fantasy

Alison Wilcox

Routledge
Taylor & Francis Group

LONDON AND NEW YORK

First published 2016
by Routledge
2 Park Square, Milton Park, Abingdon, Oxon OX14 4RN

and by Routledge
711 Third Avenue, New York, NY 10017

Routledge is an imprint of the Taylor & Francis Group, an informa business

British Library Cataloguing in Publication Data
A catalogue record for this book is available from the British Library

Library of Congress Cataloging in Publication Data
Names: Wilcox, Alison, author.
Title: Descriptosaurus : fantasy / Alison Wilcox.
Description: New York, NY : Routledge, 2016.
Identifiers: LCCN 2015045831| ISBN 9781138858749 (hardback) | ISBN 9781138858756 (pbk.) | ISBN 9781315717784 (ebook)
Subjects: LCSH: Creative writing (Elementary education) | Literary form—Study and teaching (Elementary) | Fantasy fiction.
Classification: LCC LB1576 .W487575 2016 | DDC 372.62/3—dc23
LC record available at http://lccn.loc.gov/2015045831

ISBN: 978-1-138-85874-9 (hbk)
ISBN: 978-1-138-85875-6 (pbk)
ISBN: 978-1-315-71778-4 (ebk)

Typeset in Myriad Pro
by Keystroke, Station Road, Codsall, Wolverhampton

Contents

Acknowledgements

My name might be on the front cover, but to complete this book took the help and support of a great many people. Without the unerring belief and support of my family and friends, I might never have reached the finishing line. Thanks to Andrew, Robert and Kitty for their patience and understanding; to my loyal black labradors, Alfie and Monty; to my wonderful parents, Ann and John, and to my friends, Gail and Jinny.

The inspirational performance of my sister, Trish, and her Welsh netball team at the Netball World Cup served as a timely reminder of the benefits of teamwork.

Bruce Roberts at Routledge has been the mastermind behind the *Descriptosaurus* series, and as always, I owe him an immense gratitude for his wise words, guidance and support. Sarah Richardson's efforts have been tireless and I am extremely grateful for her input and support.

Maggie Lindsey-Jones and her team at Keystroke have been exceptional.

The work of the National Literacy Trust is absolutely essential in helping to raise standards in literacy and their involvement was vital in creating the momentum to get the project started.

To Katie and Tom. I hope you enjoy reading about your adventures!

Introduction

When I first decided to write *Descriptosaurus* it was because my experience of teaching creative writing to children had revealed that many had great imaginations and lots of ideas, but did not have the descriptive vocabulary to communicate these effectively. This was partly due to a lack of reading or a passive involvement with a text so that the techniques and vocabulary were not absorbed. I have been delighted with the response to the original work and have seen many fabulous examples of descriptive writing.

After writing *Descriptosaurus,* I returned to the classroom to conduct further research on different ways to use the resource. It became evident that one of the weaknesses in children's texts was the way they connected their writing. Often the pace of their writing was dramatically slowed by lengthy, unnecessary detail because they didn't have the vocabulary to move the story on to another scene. I also found that displaying the text on the whiteboard and modelling the process was extremely effective. This was why the second edition included a CD and a section on connectives and adverbs.

NATIONAL LITERACY TRUST – DESCRIPTIVE WRITING COMPETITION

In 2013, I collaborated with the National Literacy Trust on a descriptive writing competition. I was astounded by the response and the quality of the entries. I think that too much attention is given to the apparent decreasing standards in schools, particularly in literacy, and not enough media attention given to the outstanding young writers and teachers in our classrooms today. The work and support of the National Literacy Trust are vital in maintaining and improving these standards.

WHY WRITE *DESCRIPTOSAURUS: FANTASY?*

As part of the process, the National Literacy Trust analysed the genres children chose in their descriptive pieces. It is important that children are given the opportunity to develop their interests and passions. To ensure that children are engaged and enthused with creative writing, it is vital that they are, where possible, given a choice. The four genres that stood out as by far the most popular were: ghost stories; adventure; fantasy; and myths and legends, which is why we have decided to concentrate on these four areas.

The original research and model for *Descriptosaurus* arose as a result of teaching a unit on myths and legends. Using *Descriptosaurus* to provide the pupils with a wealth of vocabulary and descriptive tools dramatically improved the quality of their writing. It did, however, become evident that the original model did not cater for the pupils' growing enthusiasm for fantasy, and, in particular, for *sword and sorcery*. The fantasy genre incorporates the essential skills and creative devices used in other genres, such as the *action* in adventure, *suspense* in ghost stories, and the *magic and creatures* in myths and legends, but extends to *battles and sieges*, and *magic and mystery*, which pupils find so engaging. Above all, it gives them a licence to experiment, and to unleash their formidable imaginations.

S/C-I-R: SETTING/CHARACTER, INTERACTION, REACTION

Often pupils' action scenes are just a list of various actions, with no description of the setting, other characters or emotions. I have seen excellent descriptions of settings, but the character(s) does not move (interact) through the setting. They are disjointed pieces of description. I have, therefore, been experimenting with a new system, which I have called S/C-I-R, which has resulted in cinematic writing of an exceptional standard.

The resulting work has described the setting, moved the character through the setting, and described their reactions to what they see or the events in which they are involved. A model of S/C-I-R is included at the beginning of each chapter.

CONTEXTUALISED GRAMMAR LEARNING

Another benefit of this system has been to provide a contextualised alternative to the prescriptive, repetitive focus on textbook grammar in response to the introduction of the SPAG tests. Taking a number of sentences or phrases for setting, interaction and reaction, combining them into a descriptive paragraph of a scene, and then experimenting with different ways of combining the sentences, openers and length is a very engaging way of learning about grammar and its impact on the flow, sense and expression. I have also noticed that the discussion that results from this experimentation has a dramatic impact on the quality of responses to comprehension tasks.

The exercise can be extended to changing tenses, including adverbs, or even using it to write a scene for a playscript. These exercises can be done as extended sessions, as part of the planning, or as warm-up exercises. They are also excellent for modelled and collaborative learning. Different focuses can be used. For example:

★ Giving the class three sentences all starting with pronouns, and setting them the challenge of using different ways to open their sentences.

★ Asking them to use the three sentences to produce a paragraph of five or more sentences.

★ Blending the sentences, but changing them into the first person and present tense.

PLANNING AND EDITING

The age-old problem of ineffective planning and cursory editing still remains. To aid in this process, I have included a section in the Appendix on the structure and planning of a fantasy, breaking it down into manageable parts. A plot planning sheet is also included in the Appendix. Developing a habit of using a planning sheet to brainstorm ideas will, as we all know, greatly enhance the final piece of text. Hopefully, the structure of the planning sheet will also aid in the structure of the story.

To help with the development of strong characterisation, I have also included a planning sheet for a hero, a villain and a creature.

To combat cursory editing, planning sheets are provided for setting and objects. If phrases and sentences are collected for Setting/Character, Interaction and Reaction for each of the scenes, and the process of blending, altering, reducing, practised in warm-up activities, is used, hopefully the editing will become more focused and effective.

NON-FICTION

The benefits of cross-curricular teaching are well documented, and fantasy provides a great opportunity to combine creative writing with historical enquiry, imagination and invention. For example:

★ An instruction manual for a spell or making a potion.
★ A design for a new magical potion or ointment, and a sales advert outlining its magical properties. This can be extended to a PowerPoint presentation.
★ An information booklet about the healing properties of plants, flowers, herbs (for example, lavender). This could be combined with a study of medieval medicines.
★ An Interpol 'Wanted' poster for a wizard, witch, magician, creature, gnome, dwarf, etc.
★ Diary entries for a castle under siege, based on a study of an actual medieval siege.
★ A newspaper article (along the lines of UFO reports) about shimmering lights at night (a portal), and strange sightings of fantasy creatures or characters.
★ A daily blog or video on a class 'YouTube', from a scientific exploration to a new fantasy kingdom, including new races discovered, extinct or new species of creatures and characters, strange phenomena, etc. This could be combined with reading *The Lion, the Witch and the Wardrobe*.
★ A biography of a fantasy author – Terry Pratchett, for example.

There is so much material that could have been included in this book. It was therefore necessary to judge the most effective use of the space available, and, in particular, not include topics that had already been covered in *Descriptosaurus: Myths & Legends*. The intention is that the two books are complementary and, therefore, increase the range of topics and descriptive vocabulary available as a toolkit for pupils to access when tackling these genres. Medieval history and fantasy literature are two of my great passions, so writing this book has been an 'imagination explosion', and I hope all those who use *Descriptosaurus: Fantasy* enjoy using it as much as I enjoyed writing it.

Alison Wilcox

Key elements

Whilst 'fantasy' as a separate genre is a fairly recent phenomenon, its roots can be seen in ancient mythology, and elements of the supernatural and the fantastic are also to be found in the first stories in folklore. *Beowulf*, for example, the earliest surviving epic poem written in English, contains fantasy elements, such as witches, monsters and dragons.

Lewis Carroll's *Alice's Adventures in Wonderland* (1865) and C.S. Lewis's *Chronicles of Narnia* (1949–1954) did much to secure popular interest, but it was Tolkien's *Lord of the Rings* (1954) that established the 'epic fantasy' and had the biggest and most enduring influence on the popularity of the genre.

FORM OF ENTERTAINMENT

The success of fantasy stories lies in their ability to transport the reader into a new, exciting and dangerous world, where there are strange creatures and supernatural powers. They provide a sense of excitement, action and suspense, a whirlwind of vibrant images, and they open the door to our imaginations.

The tales often include:

- ★ A brave, heroic character for whom the reader can root
- ★ An exciting undertaking involving physical danger (quest)
- ★ Elements from the Middle Ages
- ★ A journey to a dangerous, fantasy world – sometimes the plot is entirely based in that world or it switches between worlds or kingdoms
- ★ A series of trials to overcome

★ Life or death stakes should the hero fail
★ A villain or creature to fight against
★ Talking animals
★ Mythical creatures, such as dragons, unicorns, centaurs
★ Magical characters, such as elves, dwarfs, faeries, goblins, gnomes and sprites
★ Magical powers
★ A clear battle between good and evil
★ A special object or person that enables the hero to accomplish impossible challenges and quests
★ Many twists and turns
★ Fast paced drama
★ Excitement and suspense
★ Rich, descriptive vocabulary
★ Action sequences – battles, fights, sieges, chase, capture
★ Last-minute escapes and victory against all the odds.

A. THE HERO/HEROINE

A fantasy story needs a hero that the reader wants to follow, and who is capable of accomplishing awe-inspiring feats. (*For ease, I have referred to the hero (he), rather than alternating between hero/heroine.*) He should essentially be:

★ brave and clever and either have supernatural powers, or a special object, talent or assistance that gives him enhanced powers or skills – for example, a magical cloak, sword, staff, cauldron, belt, mirror, etc.

It is also important that the hero develops or changes in some way as a result of his experiences.

Get to know your hero

★ Collect ideas of heroes from myths, legends, folklore and fantasy stories you have read.
★ Decide on a name.
★ How old is he?

★ Think of details that could be used in your physical description, such as, face, eyes, voice, clothes or armour that reflect their personality, or skills.

★ Add a description of any distinctive features.

★ Who are his family and close friends?

★ What are his main interests?

★ What is his special talent/strength?

★ What is he most afraid of? What is his weakness? (This could be really important to the story, as you may want to make your hero face their worst fear or overcome their weakness as one of the obstacles they have to overcome.)

★ Does the hero or any of his family or friends have any secrets?

★ What has he got to gain by achieving the task, overcoming the challenge, or to lose by failing to do so?

Descriptions are included in this book for heroes, villains, and fantasy characters, based on physical attributes, voice and clothing. As it would be impossible to incorporate the infinite possibilities for clothing or armour, many of the items described relate to the medieval period as this has proved to be the most popular source.

B. THE ENEMY

The ancient theme of good versus evil is the basis for much fantasy, so if the hero is good and brave, he needs an enemy to fight who is the opposite. The enemy (referred to here as 'he') is usually:

(a) selfish, greedy, power-crazy
(b) hideous, vicious, evil.

It is possible that the enemy and hero share the same goal. It is their *motive* that is different.

Get to know your villain/creature

★ Collect ideas of villains from myths, legends or folklore.

★ Decide on a name(s).

★ Add a description of any distinctive features.
★ Where does he live? What type of place is it? Is it very secure, scary? Is it in an isolated location? How is it protected?
★ Who are his allies? Do they have special qualities?
★ Does he have a special talent/object/weapons?
★ Does he have any secrets/weaknesses? How can he be destroyed?
★ What has he got to lose by the hero achieving the task?
★ What does he do to people who challenge him?

C. QUEST, CHALLENGE

The hero has a problem to solve. This could be:

(a) **A challenge** – surviving encounters with dangerous creatures.
(b) **A journey** – to discover the point of entry into the fantasy world or another kingdom.
(c) **A quest** – usually to do with someone or something in danger.

In fantasy, the journey may be preordained, written in the stars, but make sure there is a good reason for making the journey or being in the setting and make the consequences of failure so severe that the reader is aware that there is no going back and that the hero will have to face the many obstacles and dangers along the way until he reaches the end.

D. A DANGEROUS JOURNEY

The hero battles for survival:

★ Against the elements, either natural or magical, such as a storm on land, sea, hurricanes, floods, fire and explosions, or hideous creatures, e.g. sea monsters that block his path across the sea; a tribe of trolls guarding the entrance to the kingdom; a fire-breathing dragon that prevents passage over a mountain.

E. FANTASY SETTING

★ An imaginary or other world or universe

★ Time travel is possible, so it could be set, for example, in medieval times.

The setting in a fantasy is where:

★ the action takes place;

★ the object or person being sought will be found;

★ the quest will be accomplished.

There may be a number of settings, including the hero's ordinary setting, as he travels to his final destination, overcoming obstacles and evading the main villain.

Key points

1. Decide why the setting is important to the story

(a)   What features are there that will help the hero?

(b)   What **barriers** are there to entering or escaping from the setting?

(c)   What **obstacles** are there to retrieving the object or person that has been hidden/stored?

(d)   Who or what lives there?

2. Think of words and phrases to help you build up the description of the setting

(a)   Imagine you have a camera and move it around the location, then zoom in to pick up extra details. Make notes of interesting settings from myths, legends and folklore from around the world.

(b)   Make a note of important obstacles or items that will assist or impede the hero's victory.

3. Be descriptive

Use figurative language such as **similes** and **metaphors**. Some chapters have ideas for similes and metaphors included in the word section.

4. Use senses to bring the setting to life for your reader

As well as sight, think about what your character can:

★ hear, smell, touch, taste.

5. To increase the tension, create a storm

Storms add atmosphere and danger to the story, can be used to indicate a super-natural presence and are useful to introduce other senses in addition to sight to add tension, such as sounds, touch and smells. For example:

> A column of shimmering air appeared around the stones. Then, out of nowhere, a blast of cold air surged towards her, bringing with it a swirling spiral of dead leaves and dust. Quickly, it became a column of black mist like a tornado, whirling at tremendous speed to engulf the sky above the altar stone.

Add detail and description to paint a picture in the reader's mind. Giving a setting an atmosphere is more than stating that, *It was dark*. For example, adding more descriptive detail could give you:

> The whole world suddenly seemed unnaturally dark, as if it had been drained of all light before the onset of a terrible storm. She looked round to see a vortex of darkness behind her, and beyond that – the unknown.

F. SUSPENSE

Chapter 1: Hooks to build interest and tension includes a number of ideas and sentences on how to create suspense and give a hint to the reader of the danger to come, or that the danger is getting closer.

(a) Entering the danger zone – what's waiting the other side of the portal, lurking in the underground kingdom?
(b) Feeling of being followed/watched.
(c) Fear of discovery in a hiding place as footsteps/voices get closer; snapping branches nearby.

(d) Use of punctuation to add suspense:

- ★ Include a sentence(s) that holds back essential information from the reader until its ending.
- ★ Use colons, commas and repeated full stops to delay the revelation.

Examples:

Entering the tunnel, she stopped dead in her tracks.

In the shadows, she heard whispering, chanting in the ancient tongue. Then, silence. Nothing. She dropped to her knees. Silhouetted in the torchlight was . . .

(e) Build a sense of tension by:

- ★ Making frequent references to time (the 'ticking clock' effect):
  - ☆ Could he make it in time?
  - ☆ He searched desperately for a way out. Frantic now . . . time was running out.
  - ☆ The next few seconds unfolded in horrifying slow motion.
  - ☆ For fatal seconds, they stared, unable to think or move. And as they faltered, the air rippled and he vanished.
- ★ Varying the length of the words, sentences and paragraphs to increase the pace and tension:
  - ☆ Use short words, e.g. *at once*, rather than, *immediately*.
  - ☆ Place several short sentences consecutively. *She ducked. He lunged.*
  - ☆ Include one- or two-word sentences. For example: *Oh no!* or *Coming closer. Too close.*
  - ☆ When the action is fastest use partial sentences, e.g. *He had to get to the gate. Had to secure it. He stumbled, scrambled. Five paces more. Hooves thudded over the drawbridge. Three paces more. He staggered. Lunged.*
  - ☆ Use short paragraphs – some may be a single line.
  - ☆ Include lots of **verbs** to convey action and create a fast pace. Use several verbs in a sentence.

G. OBSTACLES

Examples of obstacles the hero might have to face are:

- ★ Ground (muddy, icy, uneven)
- ★ Impenetrable forests, swamps, bogs
- ★ Sheer mountains, flooded caves, labyrinth of tunnels
- ★ Menacing, hideous creatures
- ★ Powerful magicians
- ★ Injuries sustained on the journey or inflicted by the villain, creature or magic.

H. EMOTION

Show how the hero reacts (emotion) to events, setting, villain/creature, challenges, etc. The basic rule is the same as any other genre – **'SHOW NOT TELL'**.

(A) Reaction

Describing how a character reacts to events in the setting brings the scene to life for the reader and enables them to empathise with the character's situation and to root for the hero. For example:

> He was terrified as he stepped into the portal.

This **tells** the reader that the character is **terrified**, but does not **show** how the character **reacts** to the situation.

Instead describe:

- ★ How he is feeling inside using, for example, heart or pulse
- ★ Facial expressions
- ★ Eyes
- ★ Voice.

For example, the same situation could be expanded to describe the character's reaction to entering the portal.

Every sense, every instinct screamed at him to stop. His forehead began to bead with sweat as he recalled the fear that had overwhelmed him the last time he had travelled through the portal. A thousand terrors flashed through his mind at once as the force of the portal pressed around his fingers, his arms, his face and cheeks. It felt as if a clenched fist had been thrust into his ribs.

> **Note:** The hero will experience many emotions during his adventure, but for the purposes of this book, the reactions for each section have been limited to mainly fear, anger and determination, as these are the common emotions that you would expect the hero to feel whilst he is overcoming his challenges and completing his quest.

(B) Interaction

To add a cinematic quality to your writing, it is essential that the action scenes include a description of the character's movements as he reacts to the events, to the villain/creature, and moves through the setting. The character may:

- ★ be frozen to the spot
- ★ move nervously, cautiously
- ★ duck behind a tree
- ★ move quickly – jump, spin, leap, whirl, dash, sprint
- ★ frantically look for a way of escape
- ★ move forward to defend himself.

Apart from enabling the reader to visualise the character's movements, their interaction is a signpost to the reader of the degree of danger and the closeness of the threat. For example:

As she walked, she felt a presence behind her. But no one knew the location of the entrance to the tunnel! She paused. Unable to help herself, she turned around.

With a new sense of urgency, she ran blindly, away from the sound. Not even daring to glance quickly over her shoulder, she plunged deeper into the tunnel, letting its shadows swallow her.

Part 1
The setting

1

Hooks to build interest and tension

Note: Apart from aiding the flow of your writing, this chapter can also be used to stimulate quick, brainstorming activities to get your creative juices flowing by asking the questions – Why? How? When? Where? Who? What happened? It is amazing how many stories can be created as a result of these quick activities.

OPENINGS

* Something terrible was about to happen – she could sense it. She wanted to get away, to run from whatever waited for her, but she knew it was her destiny to face it.
* He sensed that a decision had been made. He knew he didn't belong here any more. They treated him differently now.
* As she entered the forest, she looked up at the dark shadows between the trees and got the weirdest feeling.
* As soon as he had entered the tunnel, an eerie sensation had enveloped him and would not go away.
* He would remember this moment later. When everything was normal and he had been unaware of the approaching danger.
* Although he had no idea what it meant, he could sense that it was a warning.
* He could sense the danger prickling down his spine. Every night he dreamed of being pursued, chased by a menacing presence closing in around him, lurking in the background, but which he could never see. He didn't know how to put his unease into words as he didn't know what it was he feared.

* She woke shivering with a sense of foreboding, a premonition of doom hanging over her, as if her dreams foreshadowed terrible events to come.
* Sometimes, she wished she could just forget what she knew.
* It was days later that he would remember that moment.
* They were nervous days while she waited. She knew that there was no going back. Not now.
* The time had come, and he was terrified of what lay ahead.
* He lay awake night after night, heart filled with dread; he knew he had to make the most difficult decision of his life.
* *Nowhere was safe any more.*
* He was shaken to the core by what he had just witnessed.
* How different things would have been if she had never . . .
* She shouldn't have hacked into his emails. That was when everything started to go wrong.

WARNING OF DANGER TO COME

* He couldn't shake off a sense of unease, a vague feeling that something was wrong, that he shouldn't have come.
* It was becoming a bubbling cauldron that was about to boil over.
* She was safe for now.
* He had seen and heard enough to know that he was in grave danger.
* On the fourth day of his journey, events took a different turn.
* He had a feeling he was delivering himself into a trap, but nothing could have prepared him for what he met when he emerged from the portal.
* Out of nowhere, the hairs on his neck rose.
* There was something she couldn't quite put her finger on, something different, something not quite right.
* A dreadful sense of misgiving began to creep over him, like the chill of a cold breeze.
* She felt that she was caught in a maze without end, and round every corner lurked hideous monsters waiting to pounce.
* He had sensed something dark moving in the shadows, waiting for them and now he knew what. There was no way of warning the others what lay in wait; that they were escaping one nightmare to land in the middle of another.
* It was only just the beginning of a new chapter of dangers.
* All day she had been haunted by the feeling that something was coming; something of which she should be very afraid. She had not had enough time to prepare; she was not powerful enough to face it yet.
* She tried to make sense of what she had heard. And as the truth dawned on her, she began to shake.
* Ever since they had entered the kingdom, she'd been fighting an underlying sense of panic.

* *All was still as death and dark as the grave.*
* It was very quiet. Too quiet!
* The night had been silent and now even the dawn chorus was still.
* When the breeze stopped, everything went very still and the forest became unnaturally quiet.
* Then there was silence. Even the wind seemed to have died down.
* It suddenly seemed frighteningly quiet. The air was charged with tension.
* Suddenly, the birds fell silent. Then, one gave a high-pitched warning call.
* *An owl hooted and swept by on silent, white wings.*
* A scream from above caused his pulse to race. It was nothing more than a crow in the branches of a tree behind him.
* The wind howled. Great swirling gusts, relentless like an army of screaming banshees.
* *Shadows spread and lengthened. Their fear grew as night fell. Fear of the unknown. Fear of what lurked in the dark.*
* Twilight was closing in and she felt very uneasy.
* The last glowing embers of the fire slid into darkness.
* The shadows were now merging into one another, and the ground was being cloaked in the first shade of grey, heralding the night to come.
* It was dark, with only flitting glimpses of the moon to keep them company.
* *The mist came in with the tide, smothering everything like a giant fleece.*
* The night wind swept over them, whispering through the trees, fashioning the mists into ghostly shapes that flung flickering shadows on the inky surface in front of them.

THE TICKING CLOCK

* His plan would buy him a few hours and nothing more.
* When he opened his eyes, he guessed that a few hours must have passed. It was enough. It was time to make his move.
* He counted the time by the pace of the shadows creeping slowly across the ground.
* *The hours dragged past.*
* The minutes seemed to crawl.
* Tension mounted with every hour that passed.
* The seconds ticked away, agonisingly slowly. It seemed to be taking forever.
* An hour passed, and then another and after a while . . .
* In the long, agonising moments that followed . . .
* It was late evening when it finally happened.
* *The next few minutes were going to be vital.*
* Time was of the essence.
* He had less than a second to make a decision.
* It was too late to turn back now.

* There was no time to worry. No time to think. He had to act now. Time had run out.
* She knew she didn't have long to act. It had to be soon.
* He had only a second in which to act.
* In the single instant that it took her to glance down . . .
* The next seconds unfolded in horrifying slow motion.
* It happened so fast, she would have been dead if the dwarf had not been there.
* For fatal seconds, they stared, unable to think or move. And as they faltered, the air rippled and he vanished.
* Everything seemed to happen slowly. Too slowly.
* *The clock was ticking down.*
* She couldn't afford to wait any longer.
* He could feel the seconds ticking away.
* He knew they were running out of time. They might be too late.
* If he had arrived too late, everything he had been through had been for nothing.
* *They weren't going to make it in time.*
* But he was too late, far too late.

A DECISION/PLAN

* He knew his next move would be crucial. He ran through his options.
* The thirst to learn as much as possible grew with each passing day.
* It was an impossible task, but he refused to admit defeat.
* He was about to give up hope when . . .
* Suddenly, out of nowhere he had an idea. He knew what he needed to do next and he knew he was taking a huge risk. But he had no other choice.
* It was then that she knew what she had to do. There was nothing left to lose. She would see it through – whatever it took.
* This was the moment he had been waiting for. He knew that the greatest trial of his life was approaching, but he had come too far to turn back now.
* Somewhere, buried deep in her memory, she had a feeling she should know what she had to do next; that she had already been given some clue.
* Then came an incredible piece of luck.
* But a moment later, salvation, unexpected and unimagined, appeared.
* *It was all beginning to make sense at last.*
* With a jolt like an electric shock, he finally understood.
* In a split second, he realised what was happening.
* Just when he was thinking of giving up . . .

TOO CLOSE FOR COMFORT

* That had been close, too close. If he had been caught it would have all been over for him.
* She realised her mistake too late.
* The clinking of chain mail was all the warning she had.
* At that moment, she heard the whistle of a missile as it was launched at the wall beside her.
* *As he crouched in the ditch, he could hear the voices of the sentries close by in the shadows ahead of him.*
* After following the tunnel for a while, they heard hushed voices close by.
* He heard a voice murmuring in the room, and he was aware that there was someone or something – unseen . . . but standing very close to him.
* Then she heard something nearby, the slightest catch of breath.
* *A noise close behind him made him turn.*
* It was a very soft thud, barely audible even in the absolute silence.
* He became aware of faint, muffled sounds of movement.
* He had already turned away and didn't notice the slight rise and fall of her chest, the slight twitching of her fingers.

DON'T DO IT!

* It was as if she was being pulled into something dark and dangerous by a hand she couldn't see, couldn't stop even if she wanted to.
* Despite her fear, she was seized with an urgent need to return to Nidavellir, to the dwarf kingdom.
* Something urged him on. Every nerve in his body screamed at him to get out. But before he knew what he was doing, his legs seemed to move of their own accord.
* She didn't want to look but she couldn't seem to stop herself.
* It was like an invisible thread was pulling him towards the wizard's mountain stronghold.

2

Portals

Using portals and teleporting are easy ways to transport characters quickly to different locations without slowing down the pace of the story.

THE S/C-I-R STRUCTURE

A cascade of rainbow light lit up the stones. In the centre was a seam of blackness out of which appeared a golden, shimmering door. It stood between them and the other side like the edge of a waterfall.

The outline of the door rippled and pulsated as it slowly opened to reveal a tunnel. Kitty could not help looking at the continually changing pattern of flickering lights ahead of her and **wondering whether she would make it through in one piece; and, if she did make it through, what she would discover when she reached the other side. She could feel her courage starting to fade as thousands of terrors flashed through her mind. Quickly, she took a gulp of air, gritted her teeth** and walked through the shimmering air. In a blinding flash, she was sucked into the depths of the tunnel and vanished.

It felt like the world was spinning, as if she was being taken apart as she went through the portal and then transported bit by bit on a giant merry-go-round that was spinning faster and faster with every second. Her arms flailed as she tried to keep her balance. Her legs thrashed in the air. Her ears were filled with the hissing of the wind. **She squeezed her eyes shut, afraid to look. When the sensation suddenly stopped, Kitty was dizzy and gasping.**

SECTION 1 – SETTING

WORDS	

Nouns

Boulders, stones, rocks, altar stone

Ring, circle, arc

Tomb, mounds, barrows, warriors

Wood, tree, birch, oak, rowan

Watch, bracelet, necklace, ring

Cloak, belt, buckle

Book, manuscript, map, seal, cover, pages

Staff, dagger, sword, hilt, blade

Mirror, frame, surface, reflection, water, lake, pond, waterfall

Pictures, images, scenes

Shapes, outline, silhouette, shadows

Castle, fortress, towers, turrets, spires, minarets, domes

Signs, symbols, patterns, runes, glyphs, sigils

Portal, tunnel, hole, void, abyss, vortex

Entrance, archway, door, doorway, gate, handle, dial

Wall, bricks

Light, colours, glow, moonlight, mist, vapour, kaleidoscope

Rays, shaft, fragments, pinprick

Air, wind, breeze, gust, blast, whirlwind, tornado

Leaves, dust

**Similes/
Metaphors**

Seal like a hammer and anvil; like a shrivelled finger; spires as sharp as needles; like human statues; dark circles like door-knobs; column of black mist like a tornado; rippling door like the edge of a waterfall; like a shimmering haze on a summer's day; like a giant bubble; hung like a shimmering eye; clouded like an ice mirror; rippled like a huge, transparent sheet of cloth; like sunshine glancing off water; as if the air was dancing in the heat of a fire; pulsed like a heartbeat; pumped with energy like a heartbeat; flickered like flames; as if a piece of silk had been stretched over the entrance; shiny silver ribbon like a road; rushed up behind them like a wind tunnel; melted like mist

Adjectives	**Particular**, different
	Detailed, elaborate
	Old, ancient, archaic, long-forgotten, sacred
	Square, circular, ring-shaped, tooth-shaped, curved, arched
	Knotted, gnarled, crooked
	Iron, metal, bronze-coloured, wooden, oak, stone, chalk, silk, glass, crystal
	Large, huge, massive, enormous
	Great, heavy, strong, tremendous
	Tiny, small, slender, faint
	Cold, icy
	Dark, black, inky, shadowy
	White, silver, gold, yellow, pink, red, purple, green, blue, sapphire, rainbow
	Glowing, blinding, gleaming, glaring, dazzling, intense, fiery, fierce, powerful
	Pale, soft, bright
	Transparent, translucent, luminescent
	Strange, curious, mystical, mysterious, spectral
	Rippling, shimmering, swirling
Verbs	**Approached**, reached, appeared, emerged, revealed, faced with
	Formed, created
	Touched, opened, flicked, gripped
	Marked, showed, indicated
	Stamped with, embedded, etched, chiselled, scored, carved, shaped, sculpted, lined, covered, repeated
	Scattered, peppered, pocked
	Hung, cast, reflected
	Clouded, misted
	Listened, heard, made out
	Watched, looked, saw, spotted, glimpsed
	Rippled, shimmered, shivered, quivered, flickered, danced, swirled, twirled

Stood, rose, drifted, darted, swooped, shot, surged

Pulsed, pumped, pulsated

Changed, switched, shifted

Shone, lit up, sparkled, glinted, glowed, burnt, blazed, dazzled

Flooded, filled, engulfed

Ended, finished, stopped, terminated

Picked up, brought, blew, whirled, rushed

Faded, melted, disappeared, vanished, dissolved, swallowed up, carried away

Reformed, reconstructed

PHRASES – NOUNS AND ADJECTIVES

- ★ Never in exactly the same place
- ★ To the other kingdoms
- ★ *On every panel of the ...*
- ★ Outer circle
- ★ *Behind him*
- ★ From somewhere in front of them
- ★ Above the ...
- ★ Around the ...
- ★ In the centre of the ...
- ★ Beside the door
- ★ Against the doors
- ★ From within the ever-growing tornado
- ★ *At first*
- ★ Seconds later
- ★ Very gradually
- ★ All at once
- ★ With each second
- ★ *Two, massive, black boulders*
- ★ A ring of standing stones
- ★ Curious collection of standing stones
- ★ Black, memory stone
- ★ Huge, altar stone
- ★ Massive, ancient, stone tomb
- ★ *Seven-faced, cobra's head*
- ★ Each face of the cobra's head
- ★ *Wood of beech trees*
- ★ Gnarled, ancient oak

- ✳ A very old silver birch
- ✳ A great, knotted, white tree
- ✳ Wooded sentries of the . . .
- ✳ Portion of the bark on the tree
- ✳ *Sacred, chalk horse*
- ✳ Mounds and barrows of long-forgotten warriors
- ✳ *A pair of iron gates*
- ✳ A shattered metal gate
- ✳ Great carved oak doors
- ✳ An ancient, stone doorway
- ✳ Two, arched, bronze-coloured doors
- ✳ A strange, inky doorway
- ✳ Set of double glass doors
- ✳ Dial instead of a handle
- ✳ *Large fob watch*
- ✳ Ring on his finger
- ✳ Metal belt
- ✳ Enormous buckle
- ✳ White silk of the cloak
- ✳ Wooden box
- ✳ Crooked, bronze staff
- ✳ A small dagger
- ✳ Glass blade
- ✳ Double-edged, crystal sword
- ✳ A huge, bronze-bound book
- ✳ *Detailed carvings on all sides*
- ✳ Mystical symbols
- ✳ Mysterious sigils
- ✳ Strange carvings
- ✳ Runic symbols
- ✳ Row after row of glyphs
- ✳ Strange, wooden circle
- ✳ Large, rose carving
- ✳ Hundreds of carvings
- ✳ A heavy, black seal like a hammer and anvil
- ✳ A fiery shape
- ✳ Pentagrams and circles
- ✳ Swirling symbols and zigzag patterns
- ✳ Sets of keys
- ✳ Words from an ancient language
- ✳ *Black mirror*
- ✳ Small mirror in a simple, wooden frame
- ✳ Surface of the lake
- ✳ *A shadowy outline*

- ✱ Cluster of shapes
- ✱ A faint outline of a strange land
- ✱ *Strange glassy dome*
- ✱ Glass fortress
- ✱ Huge castle
- ✱ Gilded minarets
- ✱ Towers and turrets
- ✱ Long, crooked spires as sharp as needles
- ✱ Curved domes of glass and marble
- ✱ Shimmering white and silver spires
- ✱ Underground kingdom of . . .
- ✱ *Square, dark hole*
- ✱ Ring-shaped portal
- ✱ Great, black portal
- ✱ Two, dark circles like doorknobs
- ✱ *About the size of a man*
- ✱ Man-sized gap
- ✱ *Green mist*
- ✱ White vapour
- ✱ A huge column of black mist like a tornado
- ✱ *Glint of light*
- ✱ Silvery shimmer
- ✱ A fine gold mist
- ✱ Soft, blue light
- ✱ Pale sapphire light
- ✱ Bluish glow
- ✱ A shaft of blue light
- ✱ Pinpricks of purple light
- ✱ A slender ray of light
- ✱ Small round globes of rainbow light
- ✱ Fragments of silver, green and purple light
- ✱ *A blinding flash of light*
- ✱ White and glaring
- ✱ Ring of brilliant, white light
- ✱ An intense beam of white light
- ✱ Strange blue and purple lights
- ✱ *A cascade of rainbow light*
- ✱ Rainbow of colours
- ✱ *Sudden movement of air*
- ✱ A faint shimmer
- ✱ A column of shimmering air
- ✱ Golden, shimmering wall
- ✱ A shimmering waterfall
- ✱ Rippling door like the edge of a waterfall

- ✴ Like a shimmering haze on a summer's day
- ✴ *A blast of cold air*
- ✴ Fierce gust of air
- ✴ Cold and powerful wind from the portal
- ✴ Swirling spiral of dead leaves and dust
- ✴ *Curtain of shadow*
- ✴ Dark, then nothing
- ✴ Beyond the shadows – the unknown

PHRASES – VERBS

- ✴ As they reached the clearing
- ✴ Was just visible in the distance
- ✴ *Approached what looked like . . .*
- ✴ Looked like human statues
- ✴ Looked like shrivelled fingers
- ✴ Appeared to be a giant bubble
- ✴ *As he gripped the hilt . . .*
- ✴ When he touched the cover . . .
- ✴ As he opened the lid . . .
- ✴ *Flicked open with a dry crackle*
- ✴ Stopped at a map of the . . .
- ✴ Indicated a particular destination
- ✴ Set the dial to different locations
- ✴ *Stamped with . . .*
- ✴ Set into the wood
- ✴ Embedded with tiny gems
- ✴ Lined with symbols of buildings
- ✴ Etched in the centre
- ✴ Chiselled down the sides
- ✴ Scored into the surface
- ✴ Etched on each piece of metal
- ✴ Sculpted on the inner edges
- ✴ Carved with elaborate glyphs
- ✴ Sculpted into the shape of . . .
- ✴ Carved with the pattern of a hand
- ✴ Carved in the shape of open palms
- ✴ Set in runic patterns
- ✴ Covered with pentagrams
- ✴ *Formed the pattern of a . . .*
- ✴ Repeated over and over again
- ✴ *Burned into the grass*
- ✴ Burned in the middle of the iron door

- ✷ Peppered with scars of long-fallen branches
- ✷ *Set in an oak frame*
- ✷ Made from hammered metal
- ✷ *Hung like a shimmering eye*
- ✷ Clouded like an ice mirror
- ✷ Cast a warped reflection
- ✷ Where her reflection had been . . .
- ✷ When it misted up, suddenly he saw . . .
- ✷ Drawn into the surface of the mirror
- ✷ *Could see faint images*
- ✷ Saw shadowy outlines
- ✷ Started to take shape
- ✷ Could hear sounds
- ✷ Scene came to life
- ✷ *Watched for the entrance*
- ✷ Hard to believe that it had been enchanted
- ✷ Didn't know exactly what to look for
- ✷ Would be easy to miss . . .
- ✷ *Found themselves faced with . . .*
- ✷ Revealed a hollow cave
- ✷ Appeared on the other side of the door
- ✷ *Began to ripple . . .*
- ✷ Began to shimmer with . . .
- ✷ Rippled in the breeze
- ✷ Shivered and rippled
- ✷ Flickered in soft, blue waves
- ✷ Danced and swirled around him
- ✷ Shimmered and swirled in a rainbow of colours
- ✷ As if a piece of silk had been stretched across the entrance
- ✷ Rippled like a strange transparent sheet of cloth
- ✷ As if the air was dancing in the heat of a fire
- ✷ Shimmered and rippled across the surface
- ✷ Shimmered as he wrapped it around his shoulders
- ✷ Rippled in a kaleidoscope of colour
- ✷ Like sunshine glancing off water
- ✷ Swirled in a kaleidoscope of colour and patterns
- ✷ *Pulsed like a heartbeat*
- ✷ Pulsed and quivered
- ✷ Edges shimmered and pulsated
- ✷ Pumped with energy like a heartbeat
- ✷ *Came out of nowhere*
- ✷ Glimmered at the edge of her vision
- ✷ Glimmered among the trees
- ✷ Became visible in the distance

* Emerged gradually out of the seam of blackness
* *Burnt with a blue fire*
* Sparkled with a silver haze
* Glinted in the sun
* As the heavy, iron ring glowed . . .
* Shone on the curved metal plates
* Filled with a dazzling brightness
* Shimmered with spectral light
* Flickered like flames along the stones
* Lit up the stone
* Filled with a strong, white light
* Filled the air with its ominous, cold light
* Glowed luminescent green, red, blue, purple
* Shifted constantly between colours
* *Rose up out of the depths*
* Shimmered into view
* Appeared in the high, tooth-shaped rock
* Stood between the two trees
* Swirled around the base
* Darted up into the air
* Swooped through the air
* Shot towards the wall
* Blazed towards them
* Filled the room
* *As the portal opened . . .*
* Appeared in front of them like a hole
* Hung in the air above the . . .
* Formed a tunnel
* *Stood between them and . . .*
* Drew itself into a shining, silver ribbon like a road
* As if darkness was engulfing the sky
* Ended in a vortex of darkness
* *Heard a gust of wind*
* Drifted through the air over the water
* As the breeze swooped through the air
* Surged towards her
* Brought with it . . .
* Picked up the dust
* Swirled the leaves round and round
* Formed a tight whirlwind
* Blew the dust across the stone floor
* Whirled at tremendous speed towards them
* Rushed up behind them like a wind tunnel
* *Just before he disappeared through the mist*

* As they vanished . . .
* As the portal carried him away . . .
* Melted into the portal
* Vanished all of a sudden
* Swallowed up by the doorway
* Saw the tree through his body
* Rippled and disappeared
* Faded and melted like mist
* Dissolved and reformed just as quickly

SENTENCES

The orb filled with white vapour.

When he put the ring on his finger, the emerald glowed and filled with a green mist.

In front of him was a huge, bronze-bound book with mystical symbols and mysterious sigils on the cover.

When he touched the cover, the pages flicked open with a dry crackle. Eventually it stopped at a map of the kingdom of the giants.

The manuscript was stamped with a heavy, black seal like a hammer and anvil.

The outer circle of the watch was lined with symbols of buildings – towers, spires, minarets and domes.

The lid of the wooden box was carved with elaborate glyphs.

The crooked, white staff was about the size of a man, and towered above him.

The double-edged, crystal sword of the Pendragon burnt with a blue fire as he gripped the hilt.

In the case was a small dagger. Its glass blade sparkled with a silver haze as he opened the lid.

The metal belt glinted in the sun as it shone on the curved metal plates. The runic symbols etched on each plate were lit up. In the centre of the enormous buckle glowed an image of the glass fortress.

The white silk of the cloak shimmered as he wrapped it around his shoulders.

A ring of standing stones, each carved with the pattern of a hand, had been sunk deep into the hillside.

In the centre of the clearing was a curious collection of standing stones that looked like human statues.

The black memory stone had been carved into the shape of a seven-faced, cobra's head. Each face contained a glyph that indicated a particular destination.

There were two, massive, black boulders with hundreds of carvings depicting axe-heads, daggers, and rows of glyphs etched down the sides.

The stones that formed the entrance to the arc of stones had been carved in the shape of open palms.

Sigils had been etched on the inner edges of what looked like shrivelled, stone fingers pointing to the east.

The huge altar stone had detailed carvings on all sides.

The massive, ancient, stone tomb had a large, rose carving etched in the centre.

Pentagrams and circles had been burned into the grass in front of the tree to form the pattern of a doorway.

Around the chalk hill was a wood of beech trees, ancient, wooded sentries of the sacred horse that had been etched into the surface of the hill.

As they reached the clearing, they found themselves faced with what looked like a giant bubble.

Between the mounds and barrows of long-forgotten warriors was a gnarled, ancient oak, its bark peppered with scars of long-fallen branches and strange carvings. A portion of the tree rippled and disappeared, revealing a hollow cave large enough for a man to enter.

She watched for the entrance. It was never in exactly the same place, and it would be easy to miss if you didn't know exactly what to look for.

In front of him was a shattered metal gate, in the centre of which was a strange, wooden circle embedded with tiny gems that had been set in runic patterns.

Swirling symbols and zigzag patterns had been repeated over and over again on every panel of the great carved oak doors that led to the other kingdoms.

Instead of a handle, there was a dial that could be set so that different locations appeared on the other side of the door.

As the heavy, iron ring glowed, the two, arched, bronze-coloured doors suddenly faded and then melted like mist.

The gates were covered with pentagrams made from hammered metal and on each piece of metal, words from an ancient language had been etched.

A fiery shape burned in the middle of the iron door.

She held a small mirror in a simple, wooden frame. Until its surface started to shimmer and ripple, it was hard to believe that it had been enchanted into a portal door.

The black mirror, set in an oak frame, had sets of keys carved around the sides. It hung like a shimmering eye beside the door, casting a warped reflection into the hall.

The glass misted up and suddenly he could see faint images swirling in a kaleidoscope of colour and patterns.

His eyes were drawn into the surface of the mirror, and just before he disappeared through the mist, he saw shadowy outlines and a huge castle thrusting like a mailed fist out of a forest.

The pond was clouded like an ice mirror, rippling as the breeze swooped through the air around it.

The surface of the lake rippled as the breeze drifted through the air over it. Very gradually, an image started to take shape from a shadowy outline, until he could hear sounds and the scene came to life.

At first, she saw only her reflection, then the surface of the lake rippled and, where her reflection had been, she saw the image of the underground kingdom of the dwarfs.

Blue fire darted up into the air.

A fine gold mist quickly filled the room.

The air was suddenly filled with a dazzling brightness.

The air around him shimmered with spectral light.

Strange blue and purple lights flickered like flames along the stones.

An intense beam of white light, like a spotlight, shot towards the wall and lit up the stone.

The archway was filled with a strong, white light that blazed towards them from whatever lay beyond.

The bluish glow pulsed like a heartbeat as it rose up out of the depths.

Glimmering among the trees, she glimpsed a strange blue glow.

Suddenly, a crack appeared in the high, tooth-shaped rock and a mist swirled around its base.

A strange, inky doorway stood between the two trees.

As the stone began to ripple, a set of double glass doors shimmered into view.

He approached what looked like an ancient, stone doorway, which began to ripple as if a piece of silk had been stretched across the entrance.

Pinpricks of purple light flickered in soft blue waves against the doors.

A glint of light pierced the dark. Seconds later, everything about them shivered and rippled. It was as if the air was dancing in the heat of a fire.

The ring of brilliant, white light danced and swirled until it had filled the air with its ominous, cold light.

A cascade of rainbow light had lit up the stones. In the centre was a seam of blackness, out of which two dark circles like doorknobs gradually emerged.

A mist came out of nowhere filling the room. From somewhere in front of them, a husky voice whispered in an ancient language.

There was a sudden movement of air, like a shimmering haze on a summer's day; then, a blinding flash.

Something silvery glimmered at the edge of her vision. And then a slender ray of light and a cluster of shapes became visible in the distance.

The gates glowed luminescent green, red, blue, purple, thrumming with energy like a heartbeat, shifting between colours with each second.

Small round globes of rainbow light danced through the air above their heads.

Fragments of silver, green and purple light began to sparkle from within the ever-growing tornado.

The air shimmered and a mist swirled around them.

A column of shimmering air twirled around him and shimmered in a rainbow of colours.

The door rippled like a strange transparent sheet of cloth as the breeze swooped through the air around it.

It was as if a rippling door stood between them and the other side like the edge of a waterfall.

It was as if a golden, shimmering wall stood between them and the entrance to Nidavellir.

As she grasped a handle set within the door and prepared to pull, a column of shimmering air appeared around her.

A blast of cold air surged towards her, bringing with it a swirling spiral of dead leaves and dust.

The wind picked up the dust and swirled it round and round to form a tight whirlwind.

The wind from the portal was cold and powerful.

The fierce gust of air blew the dust across the stone floor around their feet.

He heard a gust of wind behind him and when he turned round, it was as if darkness was engulfing the sky above the house.

As the portal opened, the air drew itself into a shining, silver ribbon like a road that quivered under his feet.

A huge column of black mist like a tornado whirled at tremendous speed towards them.

A vortex hung in the air above the temple – a great, black portal that pulsed and quivered and was rushing up behind them like a wind tunnel. A faint outline of a strange land was just visible in the distance.

It appeared in front of them like a hole, its edges shimmering and pulsating as it formed a tunnel in front of them.

The tunnel ended in a vortex of darkness; a curtain of shadow and beyond that – the unknown.

The world around him twirled and shimmered in a rainbow of colours as the portal carried him away.

A moment of sparkling, cascading rainbow of lights, then dark, then nothing.

They melted into the portal – swallowed up by the doorway. As they vanished, the arch rippled in a kaleidoscope of colour and was gone.

With a blinding flash, the hole suddenly vanished.

It was now possible to see the tree through his body. Then, all at once, he was gone.

The world dissolved and reformed just as quickly, but now they had entered the kingdom of the black knight.

SECTION 2 – INTERACTION

WORDS

Nouns	**Images**, picture, scene
	Wall, stones, bricks
	Orb, staff, book, manuscript
	Water, lake, mirror
	Air, haze, mist, shadows
	Speed, force, pressure, direction
	Portal, hole, tunnel, void, abyss, vortex
	Air, wind, breeze, gust, whirlwind
	Shape, pentagram
	Ground, floor
	House, hall

Body, arms, hands, legs, feet, stomach

Head, face, cheeks, expression

Heart, blood, veins, pulse, chest, throat, breath

Sounds, noises, whistle, hiss, crash, thud

Similes/ Metaphors

In a blinding flash; as if he had been swallowed up; like someone disappearing into the side of a wave of water; as if he had been fired from a catapult; as if shot through the barrel of a rifle; pulled his cheeks back like rubber

Adjectives

Solid, stone, brick

Silver, misty, shadowy

Shimmering, flickering, rippling, distorted

Short, straight, direct

Slow, steady

Great, tremendous, fast, blinding, whirling

Odd, strange, mysterious

Facial

Dizzy, unsteady, slack-limbed

Weak, fuzzy, blurry, indistinct

Frozen, motionless

Familiar, well-known

Verbs

Creaked, crashed, thudded, cracked, split

Rippled, shimmered, danced, glimmered

Soared, surged, filled

Revealed, disclosed, unveiled

Placed, tapped, inserted, ran, held up, lowered, reached out, waved, flung, flailed, thrashed, wrapped

Looked, saw, closed, squeezed, flashed, opened

Realised, noticed, registered

Stood, moved, stepped, edged, walked, passed through, slid, paused, halted, stopped

Swallowed up, sucked into, vanished, disappeared

Shot, fired, swept, flew, spun, whirled, swirled, tumbled

Steadied, balanced

Stumbled, scrambled, pitched, buckled, fell, slumped, sprawled, collapsed

Gritted, gulped, gasped

Buzzed, rushed, travelled, surged

PHRASES – NOUNS AND ADJECTIVES

* *In an instant*
* In a blinding flash . . .
* *Around him*
* Whilst all around her . . .
* A short distance
* Between the doorway
* Towards the tunnel
* Down the whirling tunnel
* Into the mirror
* *Through the rippling air*
* Shimmering air
* A silver haze
* A curtain of flickering colours
* Flickering, distorted images and sounds
* A wave of shimmering water
* Total darkness
* *Grip of the portal*
* Weak legs
* Spinning head
* Odd facial expressions
* *His throat and lungs*
* His stomach, his head
* His hall, his stairs, his house, anything familiar

PHRASES – VERBS

* As the ground cracked . . .
* As the air shimmered . . .
* Creaked inwards
* Rippled around him
* Rippled against the wood
* Started to appear in front of him
* Revealed a misty tunnel

- *Filled with the hissing of the wind*
- As a whirlwind soared through the gap . . .
- Split around the shape of the pentagram
- As the ground disappeared beneath his feet . . .
- *Placed his hands on the . . .*
- Lowered his staff
- Tapped the solid brick wall
- Inserted his finger between the two stones
- Ran her hands over the manuscript
- Held up her hands
- Reached out his hand
- *Wrapped her arms around her head*
- Flailed with her arms
- Reached frantically for something to steady himself
- *When she looked down . . .*
- Closed her eyes
- Squeezed his eyes shut
- Could no longer see her own feet
- Could see no trace of . . .
- Could not even see . . .
- As the images flashed by . . .
- Realised that her hands were fuzzy and indistinct
- When she opened her eyes again . . .
- *Stood, frozen and motionless*
- Stopped dead in his tracks
- *Stepped towards the lake*
- Edged closer
- Moved forward
- Walked through the wall
- Passed through the bricks . . .
- Slid first one leg and then the other
- *Swallowed up by the mist*
- Disappeared into the shadows beyond
- Stepped into the silvery haze and vanished
- Passed through the solid wall
- Vanished through the door
- Sucked into the depths of the painting
- As if he had been swallowed up
- Like someone disappearing into the side of a wave of water
- *Shot through the portal*
- Spun through the air
- Tumbled over and over
- Tumbled head over heels
- Swept along by the current of air

* As if he had been fired from a catapult
* Whirled at tremendous speed
* Swirled as if caught inside a slow whirlwind
* As if shot through the barrel of a rifle
* Flew out the other end
* *Tried to keep his balance*
* Thrashed her legs in the air
* *Almost fell backwards*
* As he was pitched forward . . .
* Swept away by the storm of the portal
* Stumbled and flung his hands forwards
* *As he travelled through the portal*
* Gritted his teeth
* Took a few, quick gulps of air
* *As blood rushed to her . . .*
* Blocked out the . . .
* Could feel her whole body starting to buzz
* Felt the force surging through him
* *Gusted around him*
* Tugged at his hair
* Tears streamed down his face
* Stretched the flesh on his cheeks
* Pulled his cheeks back like rubber
* Contorted his face
* *Released by the portal all of a sudden*
* Scrambled to her feet
* Tried to push himself upright
* Almost made it to his feet
* Before his legs buckled . . .
* *Too dizzy to stand*
* Slumped forwards
* Fell back on his stomach
* Sprawled in a slack-limbed heap
* Collapsed on the ground with a loud crash
* Fell with a thud onto the tunnel floor

SENTENCES

She stood, frozen and motionless, whilst all around her the trees swirled as if caught inside a slow whirlwind.

She wrenched her leg back as the ground cracked, splitting around the shape of the pentagram.

Lowering his staff, he tapped the solid brick wall. As it rippled against the wood, a tunnel started to appear in front of him.

She stepped towards the lake and the mist swallowed her up.

He climbed, sliding first one leg and then the other into the mirror, and disappeared into the shadows beyond.

Rob placed his hands on the wooden circle. The door creaked inwards to reveal a misty tunnel. Frantically, he reached for something to steady himself as he was pitched forward towards the tunnel.

Squeezing his eyes shut, he inserted his finger between the two stones, and almost fell backwards as a whirlwind soared through the gap, and the storm of the portal swept him away.

As she held up her hands, she realised that they were fuzzy and indistinct. When she looked down, she could no longer see her own feet.

The air rippled around him. He stumbled and flung his hands forwards as the ground disappeared beneath his feet, and he vanished through the door.

He shot through the portal as if he had been fired from a catapult.

Katie wrapped her arms around her head, blocking out the flickering, distorted images and sounds that flashed by as she travelled through the portal.

He stepped into the silvery haze and vanished. It was as if he had been swallowed up by a curtain of shimmering water.

As she ran her hands over the manuscript, Kitty could feel blood rushing to her head and her whole body starting to buzz.

Tom felt the force surging through him – through his throat, his lungs, his stomach, his head – as he whirled at tremendous speed through the rippling air.

She took a few, quick gulps of air before walking through the shimmering air between the doorways.

Tom edged closer and reached out his hand. In a blinding flash, he was sucked into the depths of the painting and vanished.

A silver haze covered the wall, and Katie passed through, like someone disappearing into the side of a wave of water.

A breeze gusted around him, tugging at his hair and sending tears streaming down his face.

The flesh on his cheeks was stretched and pulled back like rubber, contorting his face into more and more odd facial expressions.

He spun through the air, tumbling over and over.

Suddenly, he was tumbling head over heels, swept along by the current of air. The darkness was so total he could not even see a short distance down the whirling tunnel.

Kitty shot through the portal as if through the barrel of a rifle and flew out the other end.

His arms flailed as he tried to keep his balance. His legs thrashed in the air. His ears were filled with the hissing of the wind.

She was moving forward, walking through the wall. She closed her eyes as she passed through the bricks. When she opened them again she was standing in the great hall.

As Rob was released from the grip of the portal, he slumped forwards and collapsed on the ground with a loud crash.

He tried to push himself upright, but he fell back on his stomach, too dizzy to stand.

He almost made it to his feet before his legs buckled and he collapsed and sprawled in a slack-limbed heap.

SECTION 3 – REACTION

WORDS	
Nouns	**Senses**, instincts, nerves, muscles, sensation, consciousness
	Mind, brain, thoughts, anticipation, expectation
	Surprise, shock, courage, horror, terror, fear
	Images, sights, vision, sounds
	Body, stomach, arms, fingers, chest, lungs, breath
	Face, expression, forehead, cheeks, eyes, look, sockets, ears
	Darkness, shroud, veil, curtain
	Light, colour, brightness
	Lake, surface
	Gap, hole, portal, passage, tunnel
Similes/ Metaphors	**Like a dark, hypnotic eye**; as if she was being transported on a giant merry-go-round; like sliding through a slippery tunnel of flashing colours; like a great weight; like a giant hand was pinning her down; like a clenched fist had been thrust into his ribs
Adjectives	**Nervous**, anxious, desperate
	Sudden, intense

Black, dark, dizzying, crushing

Hypnotic, spellbinding

Shimmering, flickering, cascading, flashing

Verbs **Stepped into**, travelled

Gazed, watched, looked, focused, exchanged, flickered, flashed, blinked, closed, squeezed, clamped

Tensed, tingled, sharpened

Wondered, anticipated, expected, recalled, remembered

Felt, stabbed, pierced, threatened, overwhelmed

Urged, warned, screamed

Spun, whirled, tumbled

Crept, pressed, pushed, pinned, pitched

Took apart, reassembled

Gripped, burned, burst, bulged

Sucked, gasped

PHRASES – NOUNS AND ADJECTIVES

* *Without warning*
* For seconds or even longer
* *Ahead of her*
* On all sides
* *Like a dark, hypnotic eye*
* Images in the surface of the lake
* Shimmering gap between the trees
* Flickering lights
* A rainbow of cascading colours
* Sudden, intense brightness
* *The force of the portal*
* Passage through the portal
* Scenes and images
* All thoughts, sights and sounds
* *Every sense, every instinct*
* Every nerve in his body
* A thousand terrors
* *A black shroud*
* Dizzy and gasping
* Sensation of crushing suffocation
* *A look of surprise and shock*

PHRASES – VERBS

★ As if the portal was summoning him
★ Stepped into the portal
★ Last time he had travelled by portal . . .
★ *Gazed into the . . .*
★ Watched with bated breath
★ Flickered to Tom's face
★ Flashed across her face
★ Exchanged a nervous look
★ Could not help looking at . . .
★ Focused on the . . .
★ *Clamped her eyes firmly shut*
★ Squeezed her eyes shut
★ Dared not open his eyes
★ Dared not look
★ Afraid to look
★ Made her blink
★ *Senses sharpened*
★ Felt her body tense
★ Tingled with anticipation
★ Emptied her mind
★ *Not sure what he expected*
★ Wondered whether . . .
★ Was ready for anything
★ *Flashed through his mind at once*
★ Fear of what would happen when . . .
★ Recalled the terror that had overwhelmed him
★ Stabbed by a splinter of fear
★ Forced his gibbering brain to ignore . . .
★ Felt his courage fading
★ Threatened to overwhelm him
★ Screamed at him to stop
★ Hoped she would make it through in one piece
★ *As if time had been fast forwarded*
★ Couldn't tell how long it had taken
★ *Felt like the world was spinning*
★ Like sliding through a slippery tunnel of flashing colours
★ Spun faster and faster with each second
★ As if she was being transported on a giant merry-go-round
★ *As if the darkness was swallowing up his body*
★ Felt like a great weight pressing down on him
★ Felt like a giant hand was pinning her down
★ Crept over every inch of his body

* Like a clenched fist had been thrust into his ribs
* Pushed down on every part of her
* Pressed around his fingers, his arms, his face and cheeks
* Pressed heavily into his stomach and chest
* *Pitched her forward down the tunnel*
* Took her apart as she went through the portal
* Reassembled her on the other side
* *As the force gripped his lungs . . .*
* Burned her chest
* Felt as if her ears were bursting
* As if her eyes were bulging out of their sockets
* *Tensed his stomach muscles*
* Sucked in a startled breath
* Gasped desperately for air
* *Started to swim*
* Fell over her vision
* Began to lose consciousness
* As a black curtain started to descend across his vision . . .

SENTENCES

She felt her body tense and her senses sharpen as she gazed into the shimmering gap between the trees.

Her eyes flickered to Tom's face and they exchanged a nervous look.

She could not help looking at the continually changing pattern of flickering lights ahead of her and wondering whether she would make it through in one piece.

Kitty emptied her mind of all thoughts, sights and sounds and focused on the images in the surface of the lake.

Every sense, every instinct, screamed at him to stop, that he was about to walk head-first into a solid barrier.

Katie was stabbed by a splinter of fear, fear of what would happen when she stepped into the portal.

A thousand terrors flashed through his mind at once, but it was as if the portal was summoning him like a dark, hypnotic eye.

His forehead began to sweat as he recalled the terror that had overwhelmed him last time he had travelled by portal. Suddenly, he felt his courage fading.

His whole body tingled with anticipation.

He was not sure what he expected, but he was ready for anything.

The passage through the portal had been like sliding through a slippery tunnel, with a rainbow of cascading colours on all sides.

Scenes and images flashed by as if time had been fast forwarded, so he couldn't tell if he had been moving through the portal for seconds or even longer.

Every nerve in his body screamed at him, as the force gripped his lungs, like a clenched fist had been thrust into his ribs.

A look of surprise and shock flashed across her face. It felt like a giant hand was pinning her down.

As a black curtain started to descend across his vision, he tensed and held his stomach muscles, forcing his gibbering brain to ignore the sensation of crushing suffocation that threatened to overwhelm him.

He dared not open his eyes; dared not look.

The sudden, intense brightness made her blink.

She squeezed her eyes shut, afraid to look.

She sucked in a startled breath.

He gasped desperately for air.

The force of the portal pressed around his fingers, his arms, his face and cheeks. It crept over every inch of his body, pressing heavily into his stomach and chest.

Her chest burned, her ears were bursting, her eyes felt as if they were bulging out of their sockets.

It felt like the world was spinning, as if she was being transported on a giant merry-go-round that was spinning faster and faster with each second.

It felt like a great weight was pushing down on every part of her, taking her apart as she went through the portal to be reassembled on the other side.

A black shroud fell over her vision as the world started to swim and she began to lose consciousness.

She was dizzy and gasping when the sensation suddenly stopped and without warning she was still again.

3

Tunnels

Rob froze; his eyes widened with shock as he stared at the path ahead of them. A crack like a thunderbolt bisected the tunnel. Beneath the crack, he saw nothing but empty darkness – a vast, misty abyss.

His stomach clenched in panic and he knew he had to think of something fast. He backed away and looked around. To his left a narrow, rickety plank stretched over the chasm. **He was all too aware that if it didn't hold their weight or they missed their footing on the slippery, rotting wood, they would plummet down into the misty void. He looked up and down the tunnel for the hundredth time. They had no choice.**

Slowly, he eased one foot onto the plank, and then the other, and edged across. He was nearly across the plank when it tilted sideways. Desperately, he tried to regain his balance. As he saw the drop yawning beneath him, he leapt towards the lip of the shaft at the other end.

SECTION 1 – SETTING

WORDS

Nouns	**City**, castle, world, empire, kingdom, land
	Mountain, mountainside, cliff
	Location, whereabouts, position, site
	Earth, ground, surface, depths
	Stone, rock
	Entrance, opening, hole, door, gate, hinges

Tunnel, maze, labyrinth, catacombs, crypt, vault, chamber, dungeons, cave

Burials, corpses, bodies, skulls

Symbols, carvings, signs, pictures, runes, glyphs

Passages, passageways, corridors, paths, stairs, stairways, staircases, walls, niches, roof, ceiling, headroom, arch, pillars

Crack, fissure, void, abyss, pit, chasm

Corner, bend, side

Light, lamp, candles, torch, beam, flames, glow, gleam

Darkness, blackness, shadows

Air, wind, breeze, gust

Sound, noise, breath, rasp, gasp, pant, murmur, sigh, hiss, whisper, howl, shriek

Feet, footsteps, boots

Scuff, scrape, crunch, thud, thump, rumble, bump, clack, crack, clang, rattle, blast

Smell, stench, waft

Dust, cobwebs, water, mould, slime, bats, rats

Vibration, shudder

Spikes, stalactites, stalagmites

Similes/ Metaphors	**The size of a small door**; straight as an arrow; as cold as a crypt; like a cold, dry mouth; like a heavy cloth; like a camera flash; pressed on his eyes like a black veil; closed in like the sides of a vice; as if the air was being sucked from the catacombs; like millions of dried leaves; sound like a blast from a mouth organ; like a chain being dropped into a coffin; like a clap of thunder; fissures like a sheet of ice
Adjectives	**Secret**, unknown, hidden, concealed
	Spider-like, labyrinthine, maze-like, serpentine
	Curving, bending, winding, twisting
	Straight, unswerving
	Endless, continuous, eternal
	Long, deep, low, narrow, steep, high
	Huge, enormous, vast

Tiny, small

Thick, solid

Blank, clear, empty, hollow

Dark, inky, gloomy, dim, shadowy, misty

Strange, odd, misshapen, ghostly, eerie, unearthly

Smooth, polished, seamless

Sharp, jagged, rocky

Damp, wet, clammy, glistening

Slippery, moss-covered, dangerous, treacherous

Rusting, corroded

Rectangular, square, circular

Domed, vaulted

Ancient, old, archaic

Mummified, preserved

High-pitched, shrill

Echoing, vibrating, resounding

Cold, icy, freezing

Warm, hot, steamy

Dead, stale, putrid, sickly

Clear, fresh

Black, silver, green, emerald, red, deep-red, sapphire, orange

Stone, iron, copper, brass, marble

Abrupt, sudden

Relentless, constant, non-stop, steady, persistent

Dying, waning, lessening, ebbing

Flickering, hissing, sputtering, flaming, burning, smoky

Loud, deafening, pounding, rumbling

Dripping, gushing

Verbs

Criss-crossed, snaked, spread, stretched

Patted, pushed, drew aside

Shut, slid, closed, covered, draped

Entered, stepped, followed

Bent, curved, wound, twisted, turned, coiled, spiralled, zigzagged

Led, opened, enclosed, branched, forked

Sloped, climbed, ascended, dropped, descended

Narrowed, widened

Found, faced with, passed, approached

Squeezed, crawled, hunched

Sculpted, carved

Lit, shone, illuminated, pierced, glistened, glimmered, polished

Flared, burst, burned, sputtered, flickered

Darkened, plunged

Listened, heard, sounded, dislodged, scuffed, rattled, crunched, snapped, crashed, boomed, rang, rippled, crackled, dripped, hissed, murmured

Echoed, magnified

Looked, saw, spotted, glimpsed, revealed

Felt, sensed, smelled

Drifted, wafted, flowed, grew, filled

Lurked, waited

Startled, disturbed, flew, fluttered

Split, cracked, fractured, splintered

Interrupted, punctuated, interspersed

Ended, reached, came to

PHRASES – NOUNS AND ADJECTIVES

- ★ *Somewhere in the distance*
- ★ From within
- ★ Ahead of them
- ★ Around them
- ★ Behind them
- ★ Below him
- ★ Beneath the crack . . .
- ★ Around the next corner
- ★ Further down the tunnel
- ★ To the side and back
- ★ At regular intervals

- From somewhere deep in the tunnels and passageways
- *Without warning*
- For a brief second
- Just moments before
- Next minute
- After only a few minutes
- Before too long
- Every once in a while
- Time after time
- With each step . . .
- *A complete, secret, underground world*
- A network of catacombs
- A spider-like network of tunnels
- A winding, underground maze of low, dark tunnels
- Labyrinth with an endless puzzle of staircases and tunnels
- Inky black maze of dangerous, slippery paths
- Labyrinthine set of passageways and niches
- Tunnels and vaults, staircases and dungeons
- *Low, dark tunnels*
- An inky black tunnel
- Narrow tunnel
- Narrow, jagged passages
- Long, twisting path
- Every corner, every bend, every opening
- *Five feet tall and four feet wide*
- Low, rocky ceilings
- Barely enough headroom
- *A hole in the rock the size of a small door*
- Two, huge, thick stone doors
- A rusting, iron gate
- *Seamless wall*
- Blocked entrances
- *Damp walls*
- Stone floor
- Blocks of ancient stones
- Smooth, polished rock
- Smooth, marble floors
- Deep-red walls
- Roof of striking, emerald copper ore
- A high, rectangular chamber
- Enormous domed ceiling
- A huge, black arch
- Thick pillars of ancient workmanship
- Iron rings

- ⁎ Strange carvings over archways
- ⁎ *Vast, misty abyss*
- ⁎ Solid earth underneath them
- ⁎ *Flights of steps*
- ⁎ Steep, stone stairway
- ⁎ Ancient, moss-covered steps
- ⁎ *Niches in the walls*
- ⁎ Chamber of crypts
- ⁎ Corpses from ancient burials
- ⁎ Mummified bodies
- ⁎ *Icy cold*
- ⁎ As cold as a crypt
- ⁎ Blast of cold air
- ⁎ Cold all around him
- ⁎ Waft of cold, dead air
- ⁎ Clammy, cold, icy to the touch
- ⁎ Like a cold, dry mouth
- ⁎ Gust of icy wind
- ⁎ *Light of one dim candle*
- ⁎ In the flickering light
- ⁎ Light from the lamp
- ⁎ Line of wall-mounted, sputtering torches
- ⁎ Brass candleholders on the wall
- ⁎ Billowing torches
- ⁎ Burning torch in the niche
- ⁎ Glow at the end of the tunnel
- ⁎ Red in the flaming torch
- ⁎ Flickering light of a flaming torch
- ⁎ A dim glow
- ⁎ Smoky, orange flames
- ⁎ Silver gleam
- ⁎ *Huge, ghostly shadows*
- ⁎ Odd, misshapen shadows
- ⁎ Ghostly light
- ⁎ *Inky blackness*
- ⁎ Dark as night
- ⁎ Pitch-black inside
- ⁎ Like a heavy cloth
- ⁎ Dark space between each dim lamp
- ⁎ Blackness ahead, blackness behind
- ⁎ *Sudden rasp*
- ⁎ Another sound, then another, in quick succession
- ⁎ Panting breaths
- ⁎ Hiss of a whispered word

* Humming sound
* Long, hissing slither
* Multitude of overlapping whispers
* A scuff, stumble, a kicked pebble
* Tiny crunch of pebbles
* With a loud thud
* A pounding thump
* Low, deep sound of . . .
* Occasional scuff of movement
* *Every movement in the tunnel*
* Every bump and scrape
* Dying echo in the freezing passage
* Between each repetition of the sounds
* *An unearthly howl*
* High-pitched shriek
* With a loud clack . . .
* A deafening crack
* Sound like a blast from a mouth organ
* Sound of metal clanging against stone
* Rattling noise
* *Sound of gushing water*
* Dripping water
* *Putrid, sickly stench*
* Waft of stale air
* Gust of putrid air
* *Vibration through the soles of her boots*

PHRASES – VERBS

* Known only to a few
* Would never have believed it existed
* *Criss-crossed the city*
* Carved in the mountainside
* Snaked under the castle
* Spread its roots beneath the surface
* *Patted the stones with the palm of her hand*
* Listened intently for any hollow sounds
* When he drew aside the bush . . .
* *Covered the gaping hole*
* Had been draped over the entrance
* *Slid aside to reveal . . .*
* Widened to reveal a stone-lined tunnel
* Opened in the cliff to reveal a tunnel

* *Led down into the earth*
* Burrowed into the depths of the mountain
* Descended into a secret world
* *Where the opening had been*
* When he looked back at the entrance
* Swung shut behind them
* Slid back into place
* All he could see was . . .
* *Entered an endless labyrinth of tunnels*
* Seemed to stretch on for ever
* Wound underground
* *As he went on . . .*
* Travelled deeper underground
* Walked deeper into the labyrinth
* Climbed down the . . .
* As he continued down . . .
* Made their way deeper into the mountain
* *Became even lower and narrower*
* Could barely walk upright
* Forced to hunch over as he walked
* *Spiralled down into the gloom*
* Led down into the hollow depths
* Snaked downwards into darkness
* Sloped downhill
* Dropped off at a sharp angle
* Descended steeply
* Stretched back, deep into the cliff
* Curved relentlessly downwards and inwards
* Couldn't see where it ended
* *Ran straight as an arrow*
* Never bent, never turned
* *Bent to the right*
* Twisted and turned like a maze
* Curved slightly
* As it turned sharply to the left . . .
* Led off in different directions
* Branched into several tunnels
* Curved so far they could no longer see the opening
* Narrowed and zigzagged sharply left and right
* *Forked ahead of her*
* Followed the left-hand path
* Came to another fork
* Turned to the right
* Turned to the left and then to the right

* *Found that she was . . .*
* Back where she had started
* No way of knowing which path they had followed
* It only took a few minutes for them to . . .
* Lost all sense of direction
* Were well and truly lost
* *Whenever he passed an open doorway*
* Faced with nothing but blank stone
* Approached with the greatest caution
* *As he entered the passage . . .*
* With each step they took . . .
* *Glimpsed a shelf of grinning skulls shrouded in cobwebs*
* Thought he saw . . .
* Caught a glimpse of a sudden movement
* Came across strange symbols and signs
* Revealed glimpses of . . .
* Covered in pictures of . . .
* Carved into the rock
* Carved into the walls and floor
* Carved with strange symbols
* Covered with rows of deeply carved runes
* Covered entirely with sculpted glyphs
* *Where water had leaked in from the rocks*
* Struck the wall beneath her and sprayed upwards
* Glistened with damp
* Polished into dangerous, slippery paths
* Sculpted into jagged blades
* *Grew darker*
* Already lost in darkness
* Plunged them into darkness
* Stretched into blackness
* Pressed on his eyes like a black veil
* Knocked out his flame
* Peered into the inky blackness
* Cast eerie shadows on the wall
* *Noticed a shadow that . . .*
* Seemed darker than the others
* Crept across the wall
* Looked like the odd, misshapen shadows were . . .
* Reached out as if to grab him
* Began to creep from the walls
* Slid into the air
* *Lurked in the dark*
* Waited to crack unsuspecting skulls

* *Torches were thinly spread*
* Set into the walls
* Shone only a few feet
* Moved in semi-darkness
* Spotted an eerie light source
* Glimmered faintly up ahead
* Seeped in through the cave entrance
* Sputtered and dwindled with every gust of air
* Cast a pale, sapphire light across the lake
* *Pointed the beam of the torch ahead*
* Had a dim light to guide his steps
* Lit only by the narrow beam of light from the torch
* Marked flickering pathways
* Crackled down the passage like a camera flash
* Pierced the shadows
* Illuminated a steep, natural stairway
* *Saw a shard of light*
* Grew brighter
* Flared to life
* Burst into sunlight
* Lit the main tunnel
* Filled the passageway
* *Rattled down a slope*
* Dislodged pebbles
* Crunched on the broken shells and bones
* *Could hear water*
* Dripped from the roof
* *Heard a faint, echoing gasp*
* Filled with the sound of hissing noises
* Sounded like millions of dried leaves
* Seemed to murmur and sigh
* Heard a clang of iron bells
* Sounded like a chain being dropped into a coffin
* *Could hear footsteps*
* Heard pounding feet
* Scuffed his boot against a rock
* Boomed like a clap of thunder
* Heard a shout echoing through the caves
* Rang with the echoes of his scream
* *Whatever was making the noise . . .*
* As if someone had . . .
* *Sounded close by*
* Sounded up ahead
* Followed soon after

* Grew louder
* Got louder and closer behind her
* Came towards them
* Shattered the silence around them
* *Spread through the tunnel*
* Heard echoes
* Echoed along the tunnel
* Echoed and crashed back at him
* Magnified sounds a hundredfold
* Filled the air with an echo
* Produced a magnified, hollow echo
* Bounced against the side of the tunnel
* Began to ebb and wane
* *Felt cold under his hands*
* Got colder and colder
* Breath changed to mist
* Felt as thick and warm as sauna steam
* *Grew clearer*
* Smelled fresher all of a sudden
* *Drifted towards him*
* Flowed across her cheek
* Crashed into them
* As if the air was being sucked from the catacombs
* *Disturbed a squadron of bats*
* Came towards them, flying in close formation
* Fluttered from every corner
* Flew out through . . .
* *Shook through the ground*
* Shook with the rumble of falling stone
* Followed quickly by another and another
* Stone shifting over stone
* Could see chunks of rock
* *Tumbled through the darkness*
* Splashed into the water
* Like the tunnel was closing in on him
* Closed in on them like the sides of a vice
* *Cracks blossomed across the earth*
* Webbed with fissures like a sheet of ice
* Bisected by a chasm
* So wide she couldn't see the other side
* Found nothing but . . .
* Saw nothing but empty darkness
* Floated in empty space
* Left her stranded on a tiny ledge

- ✴ *As the pressure built . . .*
- ✴ Could feel his ears popping
- ✴ Became aware of . . .
- ✴ Interrupted by . . .
- ✴ *Came to an abrupt end*
- ✴ Ended in . . .
- ✴ Were able to see an end to the tunnel
- ✴ Reached a door at the end
- ✴ Stretched high into the shadows
- ✴ Ended high in a vast cave
- ✴ Hidden either side of them
- ✴ Swung open on silent hinges
- ✴ Opened up on either side of them
- ✴ Opened out into an underground chamber
- ✴ *Shot out of holes in the floor and the ceiling*

SENTENCES

Eventually, the rock slid aside to reveal an inky black tunnel.

Kitty patted the stones with the palm of her hand, listening intently for any hollow sounds.

Two, huge, thick stone doors opened in the cliff to reveal a tunnel that burrowed into the depths of the mountain.

The crack widened to reveal a tunnel leading down into the earth. A rusting, iron gate covered the gaping hole.

When he drew aside the bush, it revealed a stone-lined tunnel five feet tall and four feet wide.

They had descended into a secret world that she would never have believed existed.

The city had spread roots beneath the surface – tunnels, vaults, chambers, stair-cases, workshops, stores, forges – a complete, secret, underground world, known only to a few.

A network of catacombs criss-crossed the city – a winding, underground maze of low, dark tunnels.

A spider-like network of tunnels had been carved in the mountainside to curve relentlessly downwards and inwards.

The sealed catacombs with their chamber of crypts and mummified bodies snaked under the castle.

Stone steps spiralled down into the gloom.

Ancient, moss-covered steps led down into the hollow depths.

With a whisper, the doors swung shut behind them, and when Tom looked back, all he could see was a seamless wall where the opening had been just moments before.

With a loud thud, the rock slid back into place, plunging them into darkness.

The tunnel snaked downwards into darkness. It seemed to stretch on for ever; blackness ahead, blackness behind.

Whenever he passed an open doorway, his fingers floated in empty space.

They had entered an endless labyrinth of tunnels, blocked entrances, strange carvings over archways and flights of steps stretching into blackness. At regular intervals, iron rings had been hammered into the walls.

On and on they went through the tunnel, which ran straight as an arrow, never bending, never turning.

The tunnel bent to the right and before too long it had curved so far that looking back they could no longer see the opening.

The tunnel narrowed and zigzagged sharply left and right, left and right, left and right.

It only took a few minutes for them to lose all sense of direction as they were faced with nothing but blank stone and narrow jagged passages that all looked the same.

She was well and truly lost. The tunnel forked ahead of her. Following the left path, she eventually came to another fork, and turned to the right, only to find that she was back where she had started.

She followed the right-hand path, then turned to the left and then the right. They took turn after turn until there was no way of knowing which path they had followed.

As he went on, the tunnels became even lower and narrower, so that he could barely walk upright and was forced to hunch over as he walked.

He took a step forward and then to the side and then back. Time after time, he found nothing but damp walls. It was like the tunnel was closing in on him.

Every corner, every bend, every opening had to be approached with the greatest caution.

Where water had leaked in from the rocks, the walls and floor glistened with damp.

The walls were smooth, marbled, carved over and over again with runes.

Thick pillars of ancient workmanship supported the roof.

As they walked deeper into the labyrinth, they came across strange symbols and signs that had been carved into the walls and floor – blocks of ancient stones covered with rows of deeply carved runes.

The walls were deep-red and the roof was a shimmering, emerald.

In niches carved into the walls, he caught glimpses of the corpses from ancient burials, their skulls shrouded in cobwebs.

The corridor grew darker, the air got staler.

Darkness pressed on his eyes like a black veil.

A gust of putrid air suddenly knocked out his flame and plunged him into darkness.

Peering into the inky blackness, he caught a glimpse of a sudden movement.

She noticed a shadow that seemed darker than the others, creeping across the wall.

In the flickering light it looked like the odd, misshapen shadows were reaching out to grab him.

Around them, ghostly shadows began to creep from the walls and slide into the air.

A little light seeped in through the cave entrance, but apart from that everything else was black.

Torches were thinly spread and they moved in semi-darkness.

The light from the lamp shone only a few feet and cast eerie shadows on the wall.

A line of wall-mounted torches lit the main tunnel, their smoky, orange flames sputtering with every gust of air.

Up ahead, he spotted an eerie, glimmering light source.

A line of sputtering torches filled the passageway, casting a pale, sapphire light across the lake.

When he entered the passage, torches set into the walls suddenly flared to life.

For a brief second, he thought he saw the flickering of flames further down the tunnel.

The glow at the end of the tunnel grew brighter and finally they burst into sunlight.

The tunnel was as cold as a crypt and dark as night.

With each step the air got colder and colder.

As they climbed down the steep, stone stairway, a blast of cold air crashed into them.

The temperature dropped so fast, his breath changed to mist.

It was pitch-black inside and a waft of cold, dead air flowed across her cheek.

The air felt as if it was being sucked from the catacombs.

The air grew stale as they travelled deeper underground.

The air felt as thick and warm as sauna steam.

Somewhere a long, hissing slither of dislodged pebbles rattled down a slope.

She was conscious of something nearby; a tiny crunch of pebbles on the floor.

There was another sound – the sound of flowing water.

He could have sworn that he heard a faint, echoing gasp.

From somewhere below in the darkness came the sound of hissing.

From within he heard the occasional scuff of movement, the hiss of a whispered word.

The whispering got louder behind her until it sounded like millions of dried leaves swirling in the wind.

A sudden rasp made him wheel round.

Every movement in the tunnel produced a magnified hollow echo. Every bump and scrape filled the air with a multitude of overlapping whispers that seemed to murmur and sigh with a life of their own.

Suddenly, an unearthly howl sounded close by. The howl came again, then a high-pitched shriek followed soon after, even closer this time.

The sound of metal clanging against stone echoed through the tunnel. Whatever was making that noise was coming towards them.

Every once in a while a gust of wind burst out with a sound like a blast from a mouth organ.

He could hear footsteps – a scuff, stumble, a kicked pebble. Someone else was down there!

A pounding thump shook through the ground, soon followed by another and another, each one growing louder and getting closer.

As he scuffed his boot against a rock, it bounced against the side of the tunnel with a loud clack, and then multiplied a hundredfold as it spread through the tunnel.

The entire tunnel shook with the rumble of falling stone.

Behind them the tunnel was darkening. He could feel his ears popping as the pressure built. The tunnel was closing in on them like the sides of a vice.

The tunnel shuddered; chunks of rock fell into the water. The tunnel was closing behind her, leaving her stranded on a tiny ledge.

After only a few minutes, she became aware of a vibration through the soles of her boots.

The air trembled with the low, deep sound of stone shifting over stone. The mountain was moving!

Cracks like thunderbolts appeared across the floor.

The stone floor was webbed with fissures like a sheet of ice. Beneath the crack she saw nothing but empty darkness.

Below him was a vast, misty abyss.

The floor was bisected by a chasm so wide she couldn't see the other side.

One minute there was solid earth underneath them. The next minute, nothing. They were tumbling through darkness.

A row of sharpened wooden stakes shot out of holes in the floor, the walls and the ceiling.

Around the next corner, the tunnel came to an abrupt end.

The tunnel grew larger, gradually widening, the walls opening up on either side of them. The air smelled fresher all of a sudden. Ahead of them, at the end of the tunnel, was a door.

The tunnel ended in a high, rectangular chamber that was so huge he couldn't see where it ended. Its enormous domed ceiling stretched high into the shadows.

Eventually, they were able to see an end to the tunnel: a huge, black arch that was covered entirely with sculpted glyphs.

From somewhere deep in the tunnels and passageways, he heard a bell pealing and hurried footsteps. Then, without warning, the doors hidden either side of them swung open.

SECTION 2 – INTERACTION

WORDS

Nouns	**Passage**, corridor, chamber, archway
	Entrance, opening, hole, gap, space, ledge
	Shaft, crack, fissure, chasm, void
	Path, slope, descent, incline, walls, niches, roof, ceiling, stalactites, stalagmites, floor, ground
	Ladder, rung, stairs, steps
	Footsteps, foothold, balance
	Presence, patrols, shadows, shapes

Bats, rats, skulls, cobwebs

Light, lamp, torch, beam

Rocks, boulders, stones, pebbles

Sounds, noises, voices, echoes

Arms, elbows, hands, fist, fingertips, legs, knees, feet, ankle, heels, toes, stomach, belly, back

Head, eyes

Adjectives

Long, narrow, twisting, sloping, steep, precipitous

Wide, gaping, yawning, cavernous

Damp, smooth, loose, dangerous, treacherous

Glistening, glowing, glinting, shimmering

Sharp, needle-sharp, pointed, jagged, barbed

Black, smoky, murky, sputtering

Bone-jarring, jolting

Cautious, wary

Numb, paralysed

Verbs

Knew, realised

Pulled, slid, brushed, swatted

Listened, heard

Felt, sensed

Ventured, followed, crossed, emerged

Found, passed, approached, faced with

Guided, flickered, sputtered, dwindled, died

Raised, lifted, swung

Looked, watched, searched, peered, saw, glimpsed, stared, fixed, glued

Moved, walked, stepped

Squeezed, edged, eased, inched, shuffled, slithered

Bent, crawled, ducked, flattened, crouched, huddled, hunkered, descended

Pressed, stopped, halted, backed, retraced

Turned, whirled, spun, wheeled

Darted, raced, bolted, sprinted, plunged

Braced, steadied, balanced

Leapt, lunged

Climbed, hoisted, hauled, dragged, clambered

Grabbed, clutched, held on, clung, gripped

Missed, slipped, slid, skidded, scrambled, stumbled, slithered

Fell, tumbled, pitched, spilled

Hit, jarred, jolted

Sliced, cut, tore, twisted

PHRASES – NOUNS AND ADJECTIVES

* At first . . .
* Time after time
* *With no other choice . . .*
* With a new sense of urgency . . .
* With the last of his strength . . .
* *One step at a time*
* With each footstep . . .
* One wrong step . . .
* *By her fingertips*
* With his right hand . . .
* *Entrance to the tunnel*
* Steep, damp slope
* Precipitous path
* Up dangerous, steep inclines
* Down the passage
* Into the long, sloping tunnel
* *Against the tunnel walls*
* Niches in the walls
* Rocks and pebbles
* A shard of needle-sharp rock
* Huge spikes of ice
* *Sound of voices*
* Slight noise at his back
* *In the cramped space*
* In the murky light
* *At the other end*
* Another dead end
* Nearly across the . . . when . . .

PHRASES – VERBS

- No one knew the location of . . .
- His whereabouts were only known by those in the society
- *Listened for signs that . . .*
- Felt a presence behind her
- Someone else was in the tunnel
- Moved towards him
- Appeared to be following him
- Let the patrols pass
- Found himself face-to-face with . . .
- Never saw who had seized hold of her
- *Dripped from the roof*
- Ran out of the cracks in the walls
- Plummeted from the roof
- *Squeezed through a hole*
- Ventured further in
- *Emerged into an opening*
- Emerged from the passage into . . .
- *Followed the long, twisting path*
- Led off in all different directions
- Descended a precipitous path
- Crossed a narrow ledge
- *Used the light from their torch*
- Guided their steps
- Followed the smoky light of the sputtering torch
- As the torch flickered and died . . .
- Pulled her deeper into the blackness
- *Flapped his hands in front of him*
- Felt ahead with his feet and hands
- Felt his way with his outstretched hands
- Slid his hand over the stones of the wall
- Brushed her fingers against the rock
- Swatted the air in front of him
- Groped their way forward
- Floundered around in the dark
- *Clung to each other*
- Grabbed Rob's arm to steady herself
- *Edged down the glistening stone steps*
- As she edged forward . . .
- Edged around the walls
- Eased his way between the boulders
- Inched his way down the tunnel
- Moved cautiously through the tunnel

* Made their way gingerly
* Picked their way carefully
* Squeezed along a narrow, murky corridor
* *Too steep to try walking*
* Shuffled closer on her belly
* Crawled as fast as she could
* Scraped her knees and elbows
* Hauled herself through the gap
* Impossible to bend her legs
* Pushed with her toes
* *Ducked as a swish of wings . . .*
* Flattened herself against the wall
* *Crouched low to the ground*
* As the vibrations travelled up his legs . . .
* Crouched low to keep his balance
* *Pressed his back to the wall*
* Backed away
* Shuffled backwards
* Backed into the centre of the chamber
* Walked backwards in a circle
* *Slipped into the shadows*
* Kept in the shadows
* Glided noiselessly along the walls
* Let the shadows swallow them
* Shrunk back into the shadows
* Hunkered down in the darkness
* Focused on becoming one with the shadows
* *Had gone too far*
* Couldn't have said which passage they'd just taken
* Too late by the time he realised . . .
* Backed into a dead end
* Faced with a high, stone wall
* Retraced his steps
* Tried to establish his whereabouts
* Walked part of the way down one tunnel
* Walked back to the fork in the tunnel
* Crossed to the other passage
* *Slithered to a halt*
* Too frightened to move
* Couldn't move
* Stopped dead in her tracks
* *Whirled round*
* Turned around
* Unable to help herself, she . . .

- ⭐ As he spun round . . .
- ⭐ Caused him to wheel around
- ⭐ *Scrabbled up*
- ⭐ Scrambled to her feet
- ⭐ Hurled himself out of the way
- ⭐ *Moved rapidly*
- ⭐ Darted from one archway to the next
- ⭐ Bolted down the tunnel
- ⭐ Plunged deeper into the tunnel
- ⭐ Sprinted down the passage
- ⭐ Moved lightning fast
- ⭐ *Looked behind him*
- ⭐ Looked around
- ⭐ Raised her head cautiously
- ⭐ Swung his head from side to side
- ⭐ Stopped to peer through each arch
- ⭐ Searched for a way out
- ⭐ Peered over the ledge
- ⭐ *Glued to the scene in front of her*
- ⭐ Fixed on the two shapes
- ⭐ Stared down the length of the tunnel
- ⭐ Stopped, head up, wary
- ⭐ Made his eyes widen with shock
- ⭐ *Searched below him for the ladder*
- ⭐ Found the first rung
- ⭐ Clung to the ladder
- ⭐ Started his descent
- ⭐ Scrambled down the ladder fast
- ⭐ Missed the last rung and tumbled
- ⭐ *Barely managed to hold on*
- ⭐ Knew that she would not be able to hold on much longer
- ⭐ Fingers tingled fiercely with pins and needles
- ⭐ *Found a foothold*
- ⭐ Found a toehold in the stonework
- ⭐ Gained a foothold in one of the iron rings
- ⭐ Dug her toes into the cracks
- ⭐ Squeezed her feet hard against the sides
- ⭐ Braced her elbows and feet against the walls
- ⭐ Tucked her knees close to her chest
- ⭐ *Grimaced and raised one knee*
- ⭐ Hoisted herself up
- ⭐ Hauled herself up hand over fist
- ⭐ Tried to scramble up
- ⭐ Dragged himself onto the path

- *Clambered down the slope*
- Slipped on a patch of loose stones
- *Foot scraped against . . .*
- Skidded from under her . . .
- Shifted under him
- Threatened his balance
- Too smooth to get a grip
- Missed her footing
- Slipped and slid on the damp steps
- Slipped and stumbled in the water
- Slithered back with a thud
- Felt himself tumbling
- Spilled head first down the slope
- *Stretched across the gaping chasm*
- As she saw the drop yawning beneath her . . .
- Could send her plummeting down
- Would be a very long fall
- *Tilted sideways*
- Tried to regain her balance
- Dug in her heels
- Prevented herself sliding
- *Leapt towards the lip of the shaft*
- Lunged for the wall
- Threw out his hands in front of him
- Broke his fall
- *Hit the ground*
- Hit the path with a bone-jarring thud
- *Sliced his arm*
- Tore his hands and knees
- Twisted her ankle
- Pain shot through her leg
- As the pain washed over him . . .
- Lay there gasping
- Could feel himself blacking out

SENTENCES

They followed the long, twisting path using the light from their torch to guide their steps.

Following the smoky light of the sputtering torch, they moved cautiously through the tunnel.

They edged down the glistening, stone steps – slipping and sliding on the damp, treacherous stairs.

At first, he moved quite rapidly, but then he stumbled and began to move more cautiously, his hand sliding over the stones of the wall.

Tom walked backwards in a circle, trying to establish his whereabouts. Looking behind, he couldn't have said which passage they'd just taken.

He walked part of the way down one tunnel and then back to the fork and crossed to the other.

Rob backed into the centre of the room, his gaze darting from one archway to the next.

Pressing his back to the wall, he eased his way down the tunnel. The noises appeared to be following him. By the time he realised he had gone too far, it was too late. He had backed into a dead end. With no other choice, he retraced his steps.

His foot searched below him for the ladder and eventually his foot found the first rung. He had just started his descent when the sound of voices made him freeze.

He clung to the ladder and focused on becoming one with the shadows.

She scrambled down the ladder so fast she missed the last rung and tumbled, her ankle twisting, pain shooting through her leg.

She couldn't move. Her eyes were glued to the scene in front of her.

He slithered to a halt, his breath coming in painful gasps.

They clung to each other. Too frightened to move.

Katie stopped dead in her tracks, staring down the length of the tunnel.

As she walked, she felt a presence behind her. But no one knew the location of the entrance to the tunnel. She paused. Unable to help herself, she turned around.

He slipped into the shadows and glided noiselessly along the walls, stopping to peer through each arch.

Shrinking back into the shadows, he let the patrols pass.

Hunkered down in the darkness, Tom's eyes were fixed on the two shapes moving towards him.

He ducked as a swish of wings rushed through the air and brushed his head with their furry bodies.

Rob began to edge around the walls, feeling with his feet and hands.

Gail ventured cautiously into the long, sloping tunnel, digging in her heels to prevent herself sliding.

He crouched low to the ground and edged his way through the boulders.

Rob had to crouch low to keep his balance as the vibrations travelled up his legs.

It was too steep to try walking, so Trish crawled.

She crawled as fast as she could, ignoring the stones that scraped her knees and elbows.

Katie had to haul herself through the gap by her fingertips. It was impossible to bend her legs in the cramped space, so she had to push with her toes.

Raising her head cautiously, Kitty peered over the ledge.

Frantically, Rob swung his head from side to side, searching for a way out.

With his right hand he swatted the air in front of him.

Her fingers brushed against the rock – then nothing.

As the torch flickered and died, he was left floundering around in the dark, feeling his way with his outstretched hands against the tunnel walls.

Rob shuffled backwards, one step at a time.

He backed away and looked around. As he did, his gaze stopped on something behind him, something that made his eyes widen with shock.

As Tom spun round, he found himself face-to-face with . . .

Katie whirled round but never saw who had seized hold of her.

A slight noise at his back caused Andrew to wheel around, his dagger raised.

She scrambled to her feet and bolted down the tunnel.

Panic-stricken, he scrabbled up, hurling himself out of the way.

With a new sense of urgency, they plunged deeper into the tunnel, letting its shadows swallow them.

She sprinted down the passage. At the end, she was faced with a high, stone wall. It was another dead end.

Moving lightning fast, Trish lunged for the wall, flattened herself against it, just as huge spikes of ice began to plummet from the roof.

Trish gained a foothold in one of the iron rings set into the stonework, and hoisted herself up.

At times they climbed, hauling themselves hand over fist up steep inclines, or scrambling, tearing hands and knees when they crawled.

He tried to scramble up, but the sides were too smooth to get a grip, and time after time he slithered back with a thud.

Gail braced her elbows and feet against the walls, knees tucked close to her chest, all too aware that a missed footing could send her plummeting down into the misty void.

Digging her toes into the cracks, Kitty squeezed her feet hard against the sides and hauled herself up, knowing that she would not be able to hold on much longer.

He was barely managing to hold on. His fingers were already numb, his arms tingling fiercely with pins and needles.

Swinging his feet, he found a foothold. Then, with the last of his strength, he dragged himself onto the path and lay there gasping.

As she clambered down the slope, Kitty stepped on a patch of loose pebbles and slipped.

Trish grabbed Rob's arm to steady herself as her foot skidded from under her.

With each footstep, rocks and pebbles shifted under him, threatening his balance.

They had to pick their way carefully, their feet slipping and sliding. One wrong step and it would be a very long fall.

As his foot scraped against something on the floor, he felt himself tumbling and tried to throw out his hands in front of him to break his fall, but it was too late.

He fell, pitching head first down the slope. On the way down, a shard of needle-sharp rock sliced his arm. Then he hit the ground with a bone-jarring thud. As the pain washed over him, he could feel himself blacking out.

She was nearly across the plank that stretched across the gaping chasm when it tilted sideways. Desperately, Gail tried to regain her balance. As she saw the drop yawning beneath her, she leapt towards the lip of the shaft at the other end.

SECTION 3 – REACTION

WORDS

Nouns	**Brain**, heart, chest, throat, breath, gasp
	Neck, shoulder, hands, palms, shins, ankle
	Face, forehead, eyes
	Instinct, sensation, panic
	Moment, time, minute, seconds, eternity
	Ceiling, hole, ridges
	Sound, noises, footsteps, rats, clang, scream

Darkness, brightness

Gust, breeze

Adjectives   **Dry**, ice-cold, tingling, lingering

Fast, fierce, feverish, desperate

Hundredth, thousandth

Grim, dreadful, frightful, horrific

Painful, torturous, excruciating

Echoing, scuttling

Verbs   **Knew**, realised, remembered

Felt, sensed, crawled, shuddered

Startled, shocked

Tensed, bit back, fought

Stopped, clenched, squeezed, banged, pounded, thudded, raced

Used to, adjusted, accustomed

Looked, saw, glanced, flickered, peered, darted, probed, searched, stared, watched, fixed

Bubbled, swallowed, gulped, choked, gasped, winced, gritted

Trickled, dripped, slithered

Felt, groped, floundered

Dug into, scratched, scraped, tore, ripped

PHRASES – NOUNS AND ADJECTIVES

* ★ Way out of the maze of tunnels
* ★ *Every time*
* ★ With every step . . .
* ★ For a dreadful moment
* ★ For the hundredth time
* ★ *Little sounds*
* ★ Painful gasps
* ★ Sound of echoing footsteps
* ★ Scuttling rats
* ★ *A fierce gust*
* ★ Touch of cobwebs on his face

- ⋆ Like the touch of a cold finger
- ⋆ *Dry throat*

PHRASES – VERBS

- ⋆ As he neared his destination . . .
- ⋆ As a shadow fell across the entrance to the tunnel . . .
- ⋆ By the time she had reached the bottom of the slope . . .
- ⋆ As the minutes stretched into an eternity . . .
- ⋆ *Heard nothing*
- ⋆ Listened for the clang of metal to start again
- ⋆ Dripped from the ceiling
- ⋆ Came out of nowhere
- ⋆ Getting closer by the minute
- ⋆ *Sensed that he wasn't alone*
- ⋆ Felt as if there were eyes everywhere
- ⋆ Could sense someone there
- ⋆ *As if the darkness was alive*
- ⋆ Breathing, watching, waiting
- ⋆ Following his every move
- ⋆ *Knew he had to think of something fast*
- ⋆ Tried desperately to remember the way they had come
- ⋆ Mind worked with feverish haste
- ⋆ Realised that the noises were only . . .
- ⋆ *Had a tingling sensation*
- ⋆ Had a lingering chill
- ⋆ As if someone was stabbing him with ice-cold needles
- ⋆ Was alert for the slightest sound or movement
- ⋆ Skin crawled at the thought of . . .
- ⋆ *Had to fight hard to . . .*
- ⋆ Bit back a sense of rising panic
- ⋆ Fought her body's natural instinct to run
- ⋆ *Remained on edge*
- ⋆ Was not sure whether it was a trap
- ⋆ Tensed his muscles in anticipation
- ⋆ Felt a sense of increasing apprehension
- ⋆ *Heart almost stopped*
- ⋆ Clenched in panic
- ⋆ Banged against his ribs
- ⋆ Raced faster and faster
- ⋆ *Swallowed, his throat suddenly dry*
- ⋆ Took his breath away
- ⋆ Choked back a gasp

* ⋆ Panic bubbled in his throat
* ⋆ Winced and gritted her teeth
* ⋆ Trickled down his forehead
* ⋆ *Took her eyes a moment to …*
* ⋆ Adjusted to the brightness
* ⋆ Glanced behind him constantly
* ⋆ Glanced back over her shoulder
* ⋆ Fixed his eyes on the opening
* ⋆ Stared at the dark tunnel
* ⋆ Peered out
* ⋆ Squinted into the darkness
* ⋆ Watched and waited
* ⋆ Darted left and right
* ⋆ Probed the tunnel for a flicker of movement
* ⋆ Looked up and down the tunnel
* ⋆ Saw a sight that sent a shiver down his spine
* ⋆ *Felt his way*
* ⋆ Floundered around in the dark
* ⋆ Groped through the darkness
* ⋆ *Rolled down his spine*
* ⋆ Landed on the nape of his neck
* ⋆ *Slithered to a halt*
* ⋆ Dared not move
* ⋆ Squeezed through the hole
* ⋆ Like they were descending into a volcanic pit
* ⋆ *Dug into the sharp ridges*
* ⋆ Scraped her shins
* ⋆ Ripped jagged cuts into her palms

SENTENCES

Little sounds startled him at first, until he realised that they were nothing but the scuttling of rats.

He had a lingering chill, as if someone was stabbing ice-cold needles into the back of his neck.

His skin crawled at the touch of cobwebs on his face.

He shuddered at the thought of groping through the darkness.

For a dreadful moment, he had a sense that they were descending into a volcanic pit.

Water dripped from the ceiling, sometimes landing on the nape of his neck and rolling down his spine like the touch of a cold finger.

She tensed, fighting her body's natural instinct to run, and was having to fight hard to do so.

Her mind was working with feverish haste as she tried desperately to remember the way out of the maze of tunnels.

As the minutes stretched into an eternity, Gail had to bite back a sense of rising panic. Still she dared not move.

She remained on edge, alert for the slightest sound or movement.

She heard nothing. But she knew she wasn't alone. She could sense it. It was as if the darkness was alive – breathing, watching, waiting.

His heart banging against his ribs, he squeezed through the hole.

With every step, his heart raced faster and more sweat trickled down his forehead.

Suddenly, all her senses were on high alert. She felt as if there were eyes everywhere, following her every move.

His stomach clenched in panic and he knew he had to think of something fast. The sound of echoing footsteps was getting closer by the minute.

It took her eyes a moment to adjust to the brightness.

He fixed his eyes on the opening and his muscles tensed in anticipation.

He stared at the dark tunnel, feeling a sense of increasing apprehension. He was still not sure whether it was a trap.

He watched and waited. Slowly, Rob peered out and squinted into the darkness.

His eyes darted left and right, probing the tunnel for a flicker of movement.

Tom kept glancing behind him, listening for the clang of metal to start again.

She looked up and down the tunnel for the hundredth time.

As he neared his destination, he saw a sight that took his breath away.

He swallowed, his throat suddenly dry.

A fierce gust came out of nowhere and took Rob's breath away.

She choked back a gasp as a shadow fell across the entrance to the tunnel.

Panic bubbled in his throat as suddenly he saw two, piercing, violet eyes like candles shining in the dark with some sort of strange power.

Every time her knees dug into the sharp ridges, Trish winced and gritted her teeth. By the time she had reached the bottom of the slope, her shins were scraped and jagged cuts had been ripped into her palms.

Part 2
Fantasy characters

4

Height and shape

As Monty approached the ancient oak, **he hoped he wasn't too late. With a sigh of relief**, he noticed that the air was filled with swirling, golden motes that flitted like moths above his head. For a moment, he thought he could see a head, just visible through the dancing sprites. He squinted into the sunlight, but **he was not sure**. It was too late to turn back now, so he slumped down onto the ground, leant against the tree and waited.

He didn't have to wait long before the sprites vanished, and he spotted the elf sitting on a branch, his round face and leaf-shaped ears now clearly visible. In the shadow of the tree, his skin seemed to have a purplish tinge. Monty scrambled to his feet, **beaming from ear to ear**.

When he spotted Monty, the elf opened his mouth in a wide smile and shinned down the tree. **Monty chuckled**. The elf was wearing his billowing, rainbow-coloured trousers and a sleeveless, leather vest he knew showed off the muscles on his arms and chest. His blond hair was even more wild than normal and fluffed out from his head like a dandelion.

WORDS

Nouns	**Faerie**, elf, dwarf, gnome, goblin, sprite, giant, troll
	Magician, wizard, witch, demon
	Build, stature
	Body, back, legs, hips, shoulders, chest, stomach, belly, arms, hands
	Chin, neck, face
	Skin, pouch, folds, muscles

Similes/ Metaphors	**Like a well-padded cushion**; as broad as a bull; built like a wrestler; as strong as an ox; straight-backed like a soldier; like a ballet dancer; like a china doll; scrawny like a plucked chicken; crooked as a walking stick; hunched like a question mark
Adjectives	**Short**, small, little, tiny, elfin, diminutive
	Average, medium
	Tall, big, large, lanky
	Huge, massive, enormous, gigantic, towering
	Broad, square, burly, strong, powerful, muscular
	Squat, stocky, thickset, sturdy, solid
	Chubby, plump, dumpy, pot-bellied, flabby, fleshy, obese
	Slim, slender, slight, petite, dainty
	Athletic, graceful, fast
	Bony, skinny, weedy, scrawny, spindly, skeletal, gaunt, emaciated, haggard
	Stooped, hunched, crooked, disfigured
	Upright, straight-backed
Verbs	**Towered**, loomed
	Stood, walked, moved, ran
	Shuffled, hobbled, limped
	Hung, wobbled, flapped, slumped
	Hunched, stooped

PHRASES – NOUNS AND ADJECTIVES

* ☆ Short and squat
* ☆ Tiny man with stumpy little legs
* ☆ Tiny, elfin girl
* ☆ Diminutive man, no taller than Kitty's forearm
* ☆ *Slim and dainty*
* ☆ Delicate form of a faerie
* ☆ Like a ballet dancer
* ☆ Small, slight body
* ☆ Petite, dainty sprite
* ☆ Like a china doll
* ☆ *Tall and lanky*

* Tall figure
* A towering figure
* An enormous giant of a man
* Legs like tree trunks
* *As broad as a bull*
* Burly men in chain mail
* A figure of menacing power
* Square shoulders
* Built like a wrestler
* Strong and muscular
* As strong as an ox
* Powerful, with broad, muscular shoulders
* Heavily muscled arms and legs
* *Athletic build*
* Tall and slender
* Straight-backed soldier
* *Short, pot-bellied dwarf*
* Small and dumpy
* Short and plump
* Like a well-padded cushion
* Like an enormous, skin pouch
* *Thin as a rake*
* Tall and scrawny
* Painfully thin
* Tall, thin stick of a man
* Scrawny like a plucked chicken
* Spindly arms and legs
* Emaciated and gaunt-looking
* *Crooked as a walking stick*
* Old and stooped
* Hunched like a question mark

PHRASES – VERBS

* Stood on his outstretched hand
* *Towered above him*
* Loomed over him
* Stepped out of the shadows
* *Wielded a double-edged sword*
* Air of someone who was used to being obeyed
* *Wobbled when he walked*
* Hung over his trousers
* *Built for speed*

* Walked gracefully
* *Looked like a walking skeleton*
* Looked like a gust of wind would bend him in half
* Hips stood out like tusks
* Skin hung in folds
* Looked as if he had shrunk inside his skin
* Stooped badly
* Could only walk with the aid of a staff

SENTENCES

The troll was an enormous giant of a man, with huge, powerful shoulders and legs like tree trunks.

He shivered as he looked up at the human pyramid towering over him.

The tiny, elfin girl was small enough to stand on Katie's outstretched hand.

The dwarf was short and plump, and cosy like a well-padded cushion.

For someone so short and dumpy, he was very fast on his feet.

The elf was slim and dainty.

She may have had a slim body, but she had broad, powerful shoulders and muscular arms and legs.

She was old, stooped and painfully thin. Every step, every painful shuffle, took every ounce of her strength.

An old, frail figure of a white-haired man stepped out from the shadows.

He was tall and scrawny like a plucked chicken, with horrid, bony hands and long, clawed fingers.

He was frail, crumpled and hunched like a question mark.

She stood erect, her head held high, with the air of someone who was used to being obeyed.

5

Head and face

WORDS

Nouns

Goblin, gnome, dwarf, elf, faerie, merfolk, mermaid, sprite, troll, wizard, witch, demon

Look, appearance, expression, mask

Forehead, brow, cheeks, cheekbones

Skull, jaw, temples, mouth, lip, eyes, eyebrows, nose, nostrils, hair

Skin, flesh, tissue, lumps, patches

Freckles, veins, shadows, bags

Wrinkles, lines, slashes, folds, flap

Sores, blisters, burns, bruise, wound, scabs

Scar, tattoo, mark, brand, pattern, design

Circles, crescents, moon, stars, pentagram, whorls, swirls, spirals, coils

Mole, wart

Neck, gills, scales, ridges

Snarl, squint, stare, smile

Width, length

Similes/ Metaphors

Long, pointed face like a raven; like a walrus; hamster cheeks; ferret-like features; bags like giant suitcases; face like thin, crumpled paper; like a china doll; as pale as bone; yellow skin like candle wax; as hard as leather; like beaten leather; like the skin of a lizard; creased like parchment; wrinkles like cruel slashes; cheekbones as sharp as blades; like a lightning bolt

Adjectives	**Oval**, round, square, rectangular, heart-shaped
	Wide, broad, full, plump, fleshy
	Narrow, thin, long, high, lean, bony, sunken, hollow
	Pointed, sharp, angular, vertical
	Drooping, sagging
	Pale, grey, ashen, white, pallid, deathly, colourless, translucent, sallow
	Red, pink, ruddy, bronze-coloured, sunburned, tanned, black, brown, olive-skinned
	Purple, blue, green, yellow
	Tough, leathery, rock-like
	Bald, smooth, shiny, slick
	Scarred, seared, burned
	Jagged, gnarled, crooked
	Skull-like, battle-scarred
	Huge, enormous
	Ugly, horrible, grisly, grotesque, hideous, deformed
	Strange, curious, haunted
	Angry, swollen, festering
	Dry, peeling, papery, flaking, blotchy
Verbs	**Looked**, gave, appeared, changed, transformed
	Scrubbed, glowed
	Lined, creased, wrinkled, crumpled
	Etched, inked, tattooed, marked, branded
	Hung, sagged, drooped
	Scarred, scabbed, marred, pocked
	Ran, covered, stretched, bisected, zigzagged
	Bulged, oozed
	Pulled, dragged, tugged, narrowed, fixed, closed, twisted, puckered, disfigured
	Burnt, scorched, singed, seared, blistered, shrivelled

PHRASES – NOUNS AND ADJECTIVES

* Square, wrinkly face
* Rectangular-shaped face
* *Narrow, pointed face*
* Oval, bony face
* Long, pointed face like a raven
* Thin, sunken face
* Sallow, scarred face
* Thin, angular face
* Hollow cheeks
* High cheekbones, as sharp as blades
* Ferret-like features
* *Broad, round face*
* Round-faced goblin
* Plump, hamster cheeks
* Wide, heart-shaped face
* *High, bald forehead*
* Bald, human-like face
* *Deathly pale*
* Pale like a porcelain doll
* Pale, almost colourless skin
* Pallid, deathly grey colour
* Pale, translucent skin
* Skin as pale as bone
* Yellow skin like candle wax
* Sickly, grey colour
* *Smooth, brown skin*
* Like beaten leather
* Tough, rock-like skin
* Ruddy, glowing face
* Round, pinkish look of a prize pig
* Deep, laughter lines in the corners of his eyes and mouth
* *Huge, pink mole*
* Enormous, wrinkled wart on her lip
* *Dark circles*
* Purple shadows under his eyes
* Bags like giant suitcases
* *Face like thin, crumpled paper*
* Papery dry skin
* Sharp, vertical lines
* Like the skin of a lizard
* Slick, green flesh as hard as leather
* *Black eye*

- Purple bruise
- Flaking skin
- Swollen, red blisters
- Mass of angry sores around his lips
- Festering, green wound
- *Thin, jagged scar*
- Hideous scar
- Ugly, wide scar
- Pattern of scars
- Crooked ridge of scar tissue
- Scarred cheekbones
- Scar above his left eyebrow
- Scarred and twisted lip
- Singed hair and eyebrows
- Mass of seared, scarred skin
- Blotched, horribly stretched skin
- Puckered, fleshy folds
- Gnarled lump of flesh
- *Black and white tattoo*
- Patterns of whorls, swirls, spirals and coils
- Circles, crescents, pentagrams
- Five-pointed star
- *Hideous, masked figure*
- Red executioner's mask
- *Flap of skin on her neck over her gills*

PHRASES – VERBS

- As his hood fell back a little way . . .
- Became visible across his cheek
- Only sign that she was from the merfolk
- Seemed to take on a purplish tinge
- *Looked like a fragile, china doll*
- Looked like a walrus
- *Creased like parchment*
- Formed slashes across his cheeks
- Stretched tight over her face
- Gave him a haunted look
- Gave him a skull-like appearance
- Sagged with wrinkles beneath her eyes
- *Sprouted two gristly hairs*
- *Etched on the side of his neck*
- Inked with a multitude of designs

- *Had a battle-scarred face*
- Ran from his temple to his jaw
- Ran across her cheek and eyebrow
- Stretched the width of his jaw
- Bisected his face
- Marred her face
- Pocked with craters
- Zigzagged across his head like a lightning bolt
- Ran the length of one side of his face
- Was just visible above his left eyebrow
- Covered his face and skull
- *Disfigured by fire*
- Oozed creamy pus
- Puckered around the wound
- Scorched into huge, pink patches
- Shrivelled into a twisted lump of flesh
- *Pulled into a permanent snarl*
- Closed in the puckered folds of a scar
- Pulled his eye into a curious squint
- Narrowed his eye in a drowsy squint
- Fixed his eye in a stare
- Twisted his lips
- Dragged his lip to meet his nostril
- Tugged her lip into a crooked smile

SENTENCES

She had a long, pointed face like a raven.

The huge, black mole on her upper lip sprouted two, long, gristly hairs.

The gnome had a very round face and plump, hamster cheeks.

The sun and wind had burned laughter lines into the skin around his eyes and mouth.

His face was oval-shaped and he had a high, bald forehead.

Her cheeks looked hollow and the flesh was wrinkled and sagging.

Her cheeks were so high, they formed two slashes across her face.

Bald, with a thin, angular face, his high, sharp cheekbones gave him a haunted look.

He was painfully thin and his face deathly pale.

Her skin was a sickly, grey colour.

His skin was yellow and creased like parchment.

He looked like a walrus with huge folds of sagging skin drooping from his face.

His pale skin was translucent. It was almost purple under her eyes and limp and sagging with wrinkles.

He had a sallow, scarred face and the haunted look of someone who had seen many battles.

With her pale, almost colourless skin, she looked like a fragile, china doll.

His colourless skin was stretched tight over his face and gave him a skull-like appearance.

The troll had tough, rock-like skin.

A sense of invincibility surrounded him.

A thin, jagged scar was just visible above his left eyebrow.

The skin around one eye had been pulled out of shape and gave her a curious squint.

As he pulled his hood back a little way, a dreadful scar became visible across his cheek.

A rough scar zigzagged like a bolt of lightning across the man's shaved head.

As the shadows lengthened, his skin seemed to take on a purplish tinge.

His face and bald head had been inked with a multitude of designs: whorls and swirls, spirals and coils, stars and moons.

Etched on the side of his neck in faded ink were two five-pointed stars.

The only sign that she was from the merfolk was a small flap of skin on her neck that covered her gills.

 **6**

Eyes

Nouns

Eyebrows, eyelashes, eyelids

Look, glance, stare

Power, force, energy

Anger, rage, fury, sadness, laughter

Sparks, flicker, gleam, glint

Light, flames, torchlight, candlelight

Similes/Metaphors

Like sparkling diamonds; like candles in the dark; as black as coal; as big as saucers; bulging eyes like a frog; like the eyes of a reptile; like a hawk; like dangerous slits; glinted like frost; as deadly as knives; as penetrating as an arrow; as if he was in a trance; like a rabbit caught in the headlights

Adjectives

Blue, sapphire, violet, grey, slate grey, flint grey, black, green, emerald green, brown, mud brown, leaf-coloured, tawny, hazel, gold-flecked, yellow

Red, blood-red, bloodshot, pink-rimmed

Dark, pale, oyster, transparent

Big, large, huge, enormous

Wide, bulging, gaping, staring, unblinking, unflinching

Round, oval, almond-shaped

Small, little, beady, narrow

Buggy, puffy, sunken

Beautiful, bright, brilliant, sparkling, gleaming, twinkling

Soft, gentle, calm, hypnotic

Laughing, impish, mischievous

Cold, icy, ice-cold, steely, piercing, flinty

Fiery, fierce, defiant, dangerous, forceful, quelling, evil, malevolent

Strange, mysterious

Verbs

Lined, rimmed, hidden, concealed

Lit, shone, beamed, danced, leaped, filled

Sparkled, gleamed, glittered, glowed, glinted

Narrowed, widened, bulged

Burned, flared

Looked, peered, glanced, swept, flickered, flicked, darted, stared, glared, drilled, bored, pierced

PHRASES – NOUNS AND ADJECTIVES

★ As black as coal
★ Button, black eyes
★ Velvet brown
★ Leaf-coloured eyes
★ Enormous, mud-brown eyes
★ Emerald green
★ Pale, sapphire blue
★ *As big as saucers*
★ Wide, almond-shaped eyes
★ Large, round eyes of an owl
★ Beautiful, grey eyes
★ Brown eyes, deep and mysterious
★ Like sparkling, blue diamonds
★ Twinkling green eyes
★ As bright as the jewel around her neck
★ Like candles in the dark
★ *Curly, black eyelashes*
★ Lashless lids
★ *Wide, bulging eyes like a frog*
★ Big, staring eyes
★ *Flinty grey*
★ Slate grey
★ Piercing grey
★ Staring, bright, green eyes

- Unflinching, oyster pale eyes
- Two, piercing, violet eyes
- *Yellow, wolf's eyes*
- Yellow, tawny, gold-flecked eyes
- Yellow and unblinking, reptilian eyes
- Eyes like a hawk
- Fierce owl-like glitter
- Fiery eyes
- *Pure white eyes*
- Milky with blindness
- *Red pupils*
- Blood-red eyes
- Swollen and bloodshot
- *Like dangerous slits*
- Small, buggy eyes
- Little, puffy brown eyes
- *Icy blue*
- Steely blue
- Cold and almost transparent
- Cold and dangerous
- *Sparks of anger*
- Dangerous gleam
- Malevolent glint
- Forceful glance
- As deadly as knives
- A flicker of rage behind his eyes

PHRASES – VERBS

- *Filled with sadness*
- Rimmed with bulging, blue veins
- Hidden beneath huge, bushy eyebrows
- *Danced with laughter*
- Lit up his face
- Beamed with warmth
- Flames leaped and danced in his eyes
- Glowed in the candlelight
- Shone like an owl's in the light
- Shone like diamonds
- Sparkled impishly
- Peered at her from beneath long lashes
- *Shone with a strange power*
- Blinded to the world

* *Drilled into him*
* Bored into him
* Fixed her with a murderous intent
* Darted rapidly
* Took in every detail, every move
* Swept over them
* Flickered like the eyes of a reptile
* *Stared as if he was in a trance*
* Transfixed like a rabbit caught in the headlights
* *Lit his eyes*
* Narrowed for a second
* Flared with ice-cold anger
* Glinted like frost
* Burned with a cruel light
* Gleamed with rage
* Burned with a malevolent fury
* *Glared unblinking*
* Gave him a quelling look
* As penetrating as an arrow
* Were alight with challenge
* Held his gaze defiantly
* *No one dared to meet his eyes*

SENTENCES

His emerald green eyes sparkled impishly.

Curly, ink-black eyelashes feathered her beautiful sapphire blue eyes.

Her mud-brown eyes were as big as saucers and twinkled with laughter.

The faerie's eyes were like sparkling, blue diamonds and glowed in the torchlight as bright as the jewel around her neck.

Her eyes were velvet brown and beamed with warmth like candles in the dark.

Until now, her face had been covered by the hood of her cloak. The first thing that they noticed was that her blue eyes were milky with blindness.

His cold eyes were as black as coal and rimmed with bulging blue veins.

Like a hawk, her eyes were yellow and unblinking and took in every detail, every move.

Her small, pig-like eyes were hidden in the folds of her wrinkled, drooping skin.

He had wide, bulging eyes like a frog that stared as if he was in a trance.

Kitty watched as his small, buggy eyes darted rapidly from one to the other.

Her cold, blue eyes were almost transparent and made Robert shiver as they drilled into him.

As his gaze swept over them, the goblin's steely, blue eyes glinted like frost, and no one dared to meet his eyes.

Her large, staring eyes burned with a cruel light.

His narrow, flint-grey eyes were like dangerous slits.

The elf looked at Katie with unflinching eyes. His mouth smiled, but his eyes did not.

The goblin's eyes burned with malevolent fury.

Her bright blue eyes burned into Tom's, defiantly holding his gaze.

His two, piercing, violet eyes shone with a strange power; the force of his glance as penetrating as an arrow.

7
Mouth, teeth and ears

SECTION 1 – MOUTH AND TEETH

WORDS	

Nouns
Molars, fangs, stumps

Lips

Smirk, sneer, leer, pucker, sulk, smile, grin

Similes/ Metaphors
Like polished pearls; like crumbling tombstones; jutted out like fangs; like an iron portcullis; glimmered like sharp crystals

Adjectives
Narrow, thin, tight

Wide, thick, full, fleshy, flabby, plump, big-lipped

Wrinkled, dry, flaking, drooping

Beaming, impish

Stern, mirthless, dreadful, menacing, sneering, reptilian

Toothless, gap-toothed

Straight, crooked, jagged

Rotting, crumbling

White, brown, yellow, stained, grey, gold-capped

Sparkling, polished

Verbs
Rose, curved, coiled

Chipped, cracked

Jutted, protruded

Glimmered, sparkled, glinted

Pressed, pursed, pinched, puckered, shrivelled

Bared, flashed, snapped, displayed, revealed, exhibited

Stuck, fixed

Clicked, babbled, jabbered, gabbled

PHRASES – NOUNS AND ADJECTIVES

* ⋆ Wide, full mouth
* ⋆ Wide mouth and thick lips
* ⋆ Narrow mouth and thin, pursed lips
* ⋆ Wrinkled, puckered mouth
* ⋆ Plump lips
* ⋆ Thick, fleshy, drooping lips
* ⋆ Thin, stern lips
* ⋆ Thin, pale lips
* ⋆ Dry, flaking lips
* ⋆ Pinched lips
* ⋆ *Reptilian smirk*
* ⋆ Dreadful, mirthless smile
* ⋆ *Impish grin*
* ⋆ Beaming smile
* ⋆ *Teeth like polished pearls*
* ⋆ Great sheet of white, polished teeth
* ⋆ Gold-capped molar
* ⋆ *Two, jagged rows of rotting, brown teeth*
* ⋆ Like crumbling tombstones
* ⋆ Stained, chipped teeth
* ⋆ Mouth full of yellow teeth
* ⋆ Crooked teeth and cracked, flaky lips

PHRASES – VERBS

* ⋆ Rose in a perfect curve
* ⋆ Curved upwards into a wide, beaming smile
* ⋆ *Chipped diagonally in half*
* ⋆ Worn to yellowing stumps
* ⋆ Jutted out like fangs
* ⋆ Snapped outward
* ⋆ Glinted when he opened his mouth
* ⋆ Gleamed like an iron portcullis
* ⋆ Flashed in his face
* ⋆ Glimmered like sharp crystals
* ⋆ Curved down over his lower lip

* *Pressed into a tight, thin line*
* Stuck in a sneering smile
* Stuck in a permanent pucker
* Turned down at the corners in a permanent sulk
* Bared in a reptilian leer
* *Clicked when she moved her lips*
* Babbled through broken teeth

SENTENCES

He was big-lipped and gap-toothed.

As she shook Rob's hand, the elf opened her mouth in a wide, beaming smile to reveal a line of teeth like white, polished pearls.

His teeth glimmered like sharp crystals.

Her lips were pale and pressed into a tight, thin line.

Her white teeth flashed in a dreadful, mirthless smile that sent a chill down his spine.

He had a wide, full mouth that seemed stuck in a sneering smile.

A gold-capped molar glinted when he opened his mouth.

Her fang teeth suddenly snapped outward.

His teeth jutted out like fangs and curved down over his lower lip.

His teeth had worn away into yellowing stumps that looked like crumbling tombstones.

Behind the thick, fleshy lips, she could see his stained and crooked teeth.

When he snarled, he revealed two jagged rows of brown, rotting teeth.

Behind his huge lips, the troll's teeth gleamed like an iron portcullis.

SECTION 2 – EARS

WORDS

Nouns	**Earlobes**, earrings
Similes/ Metaphors	**Huge, cauliflower ears**; droopy like a basset hound; like mini satellite dishes; veined like a cabbage leaf

Adjectives	**Big**, large, huge, enormous
	Small, tiny, bat-like, leaf-shaped
	Droopy, floppy, dangling
	Prominent, protruding, bulbous
Verbs	**Jutted**, projected, stretched, veined

PHRASES – NOUNS AND ADJECTIVES

- ★ Big, droopy ears
- ★ Pointed, leaf-shaped ears
- ★ Huge, cauliflower ears
- ★ Like a basset hound
- ★ Like mini satellite dishes
- ★ Small, bat-like ears
- ★ Enormous, dangling, bone earrings

PHRASES – VERBS

- ★ Jutted out on either side of his head
- ★ Attached to either side of his head
- ★ Veined like a cabbage leaf
- ★ Stretched into long, narrow ovals

SENTENCES

The elf had pointed, leaf-shaped ears.

The huge, cauliflower ears jutted out on either side of his head.

His ears were large and veined like a cabbage leaf.

Her earlobes were stretched into long, narrow ovals by enormous, dangling, bone earrings.

His ears were so big it looked like he had two mini satellite dishes attached to either side of his head.

8

Hair and facial hair

SECTION 1 – HAIR

WORDS	
Nouns	**Ponytail**, pigtail, braids, dreadlocks, plaits, bun
	Bob, crew cut, quiff, tuft, spikes
	Mane, strands, roots, lines, streaks
	Eyebrows, eyes, ears, face, temples, neck, shoulders, back
Similes/ Metaphors	**Like liquid copper**; as white and fluffy as cotton wool; shaggy, grey-streaked like a wolf; like a hedgehog; fluffed out like a dandelion; scalp gleamed like polished bone; like a tail; like a curtain; as if he had had an electric shock; as if it had been cut by a pair of shears
Adjectives	**Black**, dark, jet black, raven black
	Grey, grey-streaked, silver, grizzled, white
	Blond, yellow, straw-coloured, fair, golden, sandy, honey, bleached
	Red, copper, ginger, orange, carrot-coloured
	Brown, chestnut, auburn
	Dark, light
	Bald, shaven, hairless
	Shiny, glossy, sleek, silken, lustrous
	Thick, heavy, bushy
	Loose, tight
	Long, shoulder length, short, scalp-hugging

Curly, frizzy, wavy, straight, spiky

Thin, straggly, sparse, limp

Stiff, knotted, matted, tangled, twisted, shaggy, unruly, wild

Dry, greasy

Verbs

Dyed, streaked, bleached, coloured

Covered, receded

Shone, gleamed, shimmered

Cut, cropped, shaved

Wore, styled, combed, sleeked, swept back

Fell, flowed, streamed, cascaded, swung, trailed

Tied, held, pulled, yanked, dragged, gathered, fastened, secured, braided, plaited

Hung, fell, sprawled, hid

Drawn back, showed, revealed

Tousled, stuck up, spiked

PHRASES – NOUNS AND ADJECTIVES

* Raven black hair
* Auburn hair like liquid copper
* Thick and chestnut-coloured
* Long, straight, golden hair
* Shiny, black hair
* Thick, wavy, brown hair
* *Shaggy, grey-streaked hair like a wolf*
* Silver streak in the front of the elf's hair
* Long, limp, grey hair
* *White hair and eyebrows*
* Hair as white and fluffy as cotton wool
* *White, sparse hair*
* Silver tufts on either side of his round head
* Lines of pure white
* Few tufts of grizzled, jet black hair
* Bald apart from a few straggly strands of greasy limp hair
* Completely bald
* Perfectly symmetrical scars
* *Heavy rope of black hair*
* Loose ponytail

* Two, long pigtails
* Long, black ponytails
* Long, flowing, white hair
* Tight bun on top of his head
* *Military, scalp-hugging crop*
* Short to the nape of her neck
* *Limp, red hair*
* Long, greasy black hair
* Unruly, orange hair
* Shaggy, frizzy, matted hair
* Shaggy mane of grey hair
* A tangled, wild stack
* Like great, twisted roots

PHRASES – VERBS

* Streaked the witch's black hair
* Shimmered slightly in the torchlight
* Bleached of any colour
* *Shaved the front section of their heads*
* Scalp gleamed like polished bone
* Losing his hair
* Receding at the temples
* Covered his entire, bald head
* *Wore her hair short*
* Cut short like a hedgehog
* Cropped tight to his head
* Stuck up in a tuft at the front
* Fluffed out like a dandelion
* Sleeked back
* Swept back behind her ears
* Combed back from his face
* *Fell in a sheet down his back*
* Flowed over her shoulders
* Cascaded down his back
* *Gathered in a loose ponytail*
* Tied in plaits
* Hung down in two, long pigtails
* Swung rhythmically from side to side
* Hung behind him like a tail
* Trailed down her back
* *Pulled tightly in a bun*
* Fastened at the back with a silver spike

* *Hung down to hide his face*
* Sprawled over her shrivelled face
* Fell around his face like a curtain
* Fell into his eyes
* Hid her wild, black eyes
* *Drawn back from his face*
* Showed that the tips of his ears were slightly pointed
* *Hung in thin, limp strands*
* Stuck up madly in all directions
* Grew at odd angles out of her head
* As if he had had an electric shock
* Looked as if it had been cut by a pair of shears

SENTENCES

Her unruly, orange hair looked like flames blazing around her head.

His blond hair fluffed out from his head like a dandelion.

Her long, white hair hung in thin, limp strands on her shrunken head.

Her long, grey hair sprawled over her shrivelled face.

Her scalp gleamed like polished bone through her white sparse hair. Just visible through the limp strands were perfectly symmetrical scars.

The elf had jet black hair that fell in a sheet down his back.

The faerie's golden hair was cut short and spiked like a hedgehog.

Lines of pure white streaked the witch's black hair.

His long, golden hair fell around his face like a curtain.

Pulled back tight to her head, her auburn hair was fastened at the back with an enormous, silver spike.

As she walked, her shiny, blond hair swung rhythmically from side to side.

He wore his hair short and swept behind his ears.

When his hair was drawn back from his face, it revealed that the tips of his ears were slightly pointed.

His thick, wavy brown hair stuck up in a white tuft at the front.

Her hair had been shaved into a military, scalp-hugging crop.

He had a mop of dreadlocks like great, twisted roots.

The mop of shaggy, frizzy, matted hair hid her wild, black eyes.

SECTION 2 – FACIAL HAIR

WORDS

Nouns	**Stubble**, shadow, tufts, whiskers
	Beard, moustache, sideburns
	Face, chin, jaw, cheeks, neck, mouth, lip, nostrils, waist, knees
Similes/ Metaphors	**As if it had been cut by a hedge trimmer**
Adjectives	**Stubbly**, unshaven
	Thin, little, narrow, goatee
	Enormous, heavy, thick, bushy, bristling, drooping
	Long, flowing
	Dark, black, silver, silvery, white, grizzled, grey
	Scruffy, grimy, tangled, unkempt
	Neat, trim
Verbs	**Grew**, sprouted, poked
	Curved, twisted, drooped
	Spread, crept, covered
	Fell, dropped, reached
	Cut, trimmed

PHRASES – NOUNS AND ADJECTIVES

- ✶ Bushy sideburns
- ✶ Dark stubble
- ✶ Grizzled tufts of hair
- ✶ *Thin, little moustache*
- ✶ Enormous, heavy moustache
- ✶ Dark moustache on her upper lip
- ✶ *Goatee beard*
- ✶ Thick, bristly beard
- ✶ Long, silvery beard
- ✶ Flowing, grey beard
- ✶ *Grimy with food*

PHRASES – VERBS

* Spread across his cheeks
* Crept down his neck
* Covered most of his face
* Poked out from her chin
* Grew in grizzled tufts from ears and nostrils
* Curved around his face
* Twisted fiercely upwards
* Drooped over his upper lip and into his mouth
* Sprouted in all directions
* *Reached down to his knees*
* Fell to his waist
* *Looked as if it had been cut by a hedge trimmer*

SENTENCES

Grizzled hair sprouted in all directions from her chin.

His black beard covered so much of his face that only his nose and green eyes were visible.

His beard was tangled and grimy with food.

The gnome's bristling red beard reached down to his knees.

His long, silvery beard fell to his waist.

A flowing, white beard hung from his ancient, pale face.

9
Hands and fingers

WORDS

Nouns	**Nails**, claws, talons
	Veins, spots, dirt, grime
Similes/ Metaphors	**Hands like a shovel**; veins like rivers on a map; like claws; felt as cold as a skeleton
Adjectives	**Bony**, skeletal, long-fingered
	Wrinkled, swollen, lumpy
	Black, sharp, dirty
Verbs	**Covered**, blackened, encrusted
	Chipped, burnt, twisted
	Felt, shook, held
	Drummed, grabbed, grasped, lunged

PHRASES – NOUNS AND ADJECTIVES

- ★ On the palm of his hand
- ★ Long, elegant fingers
- ★ Enormous, shovel-like hands
- ★ Gloved hands
- ★ *Bony, long-fingered hands*
- ★ Wrinkled hands
- ★ Swollen, arthritic hands
- ★ Swollen, lumpy veins
- ★ Veins like rivers on a map
- ★ Burnt, twisted claw
- ★ Nails like claws

- ⭐ Claw-like hand
- ⭐ Blackened talons for nails
- ⭐ Long, curved, metal hooks
- ⭐ Dangerous weapons
- ⭐ *White pentagram*
- ⭐ Black mark
- ⭐ Faint silvery sheen
- ⭐ *Filthy with dirt and grime*

PHRASES – VERBS

- ⭐ Felt as cold as a skeleton
- ⭐ Sharpened to points
- ⭐ *Wore iron knuckle-dusters*
- ⭐ Tied to the end of her gloved fingers
- ⭐ *Held out a bony hand*
- ⭐ Drummed on the table impatiently
- ⭐ Grabbed her by the wrist
- ⭐ Grasped the air in front of him
- ⭐ Lunged at him
- ⭐ *Chipped and encrusted with dirt*

SENTENCES

The gnome's nails were chipped and encrusted with dirt.

Two, enormous shovel-like hands lunged at him.

She drummed her long, bony fingers on the table impatiently.

Old and swollen, her arthritic hands were covered in lumpy blue veins like rivers on a map.

She held out a bony hand, which felt as cold as a skeleton when he shook it.

His hand was a burnt, twisted claw, with blackened talons for nails.

He backed away from the claw-like hand that was grasping at the air in front of him.

Her nails were like claws, sharpened to points and dangerous weapons.

The small, white pentagram on the palm of his hand had a faint, silvery sheen.

Long, curved metal hooks had been tied to the ends of her gloved fingers.

10
Voice

Nouns	**Whisper**, murmur, wheeze, rattle
	Scream, yell, shriek
Similes/ Metaphors	**As smooth as silk**; as sweet as syrup; smooth like polished glass; like soft rain; muttered like a sleepwalker in a trance; as raspy as sandpaper; hissed like a snake; like the words were burning his mouth; as if someone had slashed his vocal cords; like the shriek of a seagull; cracked like a whip
Adjectives	**Loud**, big, strong, booming, thunderous, deafening, piercing, theatrical
	Quiet, soft, gentle, mild, calm
	Low, low-pitched, deep, guttural
	High, squeaky, shrill, high-pitched, harsh
	Dry, rough, hoarse, husky, croaky, scratchy, throaty
	Smooth, sweet, musical, lilting, chirpy, sing-song
	Pleasant, silky, creamy, sweet, syrupy
	Whining, smug, mocking, wheedling, simpering
Verbs	**Echoed**, vibrated, drilled, droned
	Cracked, croaked, clicked, gurgled, rasped
	Shouted, snarled, barked, growled
	Yelled, boomed, thundered, bellowed
	Hissed, whispered, muttered, mumbled, murmured
	Whined, whimpered, simpered, bleated

PHRASES – NOUNS AND ADJECTIVES

- ★ *Calm, deep voice*
- ★ Quiet, low-pitched voice
- ★ Like soft rain
- ★ *Chirpy, sing-song voice*
- ★ Lilting and musical
- ★ Soft, feathery whisper
- ★ *Big, booming voice*
- ★ Thunderous voice
- ★ Rich, theatrical voice
- ★ Deep, dark voice
- ★ *High-pitched, whining voice*
- ★ Wheedling tone
- ★ High-pitched whimper
- ★ Keening howl
- ★ Blood-curdling sound
- ★ Dry, cold, high-pitched voice
- ★ Cold, thin voice
- ★ Harsh and guttural
- ★ *Dry rattle in his voice*
- ★ Cracked, old voice
- ★ Throaty wheeze
- ★ Husky murmur
- ★ Croaky whisper
- ★ Loud, rasping rattle
- ★ Like a creaking gate
- ★ Raspy and ancient
- ★ Low, crackling voice
- ★ As raspy as sandpaper
- ★ Terrible, gravelly voice
- ★ Gruff voice with a thick accent
- ★ Hoarse voice
- ★ Harsh, raspy – barely above a whisper
- ★ *A malicious mockery*
- ★ Harsh with contempt
- ★ A razor edge to his voice
- ★ An edge to his voice
- ★ A hint of a threat
- ★ A hint of danger in her voice
- ★ Unmistakable menace in her tone

PHRASES – VERBS

- *Swirled out of its mouth*
- Issued from her mouth
- *Floated out of her mouth*
- As if she was speaking through velvet
- Made the words dance in his ears
- Had a calming effect
- *Echoed around the room*
- Like he was speaking through a loudspeaker
- Seemed to vibrate in his chest
- Carried through the room
- *Spoke in a wheedling tone*
- Protested in a shrill voice
- Gave a short bark of laughter
- Hissed like a snake
- *Spoke without a trace of an accent*
- Difficult to know where he was from
- Spoke in a tongue she did not recognise
- Difficult to understand
- *Found himself drifting off to sleep*
- Closed his eyes to block out . . .
- Bored into him like a drill
- Boomed in the stillness
- *Cracked like a whip*
- Dripped acid
- Sharpened his tone
- *Clicked in an odd way*
- As if someone had slashed his vocal cords
- Sounded like the scrape of a metal blade
- Muttered like a sleepwalker in a trance
- *Could talk to almost all species of animal*

SENTENCES

She had a soft, lilting voice and could talk to almost any species of animal.

The words floated out of her mouth as a soft, feathery whisper.

He had a lilting, musical voice that made the words of the spell dance in her ears.

Her voice fell like soft rain on the hushed atmosphere.

Her voice was quiet and soft but commanded attention.

His voice had become harsh and guttural.

For someone so small, he had a big, booming voice, which echoed around the room as if he was speaking through a loudspeaker.

As she babbled in the strange language, her voice became high and harsh, like the shriek of a seagull.

The voice that came from beneath the hood spoke in a tongue she did not recognise.

Foam gathered at either corner of his mouth.

There was an edge to his voice: a hint of a threat.

His voice cracked like a whip in the stillness.

The words he chanted were as raspy as sandpaper.

His voice was harsh, raspy, as if someone had slashed his vocal cords.

He whispered threats, hissing like an old, toothless snake.

She spat out the words like they were burning her mouth.

The dry, ancient voice chilled him to the bone.

11
Clothes, armour and weapons

WORDS	
Nouns	**Figure**, rider
	Furs
	Cloak, mantle, cape, robe, coat, overcoat, jacket, tabard
	Hood, cowl, cap, helmet, visor, mask, bascinet
	Armour, chain mail, hauberk, gauntlet, bracers, greaves, back plate, breast plate
	Trousers, breeches, hose, leggings
	Shirt, smock, tunic, vest, jerkin
	Boots, shoes, sandals, spurs
	Belt, strap, chain, cord, thong, lanyard
	Keys, horn
	Shield, iron boss, kite shield, staff
	Weapons, bow, arrows, quiver, scythe, mace, axe, spear, sword, knife, dirk, dagger, scimitar, blade
Similes/ Metaphors	**Like overlapping scales**; like alligator hide; like a snarling wolf
Adjectives	**Hessian**, canvas, cotton, leather, hide, wool, fur, bearskin
	Padded, quilted, stuffed, patchwork
	Sleeveless
	Vast, large, huge, cavernous, voluminous

Monk-like, hooded, cowled

Darkly clad, black-garbed, black, red, scarlet, blue, green, brown, silver, white, golden, gilt

Long, calf-length, flowing, billowing

Rich, luxurious, opulent, exquisite

Wooden, metal, steel, brass, iron, rivet-studded, steel-tipped, double-edged

Round, circular, conical, curved, straight, spiked

Short, small

Heavy, thick, wide

Polished, burnished

Verbs

Dressed, wore, clad, garbed, decked, attired, robed

Covered, wrapped, swathed

Hid, shrouded, obscured

Shaped, fashioned, moulded, sculpted, forged, designed, stamped, engraved

Outlined, emphasised, defined, accentuated

Edged, lined, trimmed, piped, fringed, decorated

Flared, flowed, streamed, swirled

Hung, reached, dangled, tapered

Attached, tied, belted, strapped, buckled, secured, fastened

Armed, bristled

Held, pushed, pulled, grasped, clutched, gripped, carried, hitched, hefted, slung, swung

Jutted, projected

Rattled, clinked, hissed, tapped

PHRASES – NOUNS AND ADJECTIVES

- ✶ Darkly clad figure
- ✶ Black-garbed rider
- ✶ Hooded, monk-like figure
- ✶ Dark, hooded robe
- ✶ Swirling cloak
- ✶ Cowled hood

* Black robe with a cavernous cowl
* Black, bearskin cloak
* Robe of pure wool
* Rich, scarlet mantle
* Blue cloak
* Long, black coat
* *Rough, hessian smock*
* Frock coat and knee boots
* Brown tunic and hose
* *Green hose*
* Leather breeches
* Brown leggings
* Billowing, black trousers
* *Padded overcoat*
* Quilted jacket
* White tabard
* *Sleeveless leather vest*
* Blue jerkin and hose
* Rivet-studded, leather jerkin
* *Chain mail shirt*
* Chain mail jacket
* Silver, mail shirt
* White armour like overlapping scales
* Cold, metal hauberk
* Burnished steel hauberks
* *Black, metal gauntlet*
* Mail hauberk, gauntlets, bracers and greaves
* *Soft, leather shoes*
* Calf-length boots
* Spanish riding boots
* Brass-studded boots
* Knife-like spurs
* Gilt spurs
* *A black, leather belt*
* War belt
* Wide, leather belt
* Thick chain
* Black cord lanyard
* *A bunch of heavy, iron keys*
* A horn on a leather thong
* *A great, engraved helmet*
* Conical helmet
* Full face mask
* Helmet visor

* *Like a snarling wolf*
* In the shape of a snake's head
* *Iron-bossed shield*
* Thick, round shield
* *Staff of gnarled wood*
* Curved bow
* A quiver of arrows
* War axe
* Short-handled axe
* Spiked mace
* Heavy, iron mace
* Short sword with a black, leather grip
* Double-edged sword
* Short, stabbing sword
* Small, silver dirk
* Ivory-sheathed scimitar
* Crescent-shaped blade

PHRASES – VERBS

* Dressed in . . .
* Dressed all in black
* Dressed head to foot in metal armour
* Clad in mail
* *Glistened like circles of polished steel*
* Looked like alligator hide
* Outlined every muscle
* *Clad in a white robe*
* Wrapped in furs
* Swathed his body
* Edged with fur
* Flared out behind her
* Swirled around him in the rising wind
* Pulled over her head
* Hitched about his shoulders
* Belted at the waist
* *Reached to her knees*
* Hung to his knees
* Tapered in at the ankles
* *Tied with leather thongs*
* Rattled on her leather boots
* *Impossible to see his face*
* Covered her entire face

* Almost hidden by its cavernous cowls
* Covered his head and most of his face
* Partly obscured his face
* Shrouded beneath her cowl
* *Carried a helmet decorated with antlers*
* Wore a helmet in the shape of . . .
* Lost behind a visored helmet
* Fitted with a visor that ringed his eyes
* Fashioned in the likeness of . . .
* Transformed her into a figure of menacing power
* *Hung from his waist*
* Slung from their belts
* *Carried a scythe*
* Gripped in his hands
* Swung on their hips
* Jutted at his side
* Tied onto his leather belt
* Hung from a wide, leather belt
* Sheathed at their waists
* Strapped around his waist
* Slung on their backs
* Attached to his back
* Strapped to her back
* Buckled across his shoulder
* Fastened around his chest
* *Wore a circular shield on his back*
* Carried a round shield
* Hefted a round, wooden shield
* Stamped with her clan crest
* Carried a white staff
* *Armed with swords and daggers*
* Bristled with weapons
* Clutched all manner of weapons
* Pulled a dagger from . . .
* Pushed his knife into the top of his boot
* Carried a stabbing dirk
* Carried a spiked mace
* Held their steel-tipped spears vertically
* Grasped a lance in his right hand
* Dangled his axe from one hand
* Hung a sword on one side and a war axe on the other
* *Clinked as he moved*
* Tapped against his thigh as he walked
* *Swung their swords with a swift, frightening force*

SENTENCES

She wore billowing, black trousers that tapered in at the ankles, a sleeveless, leather vest and brass-studded boots.

He wore a rough, hessian smock, belted at the waist. Strapped to his back was a circular shield stamped with his clan crest.

The darkly clad figure was shrouded beneath his cowl, so it was impossible to see his face. No part of him was visible except the dark boots that showed beneath the hem of his robe, but every time he moved Kitty heard the clink of a chain mail shirt.

She was dressed head to foot in white armour. On her left arm she wore a silver, metal gauntlet. Flaring out behind her was a vivid, scarlet cloak.

He wore leather breeches and a jerkin that reached to his knees and was belted at the waist. Slung from the wide, black belt were a bunch of heavy iron keys and a horn on a leather thong.

She wore chain mail under her dark robe that had a hood she could pull over her head.

From the top of her red, riding boots, she pulled a small, silver dirk.

They were armoured beneath their fur-lined cloaks.

Their faces were lost behind visored helmets fashioned in the likeness of snarling wolves.

Hanging from their left hips were crescent-shaped blades.

Part 3
Magic

12
Magical implements and ingredients

As he entered the clearing, Alfie looked up at the dark shadows between the trees and **got the weirdest feeling: a feeling of unease and a sense of a threatening, malignant presence**.

Waiting for them by the ancient oak was a darkly clad figure. Shrouded beneath the hood of her cloak, it was impossible to see her face. **All of a sudden, Alfie felt it: the questing eye. Now, he was in no doubt that they were in great danger. It was like icy fingers had closed around his heart. But he was too slow and too late. Before he could react**, she turned sharply towards him, letting her hood fall back. **Alfie gasped** and stopped dead in his tracks. Her scalp gleamed like polished bone through her sparse, white hair. Just visible through the limp strands were two perfectly symmetrical pentagrams tattooed onto her scalp.

With surprising speed, she drew her wand, grinned menacingly at them, and then, hissing like a toothless snake, pointed it at Alfie. **He uttered an ear-splitting wail** and clutched his head with both hands. His knees buckled beneath him and he slumped to the floor.

Rob, Kitty and Andrew exchanged a brief glance, and nodded. With as much force as they could muster, they hurled light bolts at the witch.

The next few minutes unfolded in horrifying slow motion. A cone of air howled from where she had stood, darkening the air with billowing clouds of swirling, black vapour. All around them, the trees were bending, arching from side to side, as if caught inside a whirlwind. When the wind had stopped, everything went very still and the forest became unnaturally quiet. There was nothing but a pile of dust.

WORDS

Nouns

Elements, earth, air, fire, water

Magic, force, energy, spells, enchantments, curse, hex, potions, ointments, poisons

Knowledge, power, instrument, tools, weapon

Sword, spear, pentacle, wand

Staff, whip, dagger, athane

Shaft, blade, pommel, hilt, tip

Cloak, mantle, hood

Locket, necklace, chain, pendant, bracelet, watch, amulet, relics

Shells, crystal, gem, jewel

Diamond, ruby, sapphire, emerald, pearls, amethyst, onyx, topaz, coral

Book, manuscript, scroll, parchment, vellum, cover, pages, seal

Box, chest, lid, tray, hinges, sides, base, bottom, rim

Scenes, image, shapes, figures, patterns, symbols, mark, brand, tattoo, runes, glyphs, sigils, hieroglyphics

Footprint, moon, crescent, star, scarab beetle, seahorse, eye, snake, tree, cross

Words, lines, names, code, poem, rhyme

Mirror, frame, orb, crystal, pendulum, surface, reflection

Pebbles, bones, yarrow sticks

Light, candles, lamp, censer, mist, glow, haze, fire, flames, smoke, incense, oil, mercury

Circle, cone, pentagram, hexagram, octagon

Chalk, wax, iron, salt

Bottle, phial, cup, chalice, goblet, cauldron, bowl, pestle, mortar, sickle, knife, scales, tripod

Ingredients, elements, recipe

Substance, powder, fluid, liquid, brew, draught, concoction, elixir, tincture

Tree, branch, stump, bark

Oak, willow, birch, hawthorn, rowan, alder, rosewood, mahogany, ebony

Plants, herbs, roots, leaves, flowers, seeds, berries

Blood, entrails, gall, spleen, liver, bile, slime, juice, eggs, eyes, ears, nail, claws, talons, fangs, horn, feathers, quills, tongue

Snake, serpent, viper, fish, eel, jellyfish, bat, cormorant, eagle, hawk, vulture, albatross, quail, chicken, rat, porcupine, ox, bullock, lynx, worm, leech, slugs, snails, caterpillars, beetles, dragon, unicorn, phoenix

Egg white, lard, lettuce, leeks, garlic, vinegar, pepper

Water, wine, pomegranate juice, lemon, orange

Sandalwood, myrrh, frankincense, lavender, rose, vanilla, chamomile, jasmine, peppermint, mint

Basil, rosemary, oregano, parsley, dill, caraway, sage, fennel, clover, nettles, daisy

Cinnamon, ginger, cloves

Henbane, hemlock, wolf's bane, monkswood, belladonna (deadly nightshade), hellebore

Mandrake root, bryony, myrtle, mugwort, wormwood, angelica, vervain, acacia, liquorice

Similes/ Metaphors

Like a huge, almond-shaped eye; stones like human statues; like a parsnip; hung like a shimmering, omnipresent eye; pulsed like a heartbeat; like a river of energy; like a sudden, brief rainbow after a sun-shower; dry and papery like a snakeskin

Adjectives

Universal, omnipresent

Soothing, spellbinding, hypnotic

Large, huge, massive, enormous

Tiny, small, minute, minuscule

Long, short, thin, thick, light, heavy

Single, several, many, numerous

Outer, inner

Heart-shaped, almond-shaped, eye-shaped, disc-shaped, vine-shaped, bell-shaped, spindle-shaped, helmet-shaped

Rounded, curved, smooth, concentric

Twisted, crooked

Blue, sapphire, turquoise, purple, violet, green, emerald, red, ruby-red, blood-red, scarlet, golden, gilded, yellow, orange, amber, brown, black, white

Pale, faint, dim

Bright, vivid, brilliant, prismatic

Silver, gold, bronze, jewel-encrusted, steel, iron, metal, wooden, oak, rosewood, ebony, leather, silk, enamel, glass, crystal, wax, beeswax

Cold, icy, tingling

Hot, pulsing, burning, scorching

Shiny, glossy, glittering, shimmering, flickering, glinting, swirling

Curious, strange, eerie, mystical, mysterious, enchanted, mythological

Plump, fleshy, juicy

Sweet, exotic, tropical

Bitter, sharp, acidic, tart, sour

Rank, foul, rotten, rancid, unpleasant, repulsive, offensive

Medicinal, healing, therapeutic

Harmful, toxic, deadly, fatal, noxious, poisonous

Verbs

Hummed, buzzed, throbbed

Purified, cleansed

Drew, painted, chalked, carved, engraved, etched, stamped, scorched

Arranged, formed, positioned

Ran, stretched, spread, spanned, covered

Hung, dangled, swung

Held, clutched, lifted, moved, passed, shook, tossed, cast, threw, wrapped

Felt, touched, tapped

Found, located, discovered

Read, interpreted, translated, decoded, divined, foresaw, prophesied

Waited, hesitated, hovered

Lit, shone, glinted, pulsed, glowed, burned, blazed, sparkled, shimmered, blinded

Heated, smouldered

Peeled, grated, chopped, diced, minced, sliced, mashed, crushed, ground, squeezed

Added, sprinkled, tossed

Mixed, stirred, swirled, shook

Boiled, bubbled, simmered

Hissed, spat, sputtered, gave off

Sieved, strained, poured, filled, sealed

Applied, rubbed, drank, swallowed

PHRASES – NOUNS AND ADJECTIVES

* In the centre of the clearing
* Within the ring of stones
* In the outer rim of the circle
* Above the entrance
* Beside the door
* Around the edge of . . .
* Inside the pentagram
* At each octagon angle
* At the bottom of the . . .
* In his right hand
* On the table
* Inside the bottle
* Beside the symbol of . . .
* *Two, massive, black boulders*
* A ring of standing stones
* Huge, altar stone
* Curious collection like human statues
* *A black pentagram*
* A red hexagram
* Concentric circles
* *Like a river of energy beneath his feet*
* A cone of power
* *Numerous black candles*
* Silver ring of red candles
* Circle of green, beeswax candles
* Yellow candle for air in the east

- ★ Red candle for fire in the south
- ★ Blue candle for water in the west
- ★ Green candle for earth in the north
- ★ *A silver chain*
- ★ A gold bracelet
- ★ A disc-shaped bronze amulet for protection
- ★ Blue crystal pendulum
- ★ A black, onyx pendulum
- ★ A diamond like a huge, almond-shaped eye
- ★ Glittering crystal of blue topaz
- ★ Single, amethyst crystal
- ★ *Sets of crossed keys*
- ★ Eye of Horus
- ★ Scarab beetle
- ★ Cross of Hermes
- ★ Silver seahorse
- ★ Infinity snake
- ★ The tree of life
- ★ An eye-shaped tattoo
- ★ A black mark
- ★ A witch's brand
- ★ Birthmark like some kind of sigil
- ★ *Invisibility cloak*
- ★ Shimmering silk of the silver cloak
- ★ Brightly coloured feathers
- ★ *Nothing but a faint ripple in the air*
- ★ Like a sudden brief rainbow after a sun-shower
- ★ *Black mirror*
- ★ Surface of the pond
- ★ *A handful of smooth bones*
- ★ Slightly longer than a finger
- ★ *Purifying sage incense*
- ★ Rosemary water
- ★ *Cover of the thick, leather bound book*
- ★ Dry and papery, like a snakeskin
- ★ Blank scroll
- ★ Black, wax seal in the shape of a scarab beetle
- ★ Words of the ancient rhyme
- ★ *Twisted shaft of his ebony wand*
- ★ Crooked, bronze staff
- ★ Glass blade of the tiny dagger
- ★ Glass orb of swirling vapours
- ★ *Heavy scent of incense in the air*
- ★ A sharp stench of old ink and dust

* Musty parchment
* Tropical scent
* Sweet but deadly fragrance
* Incense of mercury
* Offensive smell
* *Medicinal herbs and plants*
* Exotic, noxious flowers
* Vivid orange flowers
* Clusters of dark blue flowers
* Helmet-shaped flowers
* *Green, glossy leaves*
* Vine-shaped leaves
* Prickle-like hairs
* *Black, plump, shiny berries*
* Glossy, orange berries the size of peas
* *Fleshy, spindle-shaped roots*
* Thick, bell-shaped roots
* Large, brown root like a parsnip
* *A stoppered bottle*
* A huge, black cauldron
* Highly decorated, silver cauldron
* *Numerous, mythological creatures*
* Stags, boars, winged horses
* With bright green, glass eyes
* Gilded shapes and symbols
* *Handles of the cauldron*
* Bronze mounts on the rim
* In the shape of seahorses
* *With his pestle . . .*
* With his dagger . . .
* An ash twig
* Golden eagle feather
* Phoenix feather
* *Rest of the ingredients*
* A couple of eel eyes
* Several quail eggs
* Seven bats' ears
* Crushed ginger roots
* Pomegranate juice
* Horehound juice
* Stinging nettles
* Boar bile, henbane, garlic and vinegar
* Powdered snake fangs and sliced bats' eyes
* Fish eyes, viper's tongue and sesame seeds

* Ground, rook talons, porcupine quills and bark from a rowan tree
* Sliced caterpillars, dried figs, rat spleens, minced daisy roots, sliced worms, leech juice
* Lard, clover, rose petals, soot, mugwort, vervain, benzoin tincture
* Sandalwood incense, myrrh, orris root, frankincense powder
* Dill, anise, caraway, sage, rose petals, parsley, wormwood, angelica
* Willow tree bark, vanilla extract, cinnamon, almonds
* Liquorice, willow, roses, fennel, cinnamon, ginger, cloves, cormorant's blood, white and black pepper
* Boar bile, wild lettuce, henbane, bryony, mandrake root, hemlock and vinegar, water
* Water, mistletoe berries, horned slugs and dragonfly legs
* *Amber liquid*
* Dried, blue powder
* Bright green
* A black substance
* A dark green liquid

PHRASES – VERBS

* Hummed with magic
* Could feel the enchantments
* *Cast salt around the edge of the . . .*
* Painted on the floor
* Drawn in yellow-orange chalk
* Stood in a chalk circle
* *Stretched the width of the . . .*
* Arranged in a figure of eight
* Filled with hieroglyphics and interlocking patterns
* *Hung from the ceiling*
* Swung from the ceiling
* Held dozens of red candles
* Hung like a shimmering, omnipresent eye
* *Sat on the table at her side*
* Towered above him
* Rippled in the breeze
* Swooped through the air around it
* *Dangled a black, onyx pendulum*
* Passed the pendulum through the smoke
* Purified the crystal in the sage incense
* Focused on the circle
* Used her power to move the pendulum around the circle
* Held her gaze as hypnotically as a flame

- *Held a handful of bones between his palms*
- Shook the bones in his hands
- Tossed the bones onto the mat of animal hide
- *Used his pendulum to divine the future*
- Read the formation of the scattered yarrow sticks
- Divined the outcome from the pattern of the thrown bones
- *Scorched into the centre*
- *Carved around the sides*
- Stamped with the Eye of Horus
- *Knew what was contained in . . .*
- Needed the Sigillum Mysteriorum
- Translated the code that had been written in symbols
- Was reluctant to release its knowledge and power
- *Hovered over the book*
- Touched the cover
- Crackled and flicked open
- Sent a yellow mist wafting into the air
- *As his birthmark touched the . . .*
- Tingled and pulsed
- Felt a hot, tingling sensation
- Pressed his birthmark onto the seal
- Burned as if something hot had been pressed on his tattoo
- *Set in the pommel of the sword*
- Glinted from the tip of the handle
- *Wore a bronze amulet*
- Carried a staff tipped with a crystal
- Supported himself with a curiously carved staff
- Directed the force with his ebony wand
- *As he lifted the cloak around his shoulders . . .*
- Wrapped the cloak around her . . .
- Disappeared from sight
- Vanished in a prismatic effect
- *As she swept her hand in a slow arc . . .*
- When he held the blade up to the flame . . .
- *Sparkled with a purple haze*
- Filled with brilliant white, swirling vapours
- Cast a soft glow across the room
- Gave off no more light than a handful of embers
- Gave off a dim illumination
- Surrounded by a white light
- Cast blood-red light onto the star
- Flared bright orange at the edges
- *Heated by a lamp containing . . .*
- Smouldered in a censer

- ✳ Burned to give off a scent
- ✳ Drifted through the air
- ✳ *Filled with every kind of plant*
- ✳ Found the plant eventually
- ✳ Knew that the plant could cause . . .
- ✳ *Peeled the fleshy root*
- ✳ Grated the ginger
- ✳ Sliced the fennel
- ✳ Ground the snake fangs into a fine powder
- ✳ Squeezed the juice from the . . .
- ✳ Mixed with . . .
- ✳ Mixed together the . . .
- ✳ Added the berries to the mixture
- ✳ Added a pinch of . . .
- ✳ Stirred the mixture three times anticlockwise
- ✳ *Left the potion to boil for ten minutes*
- ✳ Swirled, whirled, boiled
- ✳ Bubbled in the cauldron
- ✳ Filled with bubbling, amber fluid
- ✳ Bubbled over the sides of the golden chalice
- ✳ *Mixed with water*
- ✳ Added to a glass of wine
- ✳ *Sieved through a cloth*
- ✳ Poured into a unicorn horn
- ✳ Filled a phial with vivid, blue liquid
- ✳ Sealed with wax
- ✳ *Made into an ointment*
- ✳ Applied with a phoenix feather
- ✳ Rubbed slug slime onto the burn

SENTENCES

In the centre of the clearing was a curious collection of black standing stones that looked like human statues. Within the ring, the air hummed with magic. Rob could feel the enchantments like a river of energy flowing beneath his feet.

Numerous black candles had been arranged in a figure of eight that stretched the width of the room.

A black pentagram, filled with hieroglyphics and interlocking patterns, was painted on the floor. Hanging from the ceiling was a silver ring holding dozens of red candles that cast blood-red light onto the star.

The black mirror had sets of keys carved around the sides, and hung like a shimmering, omnipresent eye beside the door.

In his right hand, he held a silver chain from which dangled a black, onyx pendulum. Slowly, he passed it through the smoke from the sage incense to purify it.

The surface of the pond rippled as the breeze swooped through the air around it. Very gradually a shadowy outline became visible.

The scent of incense was heavy in the air. The symbol of the tree of life sat on the table at Kitty's side. Beside it were a handful of smooth bones, slightly longer than a finger.

To read the code written in the symbols, Katie knew she needed the Sigillum Mysteriorum.

The cover of the thick, leather bound book was dry and papery, like a snakeskin. A black mark, a witch's brand, had been scorched into the centre.

Kitty's hand hovered over the book, reluctant to release the knowledge and power she knew was contained in its pages.

As his hand touched the cover, the pages crackled and flicked open, sending a yellow mist wafting into the air. With it came a sharp stench of old ink, dust and musty parchment.

At the bottom of the blank scroll was a black, wax seal in the shape of a scarab beetle.

Above the entrance was an eye-shaped tattoo.

His birthmark looked like a sigil of some kind. Sometimes it tingled and pulsed, or burned as if something hot had been pressed on it.

Tom lowered his forearm and pressed his birthmark onto the seal. As he did so, the words of the ancient rhyme slowly appeared.

The crooked, bronze staff was about the size of a man, and towered above him.

A glittering crystal of blue topaz had been set in the pommel of the sword.

Above the twisted shaft of his ebony wand, a single amethyst crystal glinted from the tip of the handle.

The glass blade of the tiny dagger sparkled with a purple haze when he held it up to the flame.

A glass orb filled with brilliant white, swirling vapours swung from the ceiling.

As she swept her hand in a slow arc, the glittering crystal on top of his staff glowed. It gave off no more light than a handful of embers, but it was enough to guide her through the passage.

Around her neck, she wore a disc-shaped, bronze amulet stamped with the Eye of Horus.

The silk of the silver cloak shimmered as Rob wrapped it around his shoulders.

The brightly coloured feathers of her invisibility cloak fluttered in a prismatic effect as she lifted it around her. As she disappeared from sight, there was nothing but a faint ripple in the air.

The enormous garden was filled with every kind of medicinal herb and plant she could imagine.

From the open door of the glass house, the tropical scent of the vivid orange flowers drifted through the air – its fragrance sweet and deadly, exotic and noxious.

Eventually, Tom found the clusters of dark blue flowers. He knew that the plant could cause paralysis, so he took great care snipping the helmet-shaped flowers.

A huge, black cauldron filled with bubbling black fluid sat on a three-legged tripod.

The handles of the cauldron were shaped like seahorses.

With his pestle, he ground the green, glossy leaves into a fine powder, and then squeezed the juice from the black, shiny berries and added them to the mixture.

Rob sliced the fleshy, spindle-shaped root and added it to the cauldron, along with the boar bile, henbane, garlic and vinegar. Finally, he added the powdered snake fangs and sliced bats' eyes, stirred the mixture three times anticlockwise and left it to boil for ten minutes.

In his hand, he clasped a phial filled with vivid, blue liquid.

On the table was a stoppered bottle that had been sealed with wax. Inside the bottle he could see a black substance swirling, whirling, boiling.

13
Magical interaction and reaction

SECTION 1 – INTERACTION: ACTION

WORDS

Nouns

Air, wind, breeze, gust, clouds, storm, dust

Spell, enchantment, hex, vision, prophecy, transformation

Mind, thoughts, will, focus, concentration, trance

Movement, motion, gesture, flick, wave

Force, energy, power, resistance, shield

Circle, triangle, star, pentagram, octagon

Lines, shapes, symbols, signs, marks, sigils, runes, glyphs, hieroglyphics, birthmark, tattoo

Paper, parchment, vellum, scroll, ink, chalk

Sword, dagger, blade, tip

Staff, wand, stick, twigs

Bones, feathers, eyes

Box, casket, chest

Stone, altar, tomb, door, floor

String, rope, ribbon, chains, shackles, bonds, lock, knot

Cauldron, pot, bowl, phial, glass, jar

Ointment, potion, powder, liquid, mixture

Water, blood, wine

Bones, fangs, horn

Lard, suet, slime, salt, pepper

Plants, herbs, nettles, leaves, roots, flowers, berries

Creatures, snakes, bats, beetles, dragon, phoenix, cyclops

Light, candles, torch, lamp

Smell, scent, incense, vapour, smoke

Mist, haze, fog, shimmer, glow, sparks, bolt, flames, fire

Language, tongue, words, line, poem, names, voice, breath, call, chant, hum, whisper, roar, bellow

Arms, forearm, hands, wrist, palms, fist, knuckles, fingers, fingertips, thumb, nails, legs, feet

Head, eyes, mouth, forehead

Similes/ Metaphors

Like ripples on the surface of a lake; like a captured storm cloud; like a tight band around his chest; like water splashed on hot iron; red-hot like a poker; like heat from a furnace; spun slowly like a top

Adjectives

Old, ancient, archaic

Secret, hidden, concealed, invisible

Foreign, strange, alien, bizarre, curious, outlandish, mysterious, sinister

Protective, defensive

Three, seven, ten, twelve

Three-fingered, sharp-clawed

Quick, swift, rapid, deft, urgent

Limp, loose, slack, droopy, floppy

Soft, low, muffled, faint, distant, indistinct, inaudible

Gentle, calming, soothing

Deep, booming, loud, harsh, gruff, rasping, guttural

Pale, white, white-hot, fiery, red, blue, sapphire, turquoise, green, emerald, dark green, orange, amber, purple, violet, silver, black

Fluttering, flickering, swirling, whirling, shimmering, crackling

Verbs

Drew, wrote, scribbled, chalked, painted, carved, engraved, etched

Stood, braced, turned, spun, twirled, circled, pivoted, danced

Stretched, extended, reached out, spread, straightened

Motioned, gestured, waved, clapped, snapped

Placed, arranged, formed, touched, lay, ran, rubbed, folded, tied, sealed

Held, gripped, clutched, clasped, pressed, pushed, pulled, closed, opened

Lifted, raised, twirled, swung, flicked, pointed, aimed

Tapped, rapped, knocked, struck, rang, sounded

Tossed, flung, threw, cast, sent, hurled, launched

Lit, ignited, sparked, burned

Shot, erupted, flashed, blazed, glowed

Stamped, cracked, shattered

Bowed, lowered, rolled, tilted

Shut, focused, delved, dived, concentrated, pictured, imagined, willed, summoned

Felt, blurred, tingled, buzzed, hissed

Spoke, uttered, recited, chanted, whispered, hummed, muttered, mumbled, murmured, babbled, rambled, called out, roared, bellowed

Repeated, echoed, resonated, reverberated

Crushed, ground, peeled, sliced, chopped, stabbed, squeezed

Added, mixed, stirred, swirled

Melted, boiled, simmered, heated

Cooled, poured, stored

Rubbed, applied, drank, swallowed

Gave off, discharged, released, emitted

Rose, leaked, oozed, slid, belched, spouted, filled

Turned, changed, altered, transformed

Created, produced, conjured, appeared, parted, hid, screened, disappeared, vanished

Adverbs   **Anticlockwise**, clockwise

PHRASES – NOUNS AND ADJECTIVES

* In the rim between the two circles
* *Around her knuckles*
* From her fingers
* *A rapid flick of her fingers*
* With a quick, fluttering movement of his hand
* *Invisible shield*
* Bubble of protective energy
* *Flow of energy*
* Strange, static energy
* *Pale glow*
* Purple sparks of magic
* A bolt of red light
* Ball of blue electrical bolts
* Beam of violet light
* Small, flickering flame
* Thin tendrils of coloured fire
* Spindle of emerald fire
* Ball of white-hot flames
* Sizzling, crackling shaft of purple energy
* Like heat from a furnace
* Like blue ripples on the surface of a lake
* Crackling shaft of blue energy
* Rippling sheet of green fire
* *Sinister whispers*
* Gentle hum
* Ancient language
* Foreign tongue
* Strange language
* Secret name
* Long, strange name
* Inaudible words
* Garbled words
* Words from old magic
* An old, archaic language, long forgotten

PHRASES – VERBS

* Chalked two circles on the floor
* Drew strange symbols like hieroglyphics
* Painted a six-pointed star
* Used her athane to carve a rune on the . . .

* Pierced the circle with two parallel lines
* Tattooed on her forearm
* *Formed a triangle with the three black candles*
* Lit the candles
* Scribbled George's name on the parchment
* Folded the paper three times
* Tied the paper with a piece of ribbon
* Sealed the parchment in a casket
* Placed the casket in the centre of the triangle
* Rang the bell three times
* *Held the length of leather in his hand*
* Tied three knots down its length
* As he finished tying the last knot . . .
* Whirled the wind into strange clouds
* Billowed clouds of dust into the air
* *Tossed the vulture bones into the circle*
* Stamped on the bones
* Cracked and splintered the bones
* *Crushed the herbs into a fine powder*
* Ground the snake fangs into a powder
* Sliced the mandrake roots
* Stabbed the tip of his blade into his thumb
* Melted the . . . in the cauldron
* Added the ground herbs and powder
* Added three drops of . . . to the . . .
* Took out a handful of green powder from her wallet
* Opened the phial of dragon's blood
* Squeezed two drops of blood into the bowl
* Let a few drops of blood fall into the water
* *Swirled the mixture with an ash twig*
* Swirled the mixture around
* Stirred over a high heat for ten minutes
* Stirred the bubbling liquid three times anticlockwise
* *Held his hand over the bronze bowl*
* Placed his palms over the swirling liquid
* Tossed the powder into the fire
* *Began to turn black*
* Turned dark green
* Changed to an amber colour
* Whirled in the glass like a captured storm cloud
* Gave off a green smoke
* Rose from the cauldron
* Slid down the side
* Filled with white vapour

- ★ Filled the room with the scent of incense
- ★ *Poured the liquid into a jar*
- ★ Left the mixture to cool
- ★ Rubbed the slug slime into the burns with a phoenix feather
- ★ *Gripped the sword with both hands*
- ★ Held up his wand
- ★ Raised the sword in the air
- ★ Raised the wand in his right hand
- ★ Twirled the wand slowly through the air
- ★ Flicked her wand
- ★ Swept his wand in a slow arc
- ★ Sliced the wand through the air
- ★ Made a chopping motion with his wand
- ★ Pointed her wand at . . .
- ★ Tapped the staff into the ground
- ★ *Brought his hands together*
- ★ Pressed his hands together
- ★ Closed his hand into a clenched fist
- ★ Made a claw with his left hand
- ★ Pressed his fingers and thumb tightly together
- ★ Clasped her right hand and left hand together
- ★ *Raised his left arm*
- ★ Raised her arms above her head
- ★ Stretched out his right hand
- ★ Extended an arm, palm out
- ★ Reached out with one hand
- ★ Pushed at the air in front of him
- ★ Made a shooing motion with her hand
- ★ Waved his hand above his head
- ★ Waved her hand in a small arc in front of her
- ★ Clapped his hands above his head
- ★ Snapped his fingers
- ★ Flicked his hand
- ★ Flicked her sharp-clawed finger against the ball of her thumb
- ★ Pointed her hands at . . .
- ★ Spread and pointed her five fingers straight at . . .
- ★ Pointed his arms out in front of him and opened his palms
- ★ Opened his hands and a breeze blew up
- ★ Made a three-fingered gesture over her heart
- ★ *Bowed his head*
- ★ Head rolled forward
- ★ Tilted his head back
- ★ *Stood feet apart and braced himself*
- ★ Walked as if in a trance

- ★ *Held hands*
- ★ Formed a circle around . . .
- ★ Turned slowly
- ★ Pivoted around in a circle
- ★ Spun slowly like a top and then faster and faster
- ★ Began to spin in a circle
- ★ Twirled, turned and danced around the . . .
- ★ Launched himself into the air
- ★ *Put a finger to his throat*
- ★ Cupped his mouth
- ★ Muttered under his breath
- ★ Mumbled into his long, white beard
- ★ Murmured words from an ancient language
- ★ Muttered a spell under his breath
- ★ Whispered a spell to the . . .
- ★ Spoke the ancient spell in a whisper
- ★ Spoke some, soft, rapid words
- ★ Uttered the secret name
- ★ Began to hum softly
- ★ As they began to chant . . .
- ★ Chanted the same words over and over again
- ★ *Called out a long, strange name*
- ★ Babbled in a foreign tongue
- ★ Uttered five words in a strange language
- ★ Muttered under his breath in a strange, guttural language
- ★ Chanted several inaudible words
- ★ Rambled in a dozen languages
- ★ Nothing like any language he had ever heard
- ★ Only known by a few scholars
- ★ *Bellowed in a deep, booming voice*
- ★ Roared out something that sounded like a poem
- ★ Got louder and louder
- ★ Became stronger, more urgent
- ★ Echoed through the . . .
- ★ *Moved her lips rhythmically*
- ★ Spoke at speed
- ★ Called her name in the ancient language
- ★ Bound Kitty to his will
- ★ *Breathed slowly*
- ★ Breathed deeply
- ★ Took some calming breaths
- ★ *Reached forward with both hands*
- ★ Held her right hand to her forehead
- ★ *Closed her eyes*

- ★ Focused on the ground
- ★ Focused his mind
- ★ Reached deep inside for his power
- ★ Concentrated on visualising . . .
- ★ Summoned all his will
- ★ Drew power from deep within
- ★ Dived deep into her mind
- ★ Drew on every sense, every part of his mind
- ★ Delved into the flow of energy within her body
- ★ Focused on the seizing spell
- ★ Cast a spell of distant vision
- ★ Granted her night vision
- ★ *Pictured the shimmering, silver mist of her shield*
- ★ Conjured up a shield in front of her
- ★ Flung up a wall of resistance
- ★ Raised the shimmering shield in front of her
- ★ Screened his movements
- ★ *Willed his hand to catch fire*
- ★ Summoned the wind
- ★ Parted the air in front of him
- ★ Created a tunnel through the air
- ★ Directed the spell at the chains that bound him
- ★ Flew across the room into his outstretched hand
- ★ *Blurred her vision*
- ★ Whispered in his head
- ★ Felt like a tight band around his chest
- ★ Felt the birthmark on his forearm begin to tingle
- ★ *Waited for the vision to appear*
- ★ Could feel the force radiating from him
- ★ *Touched the surface of the . . .*
- ★ Placed his palm on . . .
- ★ Lay his hand on her forehead
- ★ Touched the . . . with his fingertips
- ★ Ran her hands over the . . .
- ★ As his fingers touched . . .
- ★ *Crackled with power*
- ★ Produced a sphere of light
- ★ Lit up the runes with an eerie glow
- ★ Shot shards of ice
- ★ Erupted from the end of . . .
- ★ Flashed from his staff
- ★ Blazed like a candle
- ★ Like water splashed on hot iron
- ★ Glowed red-hot like a poker

* *Summoned her dagger*
* Cast a bolt of green energy from her wand
* Parried the red bolt
* *Transformed himself into a . . .*
* Vanished into the mist

SENTENCES

The procession of hooded figures walked as if in a trance, heads bowed, to form a circle around the altar stone.

Once the circle was complete, it was as if the trance had been lifted, and the figures, faces still hidden in their hoods, raised their hands and began to twirl and turn around the stone.

She drew two circles on the floor, one inside the other. Then, taking another piece of chalk, she added strange symbols like hieroglyphics in the rim between the two circles. Finally, in the centre, she drew a six-pointed star.

She could hardly lift the crooked, bronze staff that towered above her head. But, gradually, she eased it forwards to tap the side of the stone, her lips moving rhythmically as she silently chanted the same words over and over again.

He extended his arms, palms out, then turned slowly, his eyes closed and his head tilted back. He spread his fingers, felt them tingle, and saw waves of blue air ripple around him as he cast a cloak over the house to keep them hidden and protected from any spies or intruders.

She was sure that no one had followed her; that no one was aware of their meeting. But in case someone was able to listen, she wove a spell around them that would scramble any sounds and screen them in shadows. When she had finished, they each made a three-fingered gesture over their heart to ward against evil.

Tom arranged the three black candles to form the shape of a triangle. When he had lit them, he quickly scribbled George's name on the parchment and folded it three times. He knew there was no going back now, and quickly tied it with the piece of black ribbon and sealed it in the bronze casket. Then, he placed the casket in the centre of the triangle and rang the bell three times.

Holding the length of leather in her hand, Kitty carefully tied three knots down its length. As she finished tying the last knot, the wind grew stronger, whirling up in strange storm clouds, and darkening the air with billowing clouds of dust.

He took down a crystal bottle of clear fluid and poured it into the cauldron.

Holding his hand over the bronze bowl, he stabbed the small sharp tip of his blade into his thumb . . . squeezed two large drops into the bowl and with the knife blade swirled them around in the water.

As he placed his palms over the swirling water, it began to turn black and whirl in the bowl like a captured storm cloud.

She took out a handful of green powder from her purse and tossed it on the fire. Within seconds, a very sweet and heady scent filled the room.

Whilst the lard was melting in the cauldron, Kitty crushed the herbs into a fine powder, and sliced the mandrake roots. Carefully, she lifted down the phial containing dragon's blood and added three drops to the melted lard and then the ground herbs and roots. After stirring for ten minutes, she poured the liquid into the jar and left it to cool. One more day before she would be able to apply the ointment and fly!

With a sweep of his hand in the air above his head, he produced a sphere of light that moved ahead of them, lighting the way.

He spread his arms wide, as if to embrace the breeze that gusted through the clearing, whipping his white hair in tendrils around him. Tilting his head to the heavens, he chanted words in the language of the old magic.

Shouting loudly, she raised her palm and pivoted around in a circle. As her palm pointed towards the hooded figures, a sizzling, crackling shaft of green energy burst from her hand.

He put a finger to his throat and whispered, safe in the knowledge that his words would only be heard by Kitty.

He cupped his mouth, took a deep breath and bellowed in a booming voice that seemed to come from the depths of the ancient kingdom below their feet.

As she spread her arms and chanted, blue sparks of magic appeared, sizzling at her fingertips, and she shot skywards, like she'd been launched from a catapult.

Tom held up his hand and curled his fingers. For a moment, nothing happened. And then, a dagger appeared in his outstretched hand.

She spun slowly like a top, her arms outstretched but limp at the wrist, her head rolled forward as if in a trance.

Katie closed her eyes, took some calming breaths and dived deep into her mind and pictured the shimmering, silver mist of her shield. Summoning all her power, she fixed the shield in front of her and instinctively crouched behind the invisible barrier she had created.

Reaching out with his mind, he delved into the flow of energy within his body, probed the mechanism on the lock of his chains and slowly turned it to the unlocked position. With a click, the shackles clicked open.

Rob placed his palm on the tunnel walls and closed his eyes. He breathed in slowly, drawing power from deep within him. Gradually, he felt the sigil on his hand begin to tingle.

The moment he raised the staff, it crackled with power. He tapped it three times into the ground and transformed himself into a snake.

She twirled the rosewood wand in the air and then cast a bolt of green energy towards the Cyclops.

With a flick of his wand, he parried the white bolt that flashed towards him.

Kitty sliced her wand through the air and shot a blazing red bolt at the two creatures hovering above her.

SECTION 2 – INTERACTION: OUTCOMES

WORDS

Nouns

Elements, earth, air, fire, water

Force, energy, power, ability

Boost, enhancement, magnification, amplification

Magic, spells, enchantments, curse, hex, vision, prophecy, future, divination, transformation, telekinesis, cure

Shield, cocoon, barrier, protection, immunity, resistance

Mind, thoughts, will, focus, concentration, trance

Senses, sight, vision, hearing, sound, noises, voices, smell, touch, taste

Heart rate, lungs, breath, veins, muscles, nerves, sinews

Strength, speed, agility, reactions, disappearance, shape, appearance, animation, memory, forgetfulness, truth, honesty

Mirror, orb, spyglass, pond, surface, reflection

Shape, outline, silhouette, shadow, image

Movement, motion, gesture, flick, wave

Light, brightness, glow, haze, blur

Weather, wind, breeze, gust, clouds, storm, whirlwind, hurricane, lightning, dust, snow, ice

Circle, triangle, star, pentagram, octagon

Lines, symbols, signs, marks, sigils, runes, glyphs, hieroglyphics, birthmark, tattoo

Paper, parchment, vellum, scroll, ink, chalk

Sword, dagger, blade, tip

Staff, wand, stick, twigs

Bones, feathers, eyes

Phoenix, golden eagle

Ointment, potion, powder, liquid, juice, mixture, serum

Fire, flames, heat, fumes, smoke

Vapour, mist

Wounds, injuries, cuts, gash, bruises

Poison, pain, anguish, sickness, nausea, vomit

Feeling, consciousness

Arms, shoulders, hands, wrists, palm, fist, knuckles

Eyes, pupils, stare, gaze, mouth, jaw, throat, tongue

Guards, soldiers, warriors

Flowers, petals, wolfsbane, anaesthetic

Similes/ Metaphors

A snap like a shotgun blast; as fast as light; as quick as a hare; in the twinkling of an eye; eyes like a hawk; as though he was looking through a pair of binoculars; like a perfectly clear shield of glass; like a layer of invisible feathers; like vanishing behind a curtain of cascading water; like a stone statue; like a procession of statues gliding across ice; moved like robots; like the effect of an anaesthetic; as if their legs had been cut out from under them; as if trapped by an invisible net; as if she was in a harness; as if he had been shot from a catapult; as if caught inside a whirlwind; struck her like a whip; like tiny bolts of lightning; like powerful waves; like steel around his ankles; like a coiling snake; as if they were nothing more than insects; dismantled the wall like a stack of plastic building blocks

Adjectives

Incredible, impossible, unnatural

Invisible

Almighty, enormous, powerful, mighty, hefty

Orange, golden, purple, violet, green, emerald, blue, sapphire, pink, red, black, silvery, white

Brilliant, dazzling, glittering, shimmering, flickering

Rippling, whirling, swirling, billowing

Soft, faint, misty, fuzzy, blurred, indistinct, shadowy

Soothing, calming, comforting

Spell-binding, hypnotic, robotic

Sharp, ear-splitting, deafening

Blank, glazed, glassy, vacant, expressionless, lifeless

Slack, limp, loose

Bitter, acrid, sour, tart, acidic

Tingling, burning, numb

Fatal, lethal, deadly, dangerous, poisonous, toxic, noxious

Horrific, dreadful, horrendous, frightful, hideous, grisly, ghastly, gory

Fierce, severe, awful, terrible, acute, intense, stabbing, shooting

Bloody, blood-stained, blood-spattered

Verbs

Gifted, gave, granted, allowed, enabled, empowered

Read, foretold, predicted, anticipated, forecast, foresaw, divined, saw, scried

Cursed, hexed

Travelled, teleported, vanished, disappeared, appeared

Improved, enhanced, increased, magnified, amplified

Transformed, shape-shifted, animated

Conjured, produced, generated, summoned, willed

Created, moved, changed, controlled, manipulated, channelled

Talked, conversed, communicated, transmitted

Protected, shielded

Used, caused, forced, induced, inflicted

Lifted, rose, shot, launched, propelled

Flew, floated, hovered

Delved, dug, dived, probed

Felt, stirred, ignited, flicked, vibrated, surged, flooded, washed over, wrapped, enveloped, cocooned

Found, discovered

Picked up, snatched, plucked, grabbed, yanked, seized, gripped, clenched, clawed, locked, pinned

Waved, twirled, flicked, flipped, lashed, swung

Sent, threw, flung, hurtled

Pulled, lunged, pushed, slammed, hammered, hit, struck, whipped, cracked, sliced, pierced, shattered, smashed, destroyed, dismantled, scattered

Ran, darted, dashed, sprinted, bounded

Broke, distracted, escaped, responded

Backed away, jerked, rolled, ducked, dodged

Rocked, writhed, twisted

Slid, struggled, scrambled, stumbled, knocked

Stopped, stiffened, froze, paralysed

Drank, sipped, swallowed

Fell, dropped, crashed, lay, slumped, crumpled

Dangled, drooped, lolled, sagged, flopped

Fainted, collapsed, blacked out, swooned

Stung, fizzed, burned, fried, scorched, seared, singed

Took shape, became visible, revealed, unfolded

Wrinkled, rippled, swirled, shimmered, glowed, misted, darkened

Drifted, seeped, spread, gusted, formed, combined, merged, coalesced

Pulsed, flowed, shot, tore, bathed, consumed

Heard, sounded, blocked, drowned out

Spoke, slurred, tightened, strangled, gasped, howled

Widened, dilated, shut, squeezed, scrunched, fixed, stared, gazed

Glazed, misted, blurred

PHRASES – NOUNS AND ADJECTIVES

- ★ *All around her*
- ★ Beside him
- ★ *One after another*
- ★ All of a sudden
- ★ A minute later
- ★ Within a few minutes
- ★ The next few minutes

- ★ In a matter of minutes
- ★ *Without any warning*
- ★ Without so much as a single cry
- ★ *With a flick of its hand*
- ★ Strengthening potion
- ★ Speed boost
- ★ Sight magnification
- ★ Night vision
- ★ Hearing amplification
- ★ Taste enhancement
- ★ Immunity to flames
- ★ *Shrinking spell*
- ★ Animating spell
- ★ *Senses elixir*
- ★ Flying ointment
- ★ Healing potion
- ★ Burns ointment
- ★ Truth serum
- ★ Memory serum
- ★ Fatal poison
- ★ *Within his body*
- ★ A surge of invisible power
- ★ *With an almighty whack*
- ★ A snap like a shotgun blast
- ★ *With incredible speed*
- ★ In the twinkling of an eye
- ★ As fast as lightning
- ★ As fast as light
- ★ Quick as a hare
- ★ Incredible reactions
- ★ *Enhanced sight*
- ★ Eagle-eyed
- ★ Eyes like a hawk
- ★ Miles in the distance
- ★ *Swirling tongues of fire*
- ★ A streak of orange flame
- ★ *A misty curtain*
- ★ Hypnotic, swirling white vapour
- ★ *Surface of the glass*
- ★ Reflection in the surface of the . . .
- ★ *A flickering shadow*
- ★ A thrusting hand
- ★ Galloping warriors
- ★ Tens of thousands of soldiers

- *A flicker of movement*
- A soft shadow
- Nothing more than a shadow in the room
- *Echo of her voice*
- With a sharp crack
- With a thud
- *A circle of light*
- Strands of white light
- In a flash of light
- Few wisps of blue smoke
- White beams of soft light
- Blue glow
- Shimmering, golden mist
- Columns of flame
- A shield of shimmering blue light
- A bolt of dark-purple energy
- *Like a perfectly clear shield of glass*
- Like a layer of invisible feathers
- Between the fierce blast and his face
- *A funnel cloud*
- A current of air
- Powerful gust of wind
- Streaming eyes
- *A wall of force*
- Invisible force
- Invisible cord
- Like a coiling snake
- *Blasts of icy air*
- Icy daggers
- A wave of ice particles
- Tornadoes of snow
- *Spear of white light*
- An emerald ball of energy
- Bolt of pure red light
- A swathe of blue lightning
- A blue lightning bolt
- Fingers of white-hot flames
- A stream of sizzling light
- *An icy numbness*
- Like a stone statue
- *Glassy eyes*
- Slack jaw
- *Robotic movements*
- Like a procession of statues

- *Acrid taste*
- Strange tingling feeling on his tongue
- Burning sensation
- Numb sensation in her mouth
- Slurred speech
- Loss of feeling
- *Dangerously slow heart rate*
- Dilated pupils
- Blurred vision
- *Severe stomach pains*
- Projectile vomit
- A bloody gash across the side of her head
- *Barely conscious*
- Like the effect of an anaesthetic
- *With one final gasp . . .*
- With an ear-splitting scream . . .
- *A cloak of black smoke*
- Billowing clouds of swirling, black vapour
- Nothing but a pile of dust

PHRASES – VERBS

- *Enhanced all senses*
- Gifted him with incredible speed
- Ability to breathe under water
- Gave her immunity to . . .
- Protected her from . . .
- Gave her the power to separate her shadow from her body
- *Could see into the future*
- Able to scry
- Could foretell the future using a reflective object or surface
- Able to read people's minds
- Capable of moving objects and humans with his mind
- Could control the weather
- Able to raise a storm
- Manipulated the wind
- *Shape-shifted into a . . .*
- Travelled through the air
- Became invisible
- Teleported beyond the city walls
- Communicated with the animals
- *Cursed the family*
- Hexed the . . .

* Transformed the guards into frogs
* Induced forgetfulness
* Forced to answer truthfully
* Caused nausea and vomiting
* Inflicted severe pain
* *Summoned all of his strength*
* Delved into the flow of energy
* *Felt something stirring inside him*
* Surged through him
* Set every nerve on fire
* Vibrated through every sinew
* Like powerful waves rippling through his veins
* Felt the strength flooding his leg muscles
* Felt the air forming like steel around his knuckles
* *As he clenched his fist . . .*
* As strength flooded his body . . .
* When he lunged towards her . . .
* As Kitty struck his sword . . .
* *Broke out of his steel shackles*
* Grabbed his wrist and twisted
* Locked his arm straight
* Forced him to his knees
* Yanked him off his feet
* Slammed him into the wall
* Shattered his sword
* *Moved like lightning*
* Before the arrow could pierce his shoulder . . .
* Plucked the arrow out of the air
* Found footholds no bigger than coins
* Bounded down the cliff with impossible agility
* Scrambled his way to the top
* Dodged whirlwinds that assaulted him
* Managed to twist in mid-air
* Lunged for the ledge
* *Swallowed the juice*
* As the liquid flowed down her throat . . .
* Could feel the liquid surging through her veins
* *Allowed him to see things in the dark*
* No one else could see as far
* When she opened her eyes . . .
* As though she was looking through a pair of binoculars
* Granted the sight of an eagle
* Could see every feature, every detail of the rocks
* *Took a deep breath*

- ✶ Felt his lungs expand
- ✶ Filled his lungs
- ✶ Slipped under the water
- ✶ Allowed him to stay under the surface for a couple of hours
- ✶ *Flared to life in all directions*
- ✶ Slithered through the grass
- ✶ Crept around his legs
- ✶ Flicked up his body
- ✶ Engulfed him
- ✶ Felt the heat wash over him
- ✶ Merely singed the hairs on his hands and arms
- ✶ *As the breeze drifted over the pond . . .*
- ✶ Crinkled the surface
- ✶ *Swirled around the orb*
- ✶ Shimmered and rippled
- ✶ Misted up the spyglass
- ✶ *Scene came to life*
- ✶ Could see what was going on
- ✶ Started to take shape from a shadowy outline
- ✶ *As if it was drawing her eyes into the . . .*
- ✶ As her eyes became glassy . . .
- ✶ Eyes slid shut
- ✶ *Transformed the darkness into a scene of . . .*
- ✶ Thrust out of the depths of the pond
- ✶ *Could hear sounds*
- ✶ Turned to an indistinct slur of noise
- ✶ Heard roars from the giant creatures
- ✶ Sounded like . . . marching towards them
- ✶ Rode at full speed towards the city
- ✶ *Stood with her arms outstretched*
- ✶ Blew on the phoenix feather in his hand
- ✶ Felt a force
- ✶ Enveloped by tendrils of air
- ✶ Wrapped around his body
- ✶ Gusted around her
- ✶ Crackled with energy
- ✶ Appeared under his feet like a circular platform
- ✶ *Lifted her off the ground*
- ✶ Rose into the air
- ✶ Lifted up as if she was in a harness
- ✶ Shot into the air
- ✶ Launched into the sky
- ✶ As if he had been shot from a catapult
- ✶ *Used the current to . . .*

* Propelled herself high overhead
* Channelled the wind to slow his descent
* Created a cushion to break his fall
* Floated back to a vertical position high above the cliffs
* Hovered above the clearing
* *Felt like his whole body was floating*
* Made her hair stand on end
* Pulled his cheeks back like rubber
* *Peeled his shadow away from him*
* *Held up her hands*
* Realised her hands were fuzzy and indistinct
* Could no longer see her own feet
* Possible to see the trees through his body
* Obscured him from view
* Unseen but watching
* *All that remained was...*
* Where he had been standing ...
* As she rose off the ground ...
* *Formed in the air around him*
* Rippled as he vanished
* Vanished in a faint shimmer
* Like vanishing behind a curtain of cascading water
* Swallowed up by the silvery haze
* Became a purple blur
* Vanished completely
* Composed of swirling black vapour
* Left only a thin gunpowder-trail of fire
* *Moved swiftly down the corridor*
* Walked right past the guards
* *Created a cocoon*
* Sprang up before him
* Wrapped around her
* Gathered in strength and brightness
* Large enough to shield both of them
* *As the creature hit his shield...*
* Shot towards him
* As the arrow whistled through the air towards him ...
* Raised his red shield
* Emblazoned with a glittering, golden eagle
* Crouched behind his shield
* *Struck the shield*
* Could feel the bolts battering on the shield
* Exploded in his face
* Washed around his face

- ✶ Sizzled against the invisible barrier
- ✶ Absorbed the flames on impact
- ✶ Exploded into fragments of brilliant white light
- ✶ Flew into the air like tiny bolts of lightning
- ✶ Fell to the ground as ash
- ✶ Launched backwards
- ✶ *Went no further*
- ✶ No longer able to touch her
- ✶ *Could cure all things*
- ✶ When the sigil glowed . . .
- ✶ Stung her throat as she swallowed the . . .
- ✶ Could feel the liquid scorching through her veins
- ✶ Shot pulses of light upwards
- ✶ Bathed her wounds in a . . .
- ✶ Consumed him in a . . ..
- ✶ *Cuts disappeared*
- ✶ Bruises vanished
- ✶ Flowed to heal her ribs
- ✶ Healed his wounds
- ✶ *Summoned a gust of wind*
- ✶ Materialised around him
- ✶ Swirled as if caught inside a whirlwind
- ✶ Gusted faster and faster
- ✶ Like a hurricane had descended over the city
- ✶ Hammered down on their heads
- ✶ *Held out his hand*
- ✶ Murmured a few words in the ancient tongue
- ✶ Bent the branches down
- ✶ Changed the direction of the arrow
- ✶ Sent the weapon spiralling away from his head
- ✶ Sent it rocketing skyward back over the wall
- ✶ Hurtled into his outstretched palm
- ✶ Curled around him
- ✶ Pulled him from the ground
- ✶ Snatched her off the ground
- ✶ *As if he had struck some invisible barrier*
- ✶ As if the wand had been snatched up
- ✶ *Had no chance to struggle or defend themselves*
- ✶ *Leapt from his hand*
- ✶ Flew through the air
- ✶ Cracked against the wall
- ✶ *Tried to swing her blade at him*
- ✶ Raised his arm
- ✶ Jerked back

- Backed a short distance out of reach
- *Waved her hand in a small arc in front of her*
- Conjured up a jagged bolt of light
- Twirled the lightning bolt like a baton
- *Ignited with ice-white flames*
- Tore out of his face and hands
- Generated a blue lightning bolt over her palm
- Kept summoning . . . to throw at it
- Shot a blast of wintry sleet
- *Fizzed and burst into flames*
- Fried the air around him
- *Struck a tree some metres away*
- *Collapsed the wall*
- Struck the heavy, oak door
- Scattered splinters like deadly shrapnel
- Slammed the stone columns out of the way
- Dismantled the wall like a stack of plastic building blocks
- *Hit the ground between his feet*
- Shot up his legs
- Whipped forward
- Struck her like a whip
- Sent his sword skittering across the road
- *Burst into a geyser of flame*
- Seared the air
- Black smoke coalesced into . . .
- Formed a demonic fist the size of a huge boulder
- *Stumbled back*
- Flung himself to one side
- Barely rolled aside in time
- Knocked him to the ground
- *Leaped at her*
- Sent a wave of force
- Sent a spear of shadows
- *Before he could move . . .*
- While she was distracted . . .
- *Before he had gone more than a few paces . . .*
- Caught every energy stream he sent her way
- Responded with a bolt of her own
- With as much force as they could muster
- *Caught him in the stomach*
- Sliced into her arm
- Felt a savage blow strike his chest
- *Picked up the guard*
- Threw the . . . bodily back down the stairs

* Lifted off his feet like a rag doll
* Yanked her viciously off her feet
* Flipped through the air
* Blown across the room
* Knocked backwards over the chair
* Flicked them away
* Sent him hurtling backwards
* Smashed against a side wall
* Slammed her face first into the wall
* As if they were nothing more than insects
* *Slid to the floor*
* Crashed to the ground
* Lay in a crumpled heap
* Fell senseless to the ground
* *When the spell took effect...*
* Almost from the moment when she had ...
* *Seized hold of her*
* As if an unseen force had gripped him
* *Every time she struggled...*
* Grew tighter
* Spun her around
* Pinned her to the door
* Cut into her skin
* Stopped in mid-air
* As if trapped by an invisible net
* *Couldn't move*
* Grew rigid
* Unable to move
* Froze into stone
* Hung limply by his sides
* Pinned her legs in place
* Stood paralysed, unable to move a finger
* *Tried to speak*
* Mouth felt dry
* Mouth was burning
* Tongue started to feel numb
* Speech was slurred
* Had difficulty in swallowing
* Opened his mouth but no sound came out
* Tongue stuck to the roof of his mouth
* Felt his throat tighten
* As though he was being strangled
* Gasped as a wave of pain flooded through her
* Could hardly breathe

- ☆ Mouth dropped open
- ☆ Jaw was slack
- ☆ Tongue lolled out
- ☆ *Eyes were glazed*
- ☆ Scrunched her eyes tight
- ☆ Misted over
- ☆ Pupils dilated
- ☆ Vision blurred
- ☆ Struggled to focus
- ☆ Fixed in a glassy stare
- ☆ Rolled in her head
- ☆ Only the whites of his eyes were visible
- ☆ Before she blacked out
- ☆ Caught a brief glimpse of . . .
- ☆ *Writhed in agony*
- ☆ Clawed at her ears
- ☆ Tried to block out the sound
- ☆ *Could barely stand*
- ☆ Rocked backwards and forwards
- ☆ Knees buckled under him
- ☆ Fell to his knees
- ☆ Slumped onto her knees
- ☆ Slumped forward
- ☆ Crumpled to the floor
- ☆ Dropped to the floor
- ☆ Stiffened and fell to the floor
- ☆ Crashed to the floor
- ☆ Fell to each side of the . . .
- ☆ As if their legs had been cut out from under them
- ☆ Began to move forward like robots
- ☆ *Took a sip from the goblet*
- ☆ Pierced with a poisonous dart
- ☆ Could feel the poison taking root in her stomach
- ☆ Seeped through her veins
- ☆ Spread bile to the back of her throat
- ☆ *Unfolded in horrifying slow motion*
- ☆ A cone of air howled from where he had stood
- ☆ Darkened the air
- ☆ Swirled as if caught inside a whirlwind
- ☆ When the wind had stopped . . .
- ☆ Everything went very still
- ☆ Became unnaturally quiet
- ☆ Nothing remained but a pile of dust

SENTENCES

Tom delved into the flow of energy within his body and summoned all of his strength to break out of his steel shackles.

Instantly, a wave of invisible power surged through him.

Immediately he had swallowed the juice he felt the strength flooding his leg muscles.

Tom felt the air forming like steel around his knuckles as he clenched his fist.

He felt something stirring inside him, like powerful waves rippling through his veins, setting every nerve on fire and vibrating through every sinew.

Strength flooded Kitty's body. When he lunged towards her, she grabbed his wrist and twisted, locking his arm straight and forcing the giant to his knees.

Trish yanked him off his feet and slammed him into the wall.

As Kitty struck his sword with an almighty whack, there was a snap like a shotgun blast, and his sword shattered.

Rob moved like lightning and plucked the arrow out of the air before it could pierce his shoulder.

Katie bounded down the cliff with impossible agility, finding footholds no bigger than coins, dodging whirlwinds that tried to assault her.

With incredible speed, Rob managed to twist in mid-air, lunge for the ledge and claw his way to the top.

His enhanced sight allowed him to see things in the dark and storm that no one else could.

As the liquid flowed down her throat, she could feel it surging through her veins, and when she opened her eyes it was as though she was looking through a pair of binoculars. She had been granted the sight of an eagle. She could see every feature, every detail of the rocks miles in the distance.

He took a deep breath, and felt his lungs expand and fill until there was sufficient to allow him to stay under the surface for a couple of hours, and then he slipped under the water.

Swirling tongues of fire flared to life in all directions. A streak of orange flame slithered through the grass, creeping around his legs, engulfing him. He felt the heat wash over him. As he raised his arms, fire flicked up his body, merely singeing the hairs on his hands and arms.

The white vapour swirling around the orb was hypnotic, as if it was drawing her eyes into the mist.

Gradually, the spyglass misted up and then suddenly he could see what was going on underground.

The surface of the glass shimmered and rippled. Very gradually, the image started to take shape from a shadowy outline until she could hear sounds and the scene came to life.

As the breeze drifted over the pond, ripples crinkled the surface. A reflection – a hand thrusting out of the depths – suddenly caught his attention.

As her eyes became glassy, the sound of their voices turned to a slur of noise and then silence. Her eyes slid shut and, gradually, the darkness was transformed into a scene of galloping warriors, riding at full speed towards the city. She began to hear roars from the giant creatures and what sounded like tens of thousands marching towards them.

Quickly, he dropped off the edge of the roof and channelled the wind to slow his descent.

Strands of white light wrapped around his body, creating a cushion to break his fall.

As Tom floated back to a vertical position high above the cliffs, a ring of light appeared under his feet like a circular platform.

Suddenly, Kitty was enveloped by tendrils of air that lifted her up as if she was in a harness. The space around her crackled with energy that made her hair stand on end. Using the current, she propelled herself high overhead and hovered above the clearing.

Gently, Tom blew on the phoenix feather in his hand. He felt a force lift him off the ground, and he slowly rose into the air. His whole body felt like it was floating.

She stood with her arms outstretched. A breeze gusted around her. The next moment, a current of air lifted her off the ground. As she shot into the air, her cheeks were pulled back like rubber and her eyes streamed.

Rob was launched into the sky as if he had been shot from a catapult.

As she held up her hands, she realised that they were fuzzy and indistinct, and that she could no longer see her own feet.

The air rippled as he vanished.

It was now possible to see the trees through his body. Then, all at once, he was gone.

His whole body was suddenly composed of swirling black vapour.

Mist formed in the air around him, gradually obscuring him from view. When the mist cleared, there was nothing but a pile of dust.

It was like vanishing behind a curtain of cascading water as the silvery haze swallowed her and she vanished in a faint shimmer.

In a flash of light, he vanished completely.

She became a purple blur, as she rose off the ground; a flicker of movement, a soft shadow and then she was gone.

Tom vanished, leaving only a thin gunpowder-trail of fire where he had been standing, a trail that now moved swiftly down the corridor.

Rob walked right past the guards and up the path towards the entrance and none made as much as a move in his direction.

Slowly, his shadow peeled away from him and, on his command, leapt out into the open.

He was the shadow in the room, unseen but watching.

All that remained was the echo of her voice and a few wisps of blue smoke.

White beams of soft light wrapped around her, creating a cocoon like a layer of invisible feathers.

A shield of shimmering blue light sprang up before Tom, large enough to shield both of them.

As the creature hit Katie's shield, the air sizzled and, with a sharp crack, it was launched backwards.

Columns of flame shot towards him, but his armour absorbed them on impact.

As the arrow whistled through the air towards him, with one swift movement he had raised his red shield above his head and crouched behind it. The golden eagle emblazoned in the centre glittered as the sun's rays struck the surface. With a thud, the arrow struck the shield and then exploded into fragments of brilliant white light. They flew into the air like tiny bolts of lightning and fell to the ground as ash.

Magic sizzled against the invisible barrier and went no further.

A bolt of dark purple energy exploded in his face, but washed around it as if he had a perfectly clear shield of glass between the fierce blast and his face.

Gradually, her shield gathered in strength and brightness. She could feel the bolts battering on the shield but no longer able to touch her.

Gail could cure all things from acne to influenza.

The sigil glowed and she gritted her teeth as pulses of light shot upwards, bathing her wounds in a shimmering, golden mist.

A blue glow consumed him, and within a few minutes, his wounds appeared to be healed – the cuts disappeared and the bruises vanished.

The potion was bitter and stung her throat as she swallowed it. She could feel it scorching through her veins as it flowed to heal her ribs.

A funnel cloud materialised around him.

All around her, the trees swirled as if caught inside a whirlwind. A current of air snatched her off the ground.

The rain hammered down on their heads. The wind gusted faster. It was like a hurricane that had descended over the city in a matter of minutes.

Rob summoned a gust of wind that changed the direction of the arrow and sent it spiralling away from his head.

Slowly, the branches bent down, curling around him and pulling him from the ground.

Suddenly, the wand leapt from his hand. It flew through the air and cracked against the wall, as if it had been snatched up by a powerful gust of wind.

Andrew murmured a few words in the ancient tongue, and held out his hand. The grenade hurtled into his outstretched palm and, with another spell, he sent it rocketing skyward, back over the wall.

Without any warning, she conjured up a jagged bolt of light. Twirling it like a baton, she grinned menacingly at them.

Chanting, Trish waved her hand in a small arc in front of her and generated a blue lightning bolt over her palm.

A swathe of blue lightning tore out of his face and hands, frying the air around him.

With a flick of its hand, it slammed a stone column out of the way like a stack of toy building blocks.

An emerald ball of energy struck a tree some metres away. It fizzed and burst into flames.

Trish's hands ignited with ice-white flames, and she shot a blast of wintry sleet at his head. One after another, she kept summoning ice daggers to throw at him, blasts of icy air, tornadoes of snow.

A wave of ice particles struck her like a whip.

As the arrow hit the ground between his feet, fingers of white-hot flames shot up his legs.

He stumbled back as the arrow burst into a geyser of flame.

An invisible force knocked him to the ground and his sword skittered across the road.

Rob flung himself to one side as a spear of white light seared the air.

A bolt of pure red light struck the heavy oak door. It exploded, scattering splinters all around them like deadly shrapnel.

A wall of force picked up the guard and threw him bodily back down the stairs.

It sent a wave of force that picked them up and flicked them away as if they were nothing more than insects.

Like a rag doll, he was lifted off his feet and blown across the room.

Katie crashed against a side wall and slid to the floor, where she lay in a crumpled heap, groaning in pain.

Bravely, Tom leaped at her. Before he had gone more than a few paces, a stream of sizzling light caught him in the chest and sent him hurtling backwards.

Katie was thrown into the air, hurled backwards, flipped through the air like a rag doll, and smashed into the trees. She fell senseless to the ground – a bloody gash across the side of her head.

At first, Rob rushed in, but she caught every energy stream he sent her way and responded with one of her own. Desperate, he sent a spear of shadows to slice into her arm. She was distracted for a brief moment, and Rob took his chance. He yanked her viciously off her feet and slammed her, face first, into the wall.

Suddenly, he was jerked back as if he had struck some invisible barrier. He opened his mouth but no sound came out.

An invisible force seized hold of her, spinning her around and pinning her to the door.

The creature stopped in mid-air, as if it had been trapped by an invisible net.

Every time Gail struggled, like a coiling snake, the invisible cord that bound her wrists grew tighter and cut into her skin.

He couldn't move. It was as if an unseen force had gripped him. He tried to speak but his tongue stuck to the roof of his mouth.

He grew rigid; his hands hung limply by his sides; his jaw was slack and his eyes misted over.

They were unable to move. Even their eyes remained fixed in a glassy stare upon whatever they had been looking at when the spell took effect.

His eyes were glazed, his movements robotic.

Like a procession of statues gliding across ice, they began to move forward.

Her eyes rolled in her head and she slumped forward.

She writhed in agony, clawing at her ears, trying to block out the sound.

Tom felt his throat tighten as though he was being strangled. Choking, he fell to his knees.

All of a sudden, her knees buckled and she fell to the ground.

The soldiers fell to each side of the gate, as if their legs had been cut out from under them.

Without so much as a single cry, the dozen or so men stiffened and fell to the floor.

Suddenly, her mouth felt dry, and she had difficulty in swallowing. Within a few moments, she could hardly breathe, could hardly stand. Barely conscious, she crumpled to the floor, but before she blacked out, she caught a brief glimpse of the exotic, pink flowers on the shelf – wolfsbane!

Almost from the moment when she had taken a sip from the goblet, she knew that something was wrong. Her mouth was burning, starting to feel numb like the effect of an anaesthetic. A minute later, her speech was slurred, her pupils dilated, her vision blurring. She could feel the poison taking root in her stomach, seeping through her veins and spreading bile to the back of her throat. She gasped as a wave of pain flooded through her. Scrunching her eyes tight and clenching her fists, she rocked backwards and forwards. With an ear-splitting scream, she slumped onto her knees and dropped to the floor.

As he peered down at the poisonous dart in his leg, Tom had to struggle to focus. His legs buckled under him; only the whites of his eyes were visible as they rolled in his head. His mouth dropped open and his tongue lolled out. With one final gasp, he crashed to the floor.

Rob, Kitty and Andrew exchanged a brief glance, and nodded. With as much force as they could muster, they hurled light bolts at the demon.

The next few minutes unfolded in horrifying slow motion. A cone of air howled from where he had stood, darkening the air with billowing clouds of swirling, black vapour. All around them, the trees were bending, arching from side to side, as if caught inside a whirlwind. When the wind had stopped, everything went very still and the forest became unnaturally quiet. There was nothing but a pile of dust.

SECTION 3 – REACTION

WORDS	
Nouns	**Presence**, spirit, spectre, shade
	Magic, spell, enchantment
	Force, touch, weight, pressure
	Air, current, vibration
	Dark, shadows, danger

Fumes, nausea, sickness

Mind, brain, thoughts, consciousness, will, control, power

Senses, sensation, nerves, skin, sweat

Panic, dread, fear

Strength, muscles, sinews

Body, neck, spine, stomach, gut, arms, hands, fingers, legs, knees, feet, heart, pulse, veins, heartbeat

Head, temple, forehead, brow, face, eyes, vision, sockets, stare, gaze, throat, ears, hair, scalp

Cuts, wounds, gash, bruises

Voice, breath, gasp, whispers, words, language, scream, wail

Similes/ Metaphors	**Like waves of heat rippling through her veins**; rippled like warm water across his body; as if a tuning fork had been struck; as if she was sinking into a dark, murky lake; like a heat mirage; like a wintry breeze; like a mental probe; like icy fingers around her heart; a fog of sheer panic; like an electric current; as if she was coming up for air after a long dive
Adjectives	**Invisible**, unseen

Murky, gloomy, dull, misty

Questing, searching, probing, hunting

Powerful, strong, potent, formidable

Huge, enormous, massive

Shimmering, glinting, glistening, flashing, blinking

Strange, odd, unusual, bizarre, surreal

Dark, gruesome, horrific, hideous, frightful, nightmarish, monstrous

Dangerous, menacing, threatening, treacherous

Tingling, prickling, crawling, slithering, squirming, tugging, rushing, thundering

Pale, pallid, ashen-faced

Damp, sweaty, sticky, clammy

Dizzy, wobbly, faint, weak, giddy, shaky

Surging, swelling, whirling, billowing, undulating

Stabbing, gnawing, piercing, stinging, searing

Sharp, sheer, utter, intense, acute, severe, unbearable, excruciating

Shrill, ear-splitting, deafening

Verbs

Drank, swallowed, chewed, rubbed

Flowed, surged, flooded

Awakened, stirred, roused, kindled, ignited, sparked

Felt, sensed, experienced, detected, realised, understood, decided, wanted

Healed, cured, mended, repaired

Willed, urged, spurred, prompted

Linked, bound, connected

Cleared, focused, concentrated

Tingled, prickled, vibrated, pulsed, clouded

Thumped, pounded, hammered

Shuddered, shivered, trembled

Pushed, forced, pulled, tugged, jerked, wrenched

Hit, struck, banged, knocked, slammed, clawed

Burned, seared, exploded

Tensed, tightened, seized up, contracted, constricted

Swayed, tottered, staggered, lurched, toppled, tumbled, collapsed

Clutched, dug, pressed

Rose, fell, uttered, gasped, choked, heaved, winced, screamed, wailed

Closed, shut, scrunched, squeezed

Glazed over, blurred, blinded

Stared, fixed, bored, drilled, pierced, locked

Rang, popped, echoed, heard

Formed, emerged, beaded, crystallised, rolled, dripped

PHRASES – NOUNS AND ADJECTIVES

* In a matter of moments
* Without warning
* Almost at once

- ✶ *Across her neck*
- ✶ Soles of his feet
- ✶ Up his spine
- ✶ *A low humming*
- ✶ Buzzing in her head
- ✶ *An invisible hand*
- ✶ An invisible force
- ✶ Air pressure
- ✶ Powerful, shimmering force
- ✶ Like a heat mirage
- ✶ *Strong sensation*
- ✶ Tingling sensation
- ✶ A crawling sensation
- ✶ A dark and dangerous presence
- ✶ Someone else in her thoughts
- ✶ *A fog of sheer panic*
- ✶ A bead of sweat
- ✶ As cold as the freezing air
- ✶ Like icy fingers around his heart
- ✶ *A sharp pain*
- ✶ Small stabbing pain
- ✶ Like a huge weight
- ✶ Unbearable pain
- ✶ A searing pain like a mental probe
- ✶ *Sweet-smelling fumes*
- ✶ A wave of nausea
- ✶ Pale face and clammy skin
- ✶ *Huge gash in his . . .*

PHRASES – VERBS

- ✶ As the liquid flowed down her throat . . .
- ✶ *Awakened her power*
- ✶ Shuddered as the magic entered him
- ✶ As strength flooded her body . . .
- ✶ *Something stirred inside her*
- ✶ Aware of something tingling
- ✶ Noticed a small vibration in her bones
- ✶ *Set every nerve on fire*
- ✶ Surged around her body
- ✶ Vibrated through every sinew
- ✶ Moved up from his fingers, then his arms
- ✶ Flowed around her hand

⋆ Could feel it moving through her body
⋆ *Felt like an electric current*
⋆ Like waves of heat rippling through her veins
⋆ As if a tuning fork had been struck
⋆ *Echoed faintly in his ears*
⋆ Eyes glazed over
⋆ Voice rose and fell in an undulating sob
⋆ Winced as a headache began to pound behind her eyes
⋆ Gasped for air
⋆ *Felt a tugging sensation in his gut*
⋆ Could feel the air currents against her skin
⋆ Dropped so rapidly that his ears popped
⋆ *Hair rose on her head*
⋆ Stood up, brush-like
⋆ Spat out sparks of static
⋆ *Felt a rushing sensation*
⋆ Pulled at her face
⋆ Swirled and flashed
⋆ Made her feel dizzy
⋆ Blinded her
⋆ Closed her eyes
⋆ *Could hear strange whispers in her mind*
⋆ Pulsed through her mind
⋆ Connected by a current
⋆ Sensed he was in the presence of a very powerful magician
⋆ *Could not understand the whispers*
⋆ Seemed to be in a foreign language
⋆ Realised that she could detect words
⋆ Could understand the whispers
⋆ *Steadied himself*
⋆ Tried to make sense of what had just happened
⋆ *Could feel her nerves starting to jangle*
⋆ Sensed something dark
⋆ Something moving in the shadows
⋆ Waiting for him in the dark
⋆ As if she was being pulled into . . .
⋆ In no doubt that he was in great danger
⋆ Warned her not to . . .
⋆ Powerless to stop
⋆ *Sent a shiver through . . .*
⋆ Began to crystallise on his brow
⋆ Beaded his forehead
⋆ Rolled into his eyes
⋆ *Even though his legs had turned to rubber . . .*

- ✶ Willed himself to carry on
- ✶ *No time to worry*
- ✶ No time to think
- ✶ Had less than a second to make a decision
- ✶ Time had run out
- ✶ *Could feel her thundering heartbeat*
- ✶ Heart was thumping in his chest
- ✶ *Felt as if she had just been struck by . . .*
- ✶ Hit in the chest by a bucket of cold water
- ✶ Clawed at him like a wintry breeze
- ✶ *Swayed slightly*
- ✶ Pushed him to his knees
- ✶ Knocked him off his feet
- ✶ Crashed face first onto the ground
- ✶ Dropped to the floor
- ✶ *Became aware of . . .*
- ✶ Felt the questing eye
- ✶ Could feel a presence
- ✶ Sensed a presence
- ✶ Tried to close his mind
- ✶ Tried desperately to clear his thoughts
- ✶ Fought to break away from her control
- ✶ Found it harder and harder to concentrate
- ✶ *Thoughts became clouded*
- ✶ As if she was sinking into a dark, murky lake
- ✶ Pushed at his mind
- ✶ Burned in her brain
- ✶ Exploded in her temples
- ✶ Slammed through his head
- ✶ *Muscles contracted*
- ✶ Was incapable of any movement
- ✶ Knees buckled beneath her
- ✶ Toppled sideways
- ✶ *Locked on his eyes*
- ✶ Squeezed her eyes shut
- ✶ Eyelids became heavy
- ✶ Images swam in front of his eyes
- ✶ Could not drag his eyes away from her gaze
- ✶ Eyeballs rolled in their sockets
- ✶ Rolled up into the back of his head
- ✶ Began to water
- ✶ Vision was blurring
- ✶ Fluttered open
- ✶ *Clutched her head with both hands*

- ✷ Clutched her hand to her head
- ✷ Dug her fingers through her hair
- ✷ Pressed her fingers against her scalp
- ✷ *Gasped with pain*
- ✷ Uttered an ear-splitting wail
- ✷ Chest heaved
- ✷ Squeezed the breath out of him
- ✷ Tried to scream
- ✷ Couldn't find the air to make any noise
- ✷ Started to choke
- ✷ Felt a pressure on his neck
- ✷ As if someone was strangling him from behind
- ✷ Gasped for breath
- ✷ As if coming up for air after a long dive
- ✷ *Sucked the energy and life from his body*
- ✷ All he wanted to do was to sleep
- ✷ Spun the world out of control
- ✷ Made his head feel wobbly
- ✷ *Chewed on the leaves*
- ✷ Rubbed the ointment onto the cuts
- ✷ Swallowed the potion
- ✷ *Felt a warm glow*
- ✷ Rippled like warm water across his body
- ✷ Crept into his body
- ✷ Moved straight to the areas most badly injured
- ✷ Pain subsided
- ✷ Wound appeared to have healed
- ✷ Cuts disappeared
- ✷ Repaired the wound
- ✷ Regained consciousness

SENTENCES

A low humming echoed faintly in his ears, and his body shuddered as the magic entered him.

Something was stirring inside Kitty, like waves of heat rippling through her veins, moving up from her fingers, then her arms.

She noticed a small vibration in her bones, as if something deep inside her had awakened her power.

It was like an electric current was surging around her body.

As the spell set every nerve on fire, it looked like a powerful, shimmering force, like a heat mirage, was flowing around her body.

The liquid burned as it flowed down her throat. She could feel it moving through her body. Then, something stirring inside her, like powerful waves rippling through her veins, setting every nerve on fire and vibrating through every sinew. She could feel strength flooding her body.

He felt a tugging sensation in his gut.

She could feel the air currents against her skin.

The air pressure dropped so rapidly that his ears popped.

The hair rose on her head until it stood, brush-like, spitting out sparks of static.

Abruptly, she felt a rushing sensation. Something pulling at her face. Pictures and colours swirled and flashed, blinding her, making her feel dizzy.

As she closed her eyes, she could hear strange whispers in her mind that seemed to be in a foreign language. A strong sense pulsed through her mind that she was in the presence of a very powerful magician, that a current now connected them. Suddenly, she realised that she could detect words, could understand the whispers.

Gasping for air, Rob steadied himself and tried to make sense of what had just happened.

She could feel her nerves starting to jangle.

A crawling sensation across her neck warned her not to open her eyes.

It was as if she was being pulled into something dark and dangerous by a hand she couldn't see, couldn't stop even if she wanted to.

Her voice echoed in his head; her words sent a shiver through the soles of Rob's feet and up his spine.

Even in the chill air, sweat began to bead and rolled down his forehead into his eyes.

Rob willed himself to carry on, even though his legs had turned to rubber, and his heart was thumping in his chest.

There was no time to worry. No time to think. He had less than a second to make a decision. Time had run out.

Kitty could feel her thundering heartbeat under her hand.

Stay alert she warned herself, but it was hard. Her mind was a fog of sheer panic.

Fear clawed at him like a wintry breeze, as cold as the freezing air that had descended on the room.

The force knocked him off his feet and squeezed the breath out of him.

His eyes began to water and his vision was blurring.

The force of the blow sent him to his knees. Almost at once, he started to choke; his eyes rolled up into the back of his head. He swayed slightly before crashing, face first, onto the ground.

An invisible force pushed Tom to his knees. As he dropped to the floor, he felt a pressure on his neck, as if someone was strangling him from behind. The pain was unbearable. He couldn't scream. His mouth opened, but the stranglehold was so tight he couldn't find the air to make any noise.

Her black, reptilian eyes locked on his and burned into his brain. However hard he tried, he could not drag his eyes away from her gaze.

Shaking his head, he tried desperately to clear his thoughts, to break away from her control.

Without warning, he felt it – the questing eye. Now, he was in no doubt that he was in great danger. It was like icy fingers had closed around his heart.

A buzzing began in her head. She was finding it harder and harder to concentrate on what he was saying. She could feel a presence, someone else in her thoughts. Gasping with pain, she clutched her hand frantically to her head. A searing pain like a mental probe was exploding in her temples.

Suddenly, he became aware of a small stabbing pain in his temple. Then, he sensed a presence, like a huge weight pushing at his mind. When he tried to close his mind to the attack, another, sharper pain slammed through his head.

Katie tried to scream, but her body was seizing up, her muscles contracting. Her chest was heaving and her eyeballs were rolling in their sockets. Other than that she was incapable of any movement.

Kitty's knees buckled beneath her. A searing pain burned in her brain. Clutching her head with both hands, she dug her fingers through her hair to press against her scalp. She uttered a scream that quickly became an ear-splitting wail.

Her thoughts became clouded, as if she was sinking into a dark, murky lake.

The energy and life were being sucked from his body. His eyelids became heavy. All he wanted to do was to sleep.

Images swam in front of his eyes. The world spun out of control and he toppled sideways.

The sweet-smelling fumes made her head feel wobbly. A wave of nausea hit her hard. Her eyes were closed, her face pale and skin clammy.

As he chewed on the leaves, Rob felt a warm glow creep into his body and the pain subsided.

The magic rippled like water across Rob's body, moving straight to the areas most badly injured.

In a matter of moments, his wounds appeared to heal – the cuts disappeared and the huge gash in his stomach had knitted together.

Gradually, he started to regain consciousness. His eyes fluttered open, and he gasped for breath as if coming up for air after a long dive.

Part 4
Sieges and battles

14

Attacking a castle, fortress or walled city

A castle, fortress or walled city can be captured by stealth or by brute force, and by the use of many different tactics and weapons. Fantasy creatures and magic can also be included. As descriptions and vocabulary for castles, cities and fantasy creatures were included in *Descriptosaurus: Myths & Legends*, I have concentrated in this section on layout, structure and defences of the settlements and buildings, and the traditional weapons used. However, the catapults could be replaced by ogres or giants; dragons could be used instead of fire arrows and gunpowder; and armoured elephants could act as a battering ram.

This section can be linked to the history curriculum and is very useful to practise writing a narrative from different perspectives. The same vocabulary can be used to describe the siege, attack or battle from the point of view of the attacker and then the defender.

THE S/C-I-R STRUCTURE

Tom had spotted a movement; a cloud of dust on the horizon. He leaned out over the wall and froze. **Rigid with fear, he gripped the edge of the wall so hard his knuckles turned white.** Marching towards the castle were thousands of mounted soldiers, thousands more marching behind – a sea of black except for the flicker of light from their torches. He could now clearly hear the steady, rumbling rhythm of the enemy's siege engines. **Fear and adrenalin surging through his body**, he pulled his horn from its sheath and let out two harsh, urgent blasts that screamed a warning – the invaders had arrived.

Over the last few days, they had been frantically building many weapons – catapults to hurl rocks at and over the walls; mangonels with their huge, wooden arm and bowl-shaped bucket; ballistae like huge crossbows to fire lethal javelins capable of skewering several men at once; and long ladders and poles for scaling the walls. On the fifth morning, the order had eventually come to begin the attack.

Crouched inside the tortoise, **Rob's heart hammered against his ribs**. Slowly, the battering ram was rolling closer and closer to the gates. **He could almost feel the crossbows aimed at his head.**

He knew that from the turret over the archway they could expect a barrage of missiles to be dropped on them, or even boiled lead poured over the walls. A warning bell rang out from the roof of one of the towers.

Inside the cover of the tortoise, the battering ram dangled on chains, ready to pound the castle gates with its lethal head, its bronze raven-like beak thrust menacingly towards the gates. Rob turned and, through a slit in the back wall, caught a glimpse of Kitty with the rest of the troops huddled behind the shed.

The tortoise suddenly lurched, and Rob tried to grab something to hold himself upright. His hand just missed the chains securing the battering ram, and instead Rob found himself snatching at thin air. **With a cry of despair, he tumbled to the ground, stifling a scream of agony** as the huge wooden ram slammed into his leg.

With her left arm outstretched, Kitty pointed frantically at the castle wall, urging her troops carrying the long ladders and poles to sprint forward. When the last ladder had passed, Kitty gritted her teeth and pelted after them. Immediately, there was a twang from hundreds of bowstrings loosing their arrows, and a black deadly hail arced up into the air. **Kitty opened her mouth to scream a warning, but before she could make a sound** more and more of her men fell to the ground in front of her.

For a moment, Kitty froze. She didn't know which way to run. Her eyes darted from side to side in desperation, searching for cover. She gripped her shield tighter and kept running, stumbling over bodies to get to the base of the castle.

It was as if everything was happening in slow motion as she watched an arrow whistling towards her. A silent scream erupted inside her head, urging her to take cover. At the last moment, Kitty ducked into a defensive crouch and lifted her shield above her head. Only seconds later, she heard a series of thuds as arrow after arrow pierced her shield.

A horrifying crash ripped through the air as several boulders slammed into the wall, filling the air with shards of stone and splinters of wood. **Crouched on the ground, Andrew was afraid to move, terrified of raising his head.** Bells rang out from every corner – a cacophony of peeling, chiming, clanging that added to the sense of chaos and destruction.

The floor under his feet rocked like the deck of a ship in a storm and many of the archers standing beside them were thrown into the streets below. Cries of fear and pain filled the air. Andrew scrambled to his feet, **not sure which way to go, only certain that he could no longer stay where he was**. It was only a matter of time before the walls were breached.

Just as he reached the stairs, **Andrew twisted in agony – a piercing pain shot through his shoulder, like hot wire being pressed into a nerve. With a gasp**, his legs buckled under him and he crashed to the floor.

SECTION 1 – SETTING

WORDS

Nouns

Settlement, city, town, village

Castle, citadel, keep, fortress, fort, stronghold, fortification

Forest, wood, trees, fields, bogs, marshes

Sea, river, stream

Cliffs, mountains, hills, valley

Moat, knives, spikes, rubbish, filth, bridge, drawbridge

Tower, watchtower, drum tower, turret, barbican, gatehouse

Portcullis, doors, gates, postern gate, sally port

Entrance, archway

Rivets, struts, spikes

Wall, curtain wall, battlements, ramparts, parapet, wall-walk, walkway, merlon, embrasure

Sides, corner, edge

Arrow slits, portholes, murder holes

Courtyard, bailey, ward

Roof, spires, minarets, domes, statues

Alarm, bells, horn, bugle, drums, chant, prayers, shouts, cheers

Lights, torch, torchlight, shadows

Tar, oil, pitch, lead, fire, water

Guards, sentries, armour, lances, javelins, spears, crossbows, bows, arrows, shields, swords

Attack, onslaught

Machines, engines, weapons, ballista, belfry, siege engine, tower, catapult, trebuchet, mangonel, battering ram, cannon, hwachas, ladders, pole arms

Wheels, carriage, arm, beam, fulcrum, head, bucket, pouch, sling, chains, ropes, poles, levers, pulleys, weights

Shelter, protection, tortoise, gallery, shed

Plates, hides, skins, wool, vinegar, urine

Missiles, objects, stones, rocks, boulders, sticks, dung, bodies, heads, animals, snakes, disease

Pieces, fragments, shards, shrapnel, debris, rubble, dust

Twang, ripple, creak, rattle, shriek, whistle

Smell, stench, reek

Hole, gap, breach

Similes/ Metaphors

Statues like pieces on a chessboard; enormous rocks the size of barrels; great, spoon-like arm; frightful, wooden beast; like huge crossbows; head shaped like a raven; bronze beak; thrust like a sword; as sharp as needles; thrust like a mailed fist; as dark as flint

Adjectives

Outer, inner, front, back, side

Northern, southern, eastern, western

Round, square, rectangular, bowl-shaped, spoon-like, curved, crooked, winding

Narrow, wide, long, steep, sheer, low, deep, shallow

Solid, hollow

Metal, iron, iron-tipped, iron-bound, iron-covered, wood, wooden, marble, glass

Dark-clad, armoured

High, towering, hulking, soaring

Red, white, silver, gilded

Dark, black, grey, grim

Frightful, forbidding, menacing, sinister, eerie, macabre

Ferocious, dangerous, treacherous

Large, huge, giant, enormous, massive, immense, gigantic

Rough, rutted, jagged, spiked, needle-sharp

Dry, filthy, foul, slime-filled, foul-smelling

Deadly, lethal, murderous, venomous, destructive

Vile, severed, dead, poisonous, disease-ridden

Flickering, glinting, flaring, flashing

Many, several, lots, numerous, hundreds, thousands

Random, regular, systematic

Verbs

Marched, moved, advanced, swept

Saw, spotted, glimpsed, made out, caught sight of, revealed

Warned, alerted, signalled

Rose, soared, spiralled, erupted, reared, thrust, pierced

Loomed, stretched, blocked, shadowed, brooded

Surrounded, encircled, enclosed, ringed

Protected, defended, shielded, guarded

Built, constructed, erected, assembled

Stood, perched

Led, ran, curved, weaved

Located, set, positioned, situated

Lined, flanked, edged, bordered

Dotted, studded, peppered, interspersed

Topped, crowned, capped

Strengthened, fitted with, reinforced, fortified

Sunk, inserted, fixed, lodged, embedded

Rang, tolled, chimed, pealed

Watched, viewed, observed, surveyed

Raised, lifted, lowered, shut, locked, barred, sealed

Posted, placed, positioned, stationed, deployed

Stood, manned, marched, patrolled

Wielded, brandished

Hid, concealed, camouflaged

Prepared, poised

Shaped, moulded, sculpted

Thrust, aimed, directed, trained, levelled

Dangled, hung, suspended, swung, swayed

Dragged, hauled, heaved, yanked, lugged

Sent, tossed, flung, scattered, showered, sprayed, spattered

Shook, shivered, shuddered, juddered

Cracked, crushed, crumbled, splattered, flattened, collapsed

Resisted, withstood

Surged, poured, rushed, streamed

Covered, sheltered

Prevented, stopped

Glistened, glimmered, glinted

Soaked, dipped, doused, rinsed

Stuffed, filled, packed

Gaped, opened, yawned

Fixed, attached, fastened, bolted

Loaded, stacked, piled, extended

Mounted, launched, attacked, assaulted

Released, discharged, ejected

Hurled, pitched, hurtled, propelled

Battered, pounded, punched, hammered, crashed, slammed, pummelled, rattled

Rained, hailed, dropped, descended, plunged, plummeted

Echoed, beat, rang, chanted, prayed, shouted, cheered, jeered

PHRASES – NOUNS AND ADJECTIVES

* In the distance
* Across the . . .
* Just beyond the . . .
* On the edge of . . .
* Away to the right

- ⭑ Ahead of them
- ⭑ In front of them
- ⭑ All around
- ⭑ Every so often
- ⭑ At regular intervals
- ⭑ At random intervals
- ⭑ *Within sight of the watchtower*
- ⭑ Through a break in the trees
- ⭑ In the valley below them
- ⭑ On top of sheer, black cliffs
- ⭑ Visible over the high walls
- ⭑ *Fields to the south*
- ⭑ Treacherous bogs and marshes to the north
- ⭑ *A narrow, rutted road*
- ⭑ Long, winding, sheer road
- ⭑ *A vast, towering fortress*
- ⭑ Silhouette of a huge, dark castle
- ⭑ A grey, forbidding castle
- ⭑ Dark, macabre castle
- ⭑ A huge citadel
- ⭑ Massive keep
- ⭑ *Around the castle*
- ⭑ Outside the city
- ⭑ Round the edge of the castle
- ⭑ Across the narrow, foul-smelling moat
- ⭑ On three sides
- ⭑ At each corner
- ⭑ On either side of the entrance
- ⭑ From the tops of the towers
- ⭑ Between the towers
- ⭑ From the battlements on the city walls
- ⭑ Around the outer side of the wall-walk
- ⭑ Behind the portcullis
- ⭑ *A series of turrets*
- ⭑ Grim, forbidding towers
- ⭑ Square turrets
- ⭑ Round, drum towers
- ⭑ Iron ramparts
- ⭑ Two-storey, square tower
- ⭑ Central structure with two towers, four storeys high
- ⭑ Hulking towers and turrets
- ⭑ Towers and turrets as dark as flint
- ⭑ Numerous, menacing towers
- ⭑ Wooden watchtowers

* *Soaring towers*
* Grey towers and red-tiled roofs
* Long, crooked spires as sharp as needles
* Shimmering white and silver spires
* Gilded minarets
* Curved domes of glass and marble
* Statues like pieces on a chessboard
* *High walls*
* Massive, curtain walls
* Grey, fortified walls
* Battlements on the walls
* Walkway on top of the walls
* Parapet at the top of the fortification
* *Over the twelve-foot-high walls*
* In front of the northern wall
* Above the towering wall
* Behind the city walls
* *A dry moat*
* Steep-walled moat
* Slime-filled moat
* Hidden dangers beneath the surface of the moat
* *Narrow, rickety bridge*
* Huge planks
* *Outer gate*
* Inner gate
* South gate
* At the gates
* Above the gate
* Behind the portcullis
* *Towering, heavy, city gates*
* Wooden gates
* Heavy, double doors
* Solid iron gates
* Giant, iron doors
* Massive, iron-bound gate
* Sharp, metal spikes
* Two iron portcullises
* *Hollow slits either side of the doors*
* Archers' nests
* Arrow slits in the form of crosses
* *A warning bell*
* Bells of the city
* Creak of leather
* *Sputtering torches*

* Flickering lights of the city
* *Extra guards*
* Sentries in dark-clad armour
* Soldiers in black armour
* Archers on top of the walls
* Lethal, pointed lances
* *Enormous machines*
* Biggest siege engine ever
* Frightful wooden beast
* Wheeled, siege engines
* Square tower over ten storeys tall
* Twelve, massive, iron-covered wheels
* Portholes in the front of the machine
* *Menacing mangonels*
* Huge, spoon-like, wooden arm
* Bowl-shaped bucket
* Ballistae like huge crossbows
* Long ladders and poles
* *Battering ram*
* Huge tree trunk
* Bands of iron
* Lethal, metal head
* Bronze beak
* *Huge trebuchets with their enormous levers and slings*
* Upright beam
* Sixty-foot wooden arm
* Leather pouch
* *Enormous missiles*
* Heavy loads
* Deadly missiles
* Massive, heavy boulder
* Enormous rocks the size of barrels
* Over three thousand stones and rocks
* An explosion of stone and dust
* *Lethal javelins*
* Flights of arrows
* Fragments of needle-sharp iron
* Vile objects – dung, dead animals, nests of poisonous snakes
* Severed heads of prisoners
* Disease-ridden bodies
* Dead bodies and body parts
* *Inside the cover of the tortoise*
* Towards the gates
* To the right of the gatehouse

- From the city walls
- *Tell-tale glint of hundreds of arrows*
- Line of flickering torchlight
- *A low, whistling shriek*
- With a chorus of prayers, shouts and cheers

PHRASES – VERBS

- As they marched closer to the city
- As they left the forest
- As the gloom lifted
- *Could just make out . . .*
- Glimpsed . . . in the distance
- Could see the lights of the city
- *Alerted them that they were within sight of . . .*
- Warned them of . . .
- *Loomed into sight*
- Loomed ahead of them
- Erupted out of the land
- Reared out of the hills
- Pierced the sky
- Thrust like a mailed fist above the . . .
- *Shadowed the horizon*
- Created a jagged pattern on the horizon
- Stretched across the landscape in front of them
- *Surrounded by a dense wood*
- Shadowed by three huge, jagged mountains
- Protected by the river to the south
- Peppered with lethal bogs and marshes
- *Built on a high hill*
- Perched on a massive, table-like rock
- *Led to the city*
- Curved up the hillside towards the city
- Weaved in and out of the hillside
- *Revealed an enormous castle*
- Rose a huge citadel
- *Soared into the clouds*
- Lost in wisps of cloud
- *Flanked by high, stone walls*
- Ringed by high, black, fortified walls
- *Peppered with arrow slits*
- Studded with archers' nests
- Lined with rectangular arrow slits

- *Built of immense blocks of black stone*
- Peppered with round, drum towers
- Strengthened with many towers
- Topped with a series of turrets
- Topped with a walkway
- Crowned with iron ramparts
- Topped by long, crooked spires as sharp as needles
- *Rose at each corner*
- Perched on the edge of the turrets
- Looked out over the city walls
- *Leading to the gate was a drawbridge*
- Lined at random intervals with huge knives
- Sunken metal tips pointed upwards
- *Surrounded the castle*
- Protected the base of the castle
- Strewn with filth from the castle latrines
- Although the water in the moat wasn't deep
- Knew that beneath the surface lay hidden dangers
- Embedded in the ground were iron-tipped spikes
- *Filled with rocks*
- Positioned huge planks over the moat
- Allowed smooth access for the siege engines
- *Positioned between two large towers*
- Flanked by two towers
- Rose an enormous archway
- Towers buttressed the barbican
- *Built a turret over the archway*
- Projected out beyond the wall of the building
- *Enabled missiles to be dropped*
- Allowed boiled lead to be poured down on invaders
- *Mounted on either side of the entrance were ballistae*
- Filled with bristling arrows
- *Built the doorway twelve feet above the ground*
- Could only be reached by a series of wooden steps
- Hauled the steps back up to the huge door
- *Doors looked thicker than the biggest tree trunks in the forest*
- Set between two large towers
- Reinforced with huge metal struts
- Studded with huge spiked rivets
- Topped with sharp metal spikes
- Impaled anyone who tried to charge it
- *Blazed from the tops of the towers*
- Flickered on top of the ramparts
- Glittered in the torchlight

- ★ Glinted in the bright sunlight
- ★ Cast eerie shadows
- ★ *Rang out from the roof of one of the towers*
- ★ Tolled frantically to warn of the enemy's approach
- ★ Heard the sound of rattling chains
- ★ *As they watched and waited . . .*
- ★ As the drawbridge was raised . . .
- ★ As the portcullis was lowered . . .
- ★ Sealed the great gates
- ★ *Posted at the southern gate*
- ★ Stood guard on the top of the walls
- ★ Manned by sentries with mounted crossbows
- ★ Marched back and forth
- ★ Wielded iron-tipped lances
- ★ *Had built many weapons*
- ★ Lined up outside the city walls were . . .
- ★ Hidden from view
- ★ Ready to mount a surprise attack
- ★ *Hurled rocks at and over the walls*
- ★ Battered the walls
- ★ Discharged enormous missiles
- ★ Fired lethal javelins
- ★ Capable of skewering several men at once
- ★ *Used the huge trunk as a battering ram*
- ★ Reinforced with bands of iron
- ★ Fitted with a metal head
- ★ Shaped like a ram
- ★ Thrust like a sword towards the gates
- ★ Dangled on chains inside the tortoise
- ★ Swung on its carriage
- ★ Dragged back and forth to batter the gates
- ★ Pounded the castle gates with its lethal metal head
- ★ Pounded, punched and hammered again and again
- ★ Sent fragments of needle-sharp iron to shower the guards
- ★ *Protected the tortoise from fire hurled from the castle walls*
- ★ Glistened with wet hides that had been soaked in vinegar
- ★ *Had taken weeks to construct*
- ★ Ready to pound the city into dust
- ★ Would not be able to withstand the ferocious, destructive pounding from such a machine
- ★ *Covered in metal plates on three sides*
- ★ Gaped from the front of the machine
- ★ Covered with skins

- Stuffed with wool
- Prevented it being destroyed by fire or boiling oil
- Sprang into action
- *Heard a twang, then another, and another*
- Fixed the heavy weights to the short end of the trebuchet's arm
- Placed the stone in the leather pouch
- Released the upright beams
- Propelled the long end upward
- Hurled the stone towards the walls
- Hurled a hail of stones and rocks
- *Rattled and crashed against the walls*
- Rained down on the city
- Slammed, crashed, pounded the city
- Shook and shuddered under the onslaught
- Echoed over the castle
- Hurled at the walls from the catapults
- Smashed into the walls
- Released in just one day
- Crumbled the building inside
- *Hurled body parts over the walls*
- Splattered inside the courtyard
- Spread disease throughout the castle
- *Hauled the spoon-like arm back*
- Loaded the stone into the bowl-shaped bucket
- Released the ropes
- Hurtled through the air
- Collapsed in an explosion of stone and dust
- *As the drums renewed their beat*
- Rose among the ranks massed in front of the gates
- Raised their swords and spears over their heads
- Surged through the gap
- Stationed on the parapet
- *Rained down onto the square*
- *Raised shields above their heads*
- Made it through the gap

SENTENCES

Every so often, a spire pierced the sky, alerting them that they were within sight of the watchtowers.

Stretching across the landscape in front of them was a wall, peppered with round, drum towers and crowned with iron ramparts.

The gloom lifted to reveal a castle, built on a high hill and surrounded by a dense wood.

On top of the sheer black cliffs was a dark, macabre castle perched on a massive, table-like rock.

A dark, jagged pattern shadowed the horizon. In the valley below them, they could just make out the silhouette of a huge, dark castle with high walls, grim, forbidding towers and long, crooked spires as sharp as needles.

A grey, forbidding castle loomed into sight through a break in the trees, thrusting like a mailed fist above the woods.

Hulking towers and turrets soared into the clouds, the only thing visible over the twelve-foot-high walls.

Above the towering wall, rose forbidding towers and long, crooked spires as sharp as needles.

The central structure had two towers, four storeys high, and was topped with a series of turrets.

As they marched closer to the city, numerous menacing towers erupted out of the land, their tops lost in wisps of cloud.

Towers and turrets as dark as flint blocked the horizon.

Away to their right, rearing out of the hills, was a vast, towering fortress with square turrets at each corner.

Looking out over the city walls were eerie statues, like pieces on a chessboard, perched on the edge of the turrets.

Flanked by high stone walls, the narrow, rutted road curved up the hillside towards the city.

The north was protected by the river, and the fields to the south peppered with lethal bogs and marshes.

As they left the forest, suddenly they could see the lights of the city in the valley below them.

The flickering lights of the city could be seen in the distance. They could just make out the grey towers and red-tiled roofs.

Ahead of them, glinting in the bright sunlight, were shimmering white and silver spires, gilded minarets, and curved domes of glass and marble.

The city walls weaved in and out of the hillside.

The city was ringed by high, grey, fortified walls that had been peppered with arrow slits.

Around the castle were massive curtain walls, studded with archers' nests.

Wooden watchtowers rose at each corner, manned by sentries with mounted crossbows.

Round the edge of the castle ran high walls, ten feet thick, They had been strengthened with many towers, lined with rectangular arrow slits and topped with a walkway for sentries.

A dry moat surrounded the castle, lined at random intervals with huge knives, sunk point-upwards.

A moat strewn with filth from the castle latrines protected the base of the castle.

The water in the moat wasn't deep, but they knew that beneath the surface iron-tipped spikes were embedded in the ground.

Across the narrow, foul-smelling moat was a narrow, rickety bridge.

A drawbridge led to the gate, which was set between two large towers.

The drawbridge creaked as it was raised, and they heard the sound of rattling chains as the portcullis was lowered.

The drawbridge was up, the portcullis down, and the great gates sealed.

Torches flickered on top of the ramparts, casting eerie shadows as the sentries marched back and forth.

Torchlight blazed from the tops of the towers, from the battlements on the city walls and from each of the gates.

The towering, city gates were heavy and studded with huge, spiked rivets.

The wooden gates looked thicker than the largest tree trunks in the forest and were reinforced with huge, metal struts.

Looming before them, waiting to impale anyone who tried to charge it, was a massive, iron-bound gate, topped with sharp, metal spikes.

The doorway had been built twelve feet above the ground and could only be reached by a series of wooden steps that had been hauled back up to the door.

Ahead of them were towering gates, flanked by two towers. Between the towers rose an enormous archway.

A turret had been built over the archway, projecting out beyond the wall of the building. From there, missiles could be dropped or boiled lead poured down on invaders.

Ballistae were mounted on either side of the entrance.

A warning bell rang out from the roof of one of the towers.

The bells of the city tolled, warning of their approach.

Sentries in dark-clad armour stood guard on the top of the walls. The hollow slits either side of the doors were filled with bristling arrows.

Behind the portcullis, soldiers in black armour wielded lances, their lethal points glittering in the torchlight.

The steep-walled moat would make approaching the castle difficult, but hopefully not give the defenders enough time to prepare their defences.

All the trees and vegetation around the city had been chopped down and cleared to prevent them having access to material to construct their siege engines and fuel their camp fires.

When the moat had been filled with rocks, huge planks were positioned over the moat to allow smooth access for the wheeled, siege engines.

Lined up outside the city were massive machines for battering the walls and discharging enormous missiles.

Over the last few days, they had been frantically building many weapons: catapults to hurl rocks at and over the walls; mangonels with their huge, wooden arms and bowl-shaped buckets; ballistae like huge crossbows to fire lethal javelins capable of skewering several men at once; and long ladders and poles for scaling the walls.

The huge tree trunk had been reinforced with bands of iron and fitted with a metal head shaped like a ram to be used as a battering ram.

Inside the cover of the tortoise, the battering ram dangled on chains, ready to pound the castle gates with its lethal head.

The metal head was shaped like a raven, its bronze beak thrust like a sword towards the gates.

The walls of the tortoise glistened with wet hides that had been soaked in vinegar to protect it from fire hurled from the castle walls.

The frightful wooden beast had taken weeks to construct, and now it was ready to pound the city into dust.

It was the biggest siege engine ever built and there was no way the city walls would be able to withstand the ferocious, destructive pounding from such a machine.

The square tower was two hundred feet tall, with twelve massive, iron-covered wheels.

It was over ten storeys high and covered in metal plates on three sides.

Portholes gaped from the front of the machine, each covered with skins that had been stuffed with wool to prevent it being destroyed by fire or boiling oil.

The great spoon-like arm of the mangonel was hauled back and a massive boulder loaded into the bowl-shaped bucket.

As the ropes were released, the heavy boulder hurtled through the air and smashed into the wall to the right of the gatehouse.

The huge trebuchets were hidden from view, ready to mount a surprise attack and launch their heavy loads capable of reducing the castle to rubble.

All of a sudden, he heard a twang, then another, and another, as the trebuchets sprang into action.

He watched as the upright beams were released to hurl a hail of stones and rocks to rattle and crash against the walls.

A line of flickering torchlight lit up the deadly missiles that continued to rain down on the city.

Slamming, crashing, the trebuchets pounded the city day after day, until the walls shook, shuddered and cracked under the onslaught.

Night after night, a low, whistling shriek echoed over the castle, as enormous rocks the size of barrels were hurled at the walls from the catapults.

Over three thousand stones and rocks had been released in just one day to smash into the walls and crumble the buildings inside.

Every day more and more vile objects were hurled over the walls – dung, dead animals, nests of poisonous snakes, severed heads of prisoners.

Now, each day, the stones, rocks and boulders were joined by parts of the disease-ridden bodies of the dead.

Body parts hurtled over the walls to splatter inside the courtyard and to spread their disease throughout the castle.

The battering ram swung on its carriage as it was dragged back and forth to batter the gates.

Again and again, the battering ram pounded, punched and hammered at the metal, sending fragments of needle-sharp iron to shower the guards.

The wall collapsed in an explosion of stone and dust. Immediately, the drums renewed their beat. At the same time, a chant rose among the ranks massed in front of the wall, and with a chorus of prayers, shouts and cheers, they raised their swords and spears over their heads and surged through the gap.

Flights of arrows rained down onto the square from the archers stationed on the parapet.

With shields raised above their heads, most of them made it through the gap.

SECTION 2 – INTERACTION

WORDS

Nouns

Castle, city, walls, battlements, ramparts, gatehouse, gates, moat, trench, ditch

Army, troops, soldiers, archers, sappers

Orders, commands, directions, instructions

Silhouette, shadows

Slit

Siege engine, ram, mangonel, trebuchet, tower, wheels, arm, beam, bucket, ropes, chains, gangplank, gallery, tortoise, ladders, poles

Horses, hooves, reins

Action, barrage, onslaught, destruction

Cover, shelter, protection

Crossbows, arrows, bolts, bowstrings, swords, shields

Stones, rocks, boulders, missiles, sticks, twigs

Drums, drummers, beat, rhythm

Trumpet, blasts

Groan, creak, twang, screech, boom, cry

Desperation, pain, agony

Similes/ Metaphors

Spoon-like arm; bowl-shaped bucket; screech like rusty hinges; time limped by; as if the ... was holding its breath; as if everything was happening in slow motion

Adjectives

Massive, huge, great, enormous, gigantic

Heavy, solid

Right, left, east, west, north, south

Armoured, iron-clad

Wooden, metal, iron, bronze, steely

Relentless, persistent, continuous, endless, unremitting

Hundreds, thousands, numerous

Sharp, piercing, loud, shrill, high-pitched, harsh, deafening, ear-piercing, ear-shattering

Terrifying, ominous, deadly, lethal

Sudden, brief

Distinctive, unmistakable

Verbs	**Looked**, watched, searched, peered, exchanged, blinked

Saw, glimpsed, caught sight of

Ordered, instructed, commanded, shouted, urged

Stopped, halted, waited

Resumed, restarted, recommenced

Led, guided, steered

Moved, drew closer, lurched, lumbered, trundled, rolled, pitched

Dragged, tugged, hauled, heaved, pulled, pushed, carried, tipped, upended

Dug, tunnelled, mined, burrowed

Packed, filled, stuffed, crammed

Aimed, pointed, directed, trained, levelled

Released, loosed, launched

Arced up, climbed, sailed, flew, shot, streaked

Rained down, hailed, showered, pelted, plunged

Hit, slammed, smashed, pierced, stabbed, punctured

Reared, lunged, charged, pounced, wrestled, fought

Beat, banged, hit, struck

Blew, sounded, blasted

Rattled, crashed

Filled, echoed, resonated, reverberated

Announced, declared, proclaimed, trumpeted, signalled, heralded

Alerted, warned

Threatened, foreshadowed

Raised, lifted, lowered

Flung out, groped, fumbled, searched, scrabbled, grabbed, snatched

Stood, straightened

Turned, whirled, spun

Sheltered, dived, dropped, ducked, scrambled, crouched, huddled

Avoided, evaded, dodged, missed

Fell, stumbled, toppled, tumbled

Darted, raced, rushed, dashed, sprinted, pelted, stormed

Unsheathed, drew, grasped, clutched, gripped

Stifled, muffled, smothered, swallowed

Prayed, hoped

Gritted, clenched

PHRASES – NOUNS AND ADJECTIVES

* *Almost at once*
* Without warning
* Not enough time to . . .
* At that very moment
* All of a sudden
* At the last moment
* For a moment
* *All around him*
* Above her on the battlements
* In front of him
* Just above his head
* *Into the moat*
* Towards the walls of the castle
* Against the city walls
* From the top of the ramparts
* Near the castle walls
* To the right of the gatehouse
* Through a slit in the back wall
* Under the cover of the wheeled gallery
* Beneath the gigantic wheels
* *One of the horses*
* Enormous, armoured beasts
* *Siege engine*

* Wooden tower
* Wheels of the siege engine
* Great, spoon-like arm of the mangonel
* Bowl-shaped bucket
* Huge wooden ram
* *Steely glints*
* Cloud of arrows
* Relentless hail of arrows
* *Stones and rocks*
* A hail of sticks, stones
* An explosion of masonry and dust
* *With an enormous groan*
* Rhythmic beat of the drums
* Terrifying boom of the war drums
* Distinctive twang of the trebuchets
* With a screech like rusty hinges
* With a cry of despair

PHRASES – VERBS

* *Halted outside the city limits*
* Announced their arrival
* Threatened destruction and defeat
* *Even as he watched* . . .
* As they waited . . .
* *Time stood still*
* Time limped by while they waited for . . .
* As if the whole army was holding its breath
* As if everything was happening in slow motion
* *As the hours passed, they began to* . . .
* When the order eventually came to . . .
* *Filled with a deafening crash*
* Enormous trees were felled
* As he was leading his troops out of the wood . . .
* *Dragged along the huge, tree trunk*
* Reared up suddenly
* Struck the air with its hooves
* *Lunged at the horse*
* Wrestled desperately with the reins
* Fought to bring it under control
* Heaved, pushed, dragged and tipped rocks and boulders into the moat
* *Started to move suddenly*
* Lurched forward all of a sudden

- ★ Lumbered towards the castle
- ★ Rolled slowly towards the gates
- ★ As the tower drew closer to the walls . . .
- ★ As the siege engine stopped . . .
- ★ *Once the mangonel was ready*
- ★ Sprang into action
- ★ Hauled back the . . .
- ★ Heaved the massive boulder
- ★ Released the huge, wooden beams
- ★ As the ropes were released . . .
- ★ Filled with the twang from . . .
- ★ Released their deadly load
- ★ Aimed at the walls
- ★ Resumed their onslaught
- ★ *As soon as the gangplank was lowered*
- ★ Carried the long ladders and poles
- ★ When the last ladder had passed . . .
- ★ *Burrowed into the base of the wall*
- ★ Packed the twigs into the hole in the wall
- ★ *Alerted Rob that . . .*
- ★ Stopped dead in his tracks
- ★ Stopped abruptly
- ★ Waited nervously on the ladders
- ★ Were ready to rush onto the walls
- ★ *Straightened and looked up*
- ★ Caught a brief glimpse of a silhouette
- ★ Turned and caught a glimpse of . . .
- ★ Peered over the top of the trench
- ★ Peered out of the side of the gallery
- ★ Looked up at the battlements
- ★ Exchanged a brief look before . . .
- ★ Blinked in the sudden sunshine
- ★ Watched as the heavy boulder . . .
- ★ Squeezed his eyes shut and prayed
- ★ *Alerted him that . . .*
- ★ Just as he was starting to give up hope that . . .
- ★ Certain that everything had been checked
- ★ *Held his breath*
- ★ Gritted his teeth
- ★ Prayed that the trebuchet was not . . .
- ★ Didn't know which way to run
- ★ *Hurtled through the air*
- ★ Smashed into the wall
- ★ *Drawn crossbows were pointed towards them*

- ★ Watched the bolt coming towards him
- ★ Arced up into the air
- ★ Rained down on them
- ★ Plunged towards them
- ★ Flew past her ear
- ★ Rained down onto the roof of the gallery
- ★ Pierced the wood
- ★ Rattled and crashed
- ★ *Narrowly avoided the arrow which . . .*
- ★ Narrowly evaded an arrow
- ★ *Unsheathed his sword*
- ★ Grasped their swords
- ★ Gripped his shield tighter
- ★ Lifted their shields over their heads
- ★ With their shields raised above their heads
- ★ *Lifted her trumpet*
- ★ Blew two, sharp blasts
- ★ Beat his sword against his shield
- ★ *Turned to the drummers and raised his arm*
- ★ Lowered her arm
- ★ With her left arm outstretched
- ★ Pointed frantically at . . .
- ★ *Shouted at her men on the top level of the tower*
- ★ Ordered the men to be ready to . . .
- ★ Commanded the men to her left to . . .
- ★ Urged his men to sprint forward
- ★ *As more and more of his men fell to the ground*
- ★ *Searched for cover*
- ★ Had taken cover the moment . . .
- ★ Dropped into a defensive crouch
- ★ Crouched on the battlements
- ★ Crouched inside the tortoise
- ★ Crouched at the base of the wall
- ★ Huddled behind the . . .
- ★ Sheltered from the barrage of arrows and missiles
- ★ Flung himself down behind . . .
- ★ Ducked frantically
- ★ Ducked instinctively down behind . . .
- ★ Dived back under the gallery
- ★ Scrambled back behind . . .
- ★ *Stumbled and flung her hand out*
- ★ Grasped the pole
- ★ Groped for something to . . .
- ★ Tried to grab something

- ✳ Snatched at thin air
- ✳ *Held himself upright*
- ✳ Stopped her falling
- ✳ Stopped him being crushed
- ✳ Just missed the chains securing the battering ram
- ✳ Slammed into her leg
- ✳ Tumbled to the ground
- ✳ *Stifled a scream of agony*
- ✳ *Heaved the gates back*
- ✳ As soon as the gates began to creak open . . .
- ✳ *Darted from side to side in desperation*
- ✳ Pelted after the other troops
- ✳ Joined the others
- ✳ *Darted through the gap*
- ✳ Stormed through

SENTENCES

As the order eventually came to halt outside the city limits, Tom turned to the drummers and raised his arm. At once the terrifying boom of the war drums filled the air.

Tom unsheathed his sword and beat it against his shield in time to the rhythm of the drums. All around him, soldiers began to slam their weapons against their shields, announcing their arrival and threatening destruction and defeat.

He stopped dead in his tracks. The wood was filled with a deafening crash, then another as the enormous trees were felled.

As he was leading his troops out of the wood, one of the horses dragging along the huge tree trunk suddenly reared up and struck the air with its hooves. The trunk started to roll. Rob lunged at the horse. Wrestling desperately with the reins, he fought to bring it under control.

Hour after hour, he had heaved, pushed, dragged and tipped rocks and boulders into the moat. Just as he was starting to give up hope that the moat would ever be filled, the enormous, armoured mules arrived.

Certain that everything had been checked, Kitty lifted her trumpet, and blew two sharp blasts. With an enormous groan, the siege engine lumbered towards the castle.

With a screech like rusty hinges, the wheels of the siege engine suddenly started to move and the tower lurched forward. Katie stumbled and flung her hand out to grasp the pole, groping for something to stop her falling and being crushed beneath the gigantic wheels.

As the siege engine stopped near the castle walls, Kitty straightened and looked up. She caught a brief glimpse of a silhouette crouched on the battlements above her.

Steely glints caught the morning sun, alerting Rob that drawn crossbows were pointed towards them from the top of the ramparts. Frantically, he ducked and scrambled back behind the wooden tower.

A hail of arrows arced up into the air, and rained down on them. As one, they dropped into a defensive crouch and lifted their shields over their heads. Time stood still. It was as if the whole army was holding its breath.

It was as if everything was happening in slow motion as he watched the bolt coming towards him, and at the last moment, he ducked down behind the tortoise, narrowly avoiding the arrow that pierced the wood just above his head.

As the tower drew closer to the walls, Katie shouted to her men on the top level to be ready to lower the drawbridge.

Waiting nervously on the ladders, Rob and Kitty exchanged a brief look before grasping their swords, ready to rush onto the walls, the moment the gangplank was lowered.

They crouched inside the tortoise, sheltering from the barrage of arrows and missiles raining down on them from the walls of the castle as the battering ram slowly rolled towards the gates.

Katie turned and, through a slit in the back wall, caught a glimpse of the rest of the troops huddled behind the shed.

The tortoise suddenly lurched, and Rob tried to grab something to hold himself upright. His hand just missed the chains securing the battering ram, and instead Rob found himself snatching at thin air.

With a cry of despair, Katie tumbled to the ground, stifling a scream of agony as the huge wooden ram slammed into her leg.

Kitty watched as they hauled back the great spoon-like arm of the mangonel. Once it was ready, she lowered her arm, ordering the men to her left to heave the massive boulder into the bowl-shaped bucket.

As the ropes were released, Rob peered over the top of the trench. Blinking in the sudden sunshine, he watched the heavy boulder hurtle through the air and smash into the wall to the right of the gatehouse.

The relentless hail of arrows that had rained down onto the roof of the gallery abruptly stopped. Tom peered out of the side of the gallery and looked up at the battlements. There was no sign of the archers. They had taken cover the moment the missiles had plunged towards them.

As a spear flew past her ear, Kitty flung herself down behind the trebuchet.

The moment the hail of stones that had rattled and crashed against the city walls stopped, the archers resumed their onslaught. Kitty dived back under the gallery, just narrowly evading an arrow that flew past her face.

With her left arm outstretched, Kitty pointed frantically at the castle wall, urging her troops carrying the long ladders and poles to sprint forward.

When the last ladder had passed, Kitty raised her shield over her head, gritted her teeth and pelted after them.

Rob gripped his shield tighter as the air was filled with the twang from hundreds of bowstrings loosing their arrows.

For a moment, he froze. He didn't know which way to run. Above him, a cloud of arrows rained down. His eyes darted from side to side in desperation, searching for cover, as more and more of his men fell to the ground in front of him.

As soon as the gates began to creak open, Rob and his men stormed through, heaving them back and scattering the guards.

Suddenly, in a burst of masonry and dust, the wall collapsed. With their shields raised above their heads, Tom and Rob joined the others and darted through the gap.

15

Defending a castle, fortress or walled city

SECTION 1 – SETTING

WORDS

Nouns

Army, enemy, invaders, attackers, assailants

Soldiers, armour, spikes, wagons, beasts

Trail, dust, light, torches

Castle, city, walls, gates, doors, buildings, houses

Citizens, inhabitants

Guard towers, gatehouse, battlements, parapet, bailey, courtyard

Horn, bells, blast, toll

Ballistae, siege towers, catapults, trebuchets, hwachas, ladders, sappers, battering ram, chain, links, pole

Orders, commands

Murder holes, arrow slits

Archers, bows, crossbows, cords, string, groove, bolts, arrows, feathers

Stones, rocks, boulders, avalanche

Water, pitch, tar, lead, oil, urine

Fire container, urn, vat, cauldron, buckets, pots

Braziers, torch, fire, Greek fire, fire arrows, flames, inferno, gunpowder

Ladders, pole-arms

Weapons, pitchforks, axes, hammers, spears

Cannon, mount, wheels, touch hole, cannon balls

Echo, quiet, ripple, twangs, hisses, whistle, cries, shriek, screams

Similes/ Metaphors

Stones the size of a football

Adjectives

Outer, exterior, external, inner, interior, internal

North, south, east, west

Top, tip, peak, ground, base, foundation

Black, dark

Thousands, hundreds, dozens, groups, piles

Mounted, foot soldiers

Skilled, accurate, precise, deadly, treacherous

Quick, rapid

Bristling, bursting

Boiling, bubbling, sizzling, scalding, flaming

Glinting, blazing

Silent, eerie, alarming, terrifying, fearful

Loud, urgent, frantic, desperate

Large, huge, enormous

Brass, metal, iron, cast-iron, wooden

Verbs

Marched, advanced, tramped

Stretched, spread, expanded

Trailed, shadowed

Saw, spotted, made out, glimpsed, caught sight of, revealed

Cut off, surrounded, blocked, trapped, isolated

Breached, cracked, crumbled, fractured

Blew, sounded, tolled, chimed, clanged

Grew, increased, swelled, filled

Ordered, commanded, directed, instructed

Closed, shut, sealed, barred

Buzzed, whirred, hummed

Rushed, ran, darted, bolted, dashed

Hammered, banged, pounded

Mustered, rallied, mobilised, marshalled

Stood, positioned, manned, stationed

Watched, stared, observed, surveyed

Piled, stacked, heaped

Dropped, poured, toppled, tumbled, plunged, cascaded, plummeted

Filled, loaded

Combated, resisted, repelled

Warmed, heated, melted, boiled

Poised, prepared, braced

Winced, grimaced, flinched

Drowned, silenced, muffled

Slammed, smashed, crashed, shattered, crumbled, crushed, collapsed

Clasped, clutched, grasped, gripped

Thrown, flung, pitched, heaved, launched

Roared, bucked, exploded

Licked, flicked

Engulfed, drowned, enveloped

Melted, scorched, charred

Loaded, reloaded, pulled, yanked, hauled back, aimed, fired

Waited, hesitated, paused

Gathered, assembled

Leaned over, dangled, hung

Rained, hailed, showered, pelted

Blasted, exploded, burst

Passed, touched

Hissed, sputtered, flared

PHRASES – NOUNS AND ADJECTIVES

- ★ Outer wall of the castle
- ★ Beyond the gatehouse
- ★ On top of the east gate
- ★ Inner courtyard
- ★ Below him in the streets
- ★ *Approaching army*
- ★ A sea of black
- ★ Trail of dust
- ★ *Thousands of mounted soldiers*
- ★ Hundreds of soldiers
- ★ Groups of skilled archers
- ★ Hundreds of wagons and beasts
- ★ *Flicker of light from their torches*
- ★ Glints of armour
- ★ Bristling spikes
- ★ *Enormous siege engines*
- ★ A dozen ballistae
- ★ Massive siege towers
- ★ Taller than the city walls
- ★ Trebuchets bristling with archers
- ★ *Every few paces along the parapet*
- ★ Alongside the brass container
- ★ In the side of the building
- ★ *Out over the wall*
- ★ Through the holes in the floor
- ★ *Onto the soldiers at the base of the castle*
- ★ Onto the wooden tower
- ★ *Rolls of straw*
- ★ Piles of stones, each the size of a football
- ★ *Huge vats*
- ★ Large cast-iron pots
- ★ *Cannons on cast-iron mounts*
- ★ A pile of cannon balls
- ★ *A hail of flaming arrows*
- ★ Over two hundred fire arrows
- ★ Hwacha and bags of gunpowder
- ★ Column of flames
- ★ *A deadly hail of bolts*
- ★ An avalanche of rocks
- ★ Boiling pitch
- ★ *Eerily quiet*
- ★ Fearful echo

- Two blasts from a horn
- Ripple of twangs and hisses
- Battle cries
- A terrifying shriek

PHRASES – VERBS

- Stretched as far as the eye could see
- Marched towards the castle
- Marched behind the mounted soldiers
- Trailed behind the army
- *As the army drew nearer*
- Could make out . . .
- *Had been cut off during the night*
- Surrounded the city
- Positioned before the outer wall of the castle
- *Before relief could reach them*
- Would starve or the defences would be breached
- *Lumbered towards the walls*
- As the battering ram was brought up to the gates . . .
- Drowned out suddenly by . . .
- *Blew from the towers*
- Grew gradually louder and more urgent
- Filled the air
- Tolled to order the gate to be closed
- *Buzzed with frantic activity*
- Rushed from building to building, house to house
- Hammered on doors
- Issued orders
- Mustered the citizens to action
- *Stood shoulder to shoulder on the walls*
- Watched and waited silently
- Stared with disbelief at the approaching army
- *Manned the battlements*
- Stationed at regular intervals on the guard towers
- Posted on the walls of the outer bailey
- Waited on the battlements
- Gathered on the parapets
- Poised with their pole-arms to . . .
- Waited on top of the east gate for the siege engines to draw closer
- *Before the enemy soldiers reached the top*
- Hurled away the ladders
- *Piled against the wall*

★ Stacked beside each wheel of the cannon
★ Ready to be dropped down onto the attackers
★ Filled with urine to combat Greek fire
★ *Hung over braziers to boil the oil*
★ Warmed dozens of cauldrons over fires
★ *Clasped their weapons*
★ Grasped their bows
★ Turned their crossbows towards the invaders
★ Loaded an arrow into the groove
★ Pulled back their bowstrings
★ Leaned over the parapet
★ Fired from the walls
★ Fired at . . .
★ Shot with deadly accuracy
★ Reloaded with speed, again and again
★ Did not give their assailants any time to seek cover
★ Stopped the battering ram getting any closer to the gates
★ *Rained down on the men below*
★ Sliced down on the heads of the attackers
★ Cascaded over the wall
★ Blasted out over the wall
★ Smashed straight onto the siege ladder
★ *Bucked and exploded*
★ Slammed into the chains holding the battering ram
★ Shattered the links
★ Sent the huge, wooden pole crashing to the ground
★ Rolled over onto the men guiding it
★ Crushed the men underneath
★ *Loaded into the holes in the iron plate of the hwacha*
★ Fixed bags of gunpowder to the arrows' feathers
★ Passed a torch across the gunpowder
★ Threw a torch onto the bubbling pitch
★ *Hissed and sputtered*
★ Roared up the walls
★ Licked at the edges of the hole
★ Engulfed the soldiers in an inferno
★ Melted into screams of agony
★ *Gathered in the inner courtyard*
★ Stared at the gates
★ Winced with every pounding crash
★ Wouldn't be long before the walls collapsed

SENTENCES

Moving towards the castle were thousands of mounted soldiers, with thousands more marching behind – a sea of black except for the flicker of light from their torches.

A trail of dust, from the hundreds of wagons and beasts trailing behind the army, stretched as far as the eye could see.

As the army drew nearer, they started to make out glints of armour and bristling spikes.

The castle had been cut off during the night, with no chance of relief reaching them before they either starved or the invaders breached their defences.

The bells tolled, ordering the gates to be closed.

The horn blew, growing gradually louder and more urgent, until its fearful echo filled the air.

The city was buzzing with frantic activity. Horns blew from the towers, soldiers rushed from building to building, house to house, hammering on doors, issuing orders, mustering the citizens to action.

The city was surrounded. A dozen ballistae, massive siege towers, taller than the city walls – loaded with catapults, trebuchets and bristling with archers – were positioned before the outer wall of the castle.

The city was eerily quiet as its citizens stood shoulder to shoulder on the walls – silent, watching, waiting, staring with disbelief at the approaching army.

Hundreds of soldiers already manned the battlements, grasping their bows, their swords ready at their sides.

Groups of archers were stationed on the guard towers that rose at regular intervals.

Beyond the gatehouse, more archers had been stationed on the walls of the outer bailey.

Rolls of straw were piled against the wall alongside the brass fire container.

Every few paces along the parapet was a pile of stones, each the size of a football, ready to be dropped down onto the attackers.

Huge vats had been filled with urine to combat any Greek fire that was hurled over the walls.

Below him in the streets, soldiers were warming dozens of cauldrons over fires.

Large cast-iron pots hung over braziers to boil the oil that would be poured over the battlements onto the invaders.

Hundreds waited on the battlements, poised with their pole-arms to hurl away the ladders before the enemy soldiers reached the top.

Cannons on cast-iron mounts punctuated the towers, a pile of cannon balls stacked beside each one.

A hwacha was poised on top of the east gate, waiting for the siege engines to draw closer.

The inhabitants of the castle had gathered in the inner courtyard, where they stood, silently, staring at the gates, wincing with every pounding crash, clasping their weapons – pitchforks, axes, hammers and spears.

Hundreds of skilled archers had gathered on the parapets, and as the enormous siege engine lumbered towards the walls, they turned their crossbows towards the invaders.

They pulled back their bowstrings. The creaking of the enormous wheels was suddenly drowned out by two blasts from a horn and, with a ripple of twangs and hisses, a hail of flaming arrows were fired from the walls towards the siege engine.

As the battering ram was brought up to the gates, the archers hauled back their cords, loaded an arrow into the groove, leaned over the parapet, and, with a ripple, fired as one. A deadly hail of bolts rained down on the men gathered below, slicing down onto their heads.

The archers shot with deadly accuracy and reloaded with speed, again and again, not giving their assailants any time to seek cover and stopping them bringing the battering ram any closer to the gates.

An avalanche of rocks cascaded over the wall, smashing straight onto the siege ladder.

Boiling pitch cascaded down the walls onto the soldiers working at the bottom.

As a torch was thrown onto the bubbling pitch, a column of flames roared up the walls and engulfed the soldiers in a deadly inferno. Battle cries melted into screams of agony.

Despite the boulders and boiling oil that had been dropped and arrows that had been fired at the sappers through the holes in the floor, flames were licking at the edges of the holes in the side of the building. It wouldn't be long before the wall collapsed.

The cannons bucked and exploded, and a ball slammed into the chains holding the battering ram, shattering the links, sending the huge, wooden beam to crash into the ground, where it rolled over the men holding it, crushing them underneath.

Over two hundred fire arrows had been loaded into the holes in the iron plate of the hwacha, and bags of gunpowder had been fixed to the arrows' feathers. When the torch was passed across the gunpowder, the arrows hissed and sputtered and, with a terrifying shriek, the fire arrows blasted out over the wall onto the wooden tower.

SECTION 2 – INTERACTION

WORDS

Nouns

Horizon, air, sky, land, ground

Buildings, house, castle, keep, watchtower, bastion, walls, battlements, parapet, ramparts, merlon, gates, doors, portcullis, floor, murder hole, stairs, steps

Defences, shelter, cover, protection

Army, enemy, soldiers, attackers, invaders, opponents, assailants, sappers, archers

People, inhabitants, citizens, crowd, servants

Siege engines, assault engines, machines, catapult, trebuchet, battering ram, ladders

Cannon, touch hole, gunpowder, cannon balls

Boulders, rocks, stones, straw, masonry, dust

Buckets, cauldrons, liquid, pitch, oil, tar, petrol, handle, nozzle

Tinder box, torch, fire, flames, inferno

Weapons, swords, shields, spears, daggers, axes, hammers, pitchforks, bows, crossbows, arrows, bolts, cords, groove

Sounds, noise, crash, groan, creak, ripple, boom

Chant, drums, beat, rhythm

Horror, chaos, disarray, confusion, mayhem, bedlam, pandemonium

Fear, senses, nerves, adrenalin

Head, chin, neck, eyes, shoulder, ankle, hand, knuckles

Adjectives

Approaching, advancing

Steady, constant, unchanging, continuous

Rumbling, booming, roaring

Bubbling, boiling, hot, scalding

Orange, fiery, flaming, burning, blazing

Crumbling, falling, tumbling

Deadly, lethal, fatal, murderous

Hundreds, thousands, groups, lots, numerous, more, additional

Huge, massive, enormous

Armoured, metal-clad, iron-tipped

Desperate, urgent, wild, frantic

Harsh, shrill, deafening

Loyal, faithful, devoted

Silent, quiet, hushed, dumb, mute

Rigid, motionless, frozen, paralysed, stock-still

Nervous, tense, terrified, terror-stricken, petrified

Verbs

Warned, alerted, knew, realised, prayed, hoped

Winced, flinched, started, recoiled

Saw, spotted, glimpsed, picked out

Watched, looked, strained, peered, stared, fixed, probed, glanced

Heard, listened

Gathered, assembled, mustered, rallied

Filled, clustered

Renewed, resumed

Dug, burrowed, mined, tunnelled

Pounded, battered, pummelled

Shook, shuddered, trembled

Burst, exploded, shattered

Breached, split, bust

Crashed, rammed, cannoned

Clashed, clanged, clattered, smashed, banged

Spilled, flowed, flooded, surged, swarmed, poured

Charged, stormed, swooped

Surrounded, encircled, besieged

Loaded, filled

Lifted, heaved, hauled, tilted, pumped, sprayed

Pushed, sent, threw, hurled, launched, shot, dropped

Plunged, descended, cascaded

Torched, set light to, lit, ignited

Sprang back, rebounded, ricocheted

Stood, waited

Knocked, banged, hammered

Signalled, gestured, pointed

Blew, let out, blasted

Screamed, shrieked, howled, yelled

Dropped, ducked, dived, dodged, weaved

Knelt, crouched, huddled

Moved, stepped, shuffled, shifted, manoeuvred

Swung, turned, whirled

Leaned, bent, dangled

Rushed, raced, darted, dashed, sprinted, bounded

Lunged, sprang, leapt, pounced

Stumbled, staggered, pitched, fell

Twisted, hurt, hit, slammed

Cranked, nocked, loaded, reloaded, aimed, pointed, fired, unleashed

Unsheathed, clasped, gripped, clutched, raised, flailed, slashed

Covered, engulfed

Drove back, forced back, repelled

PHRASES – NOUNS AND ADJECTIVES

* ✻ Fear and adrenalin
* ✻ Every muscle in her body
* ✻ *Above her head*
* ✻ Beside her
* ✻ Behind him
* ✻ *Out of the shelter of the . . .*
* ✻ On the top of the watchtower
* ✻ Through the murder hole in the floor
* ✻ *Straight onto the heads of the attackers*
* ✻ Onto the soldiers working at the base of the castle
* ✻ Onto the burning straw and the enemy machines
* ✻ *A hail of quarrels*
* ✻ An orange column of flames
* ✻ A cloud of dust

- *More and more ladders*
- Hundreds of metal-clad invaders
- *With a groan*
- With a ripple of noise
- Steady, rumbling rhythm of the enemy's siege engines
- Deafening boom of the battering ram
- *Desperate throng of people*
- Loyal servants
- *Pitchforks, axes, hammers and spears*

PHRASES – VERBS

- Spotted a movement in the distance
- Rose on the horizon
- Watched as the approaching army drew closer
- *As the enemy drums renewed their beat*
- A chant rose among the soldiers massed at the gates
- Sappers burrowed into the walls
- When the assault engines were close enough
- Loaded into the trebuchet below them
- Pounded the portcullis
- Shook beneath her
- *Just in time to see that the invaders had . . .*
- As the gates burst open
- The moment the first defences were breached
- *Rose up on the walls behind him*
- Crashed down onto the battlements
- Spilled onto the wall
- Breached the wall
- Charged across the battlements towards them
- *Surrounded by devastation and chaos*
- Became more and more difficult to . . .
- *Senses were on high alert*
- Surged through her body
- Steeled himself
- Winced with every pounding crash
- Knew that time was running out
- Prayed silently that she could make it to the keep
- *Could now clearly hear . . .*
- Listened nervously to . . .
- *Lifted her head slowly*
- Kept his head down
- Strained her neck to look down

* Rose up to peer over the wall
* *Stared at the gates*
* Kept her eyes fixed on the gates
* Peered out
* Probed for any movement, any sound
* Looked over his shoulder
* Glanced nervously over the wall
* Stared at the unfolding horror
* Picked out Kitty amongst the sea of terrified faces
* *Gathered as many people as he could to fight the enemy*
* Filled the courtyard
* Formed a line
* Clustered around the buckets of boiling water
* Crouched around the buckets of hot tar
* *Stood silently in the inner courtyard*
* Waited motionless in the barbican
* Waited at the top of the battlements
* Waited nervously beside the rolls of straw
* Waited for what seemed an eternity
* Waited for the gate to burst open and the breach to be flooded
* *Was unable to move*
* Was rigid with fear
* Waited, watched . . . still could not move
* Even when a dagger clashed into the stone wall
* *Gripped the edge of the wall*
* Knuckles turned white
* Clutched desperately at the battlements
* Flailed her arms
* *Hammered on doors*
* With his arm outstretched
* Signalled with his hands to . . .
* The moment she gave the signal
* Gestured madly for him to get down
* Pointed at the massive boulder
* *Pulled her horn from its sheath*
* Let out two harsh, urgent blasts
* Screamed a warning – the invaders had arrived
* Shrieked in agony
* *As a boulder smashed into the ramparts*
* Threw herself flat
* Ducked back behind the stone wall
* Dodged crumbling masonry
* Ducked beneath the ramparts
* Crouched behind a merlon

* Crouched on all fours
* *Shifted from side to side*
* Stepped sideways
* Stepped towards the wall
* Manoeuvred around the top of the bastion
* *Leaned out over the wall*
* Leaned over the parapet
* As Kitty leaned down the stairs
* *Swung round*
* Whirled round
* Twisted to look over her shoulder
* *Poured hot tar into buckets*
* Took yet another bucket of hot tar from Rob
* Passed the bucket up to Trish
* *Lifted the huge boulder out over the edge*
* Heaved the roll of straw onto the wall
* Pushed as hard as they could
* Sent the enormous stone plunging down
* Tilted the cauldrons of boiling pitch on their sides
* Launched the straw rolls over the wall
* As the scalding liquid cascaded down
* *Were ready to fire*
* Were ready to drop them through the holes
* *Opened her tinder box*
* Clutched the flaming torch
* Placed the slow match on the touch hole
* Set light to the tube at the end of her spear
* Set the straw alight
* Threw the flaming torch onto the bubbling pitch
* Pumped furiously at the handle
* Sprayed petrol out of the nozzle
* *Shot into the mass of men gathered below*
* Sliced down onto their heads
* Hurled the flaming spear at the catapult
* Pushed the flaming missile down onto the attackers
* Engulfed the invaders below in an inferno
* Drove the invaders back
* Did not give their opponents any time to seek cover
* *As a column of flames lit the sky . . .*
* Roared up the walls
* *Rushed to lock themselves behind doors*
* Raced from building to building
* Sprinted for the stairs
* Bounded up the steps, faster and faster

- Took the stairs three at a time
- Raced along the ramparts to the cannon
- Ran in a low crouch
- Weaved in and out of the crowd
- Dragged along blindly
- *Launched himself at the ladder*
- Sent the ladders tumbling from the walls
- *Nearly fell*
- Pitched forward
- Staggered backwards
- Didn't even have time to break her fall
- Went down hard
- *Twisted her ankle*
- Slammed her chin into the ground
- *Knelt and cranked her crossbow*
- Gripped her bow tighter
- Was ready to unleash a hail of arrows
- Hauled back the cords
- Loaded a quarrel into the groove
- Let his arrow fly
- Reloaded again and again
- Pointed her arrow with deadly accuracy at every movement
- *Unsheathed his sword*
- Clasped their weapons
- Gripped her iron-tipped spear with both hands
- Raised her sword above her head
- Slashed with their swords

SENTENCES

Tom had spotted a movement in the distance and leaned out over the wall on top of the watchtower.

A cloud of dust rose on the horizon. He froze. He was unable to move. Rigid with fear, he gripped the edge of the wall so hard his knuckles turned white.

Katie watched as the approaching army drew closer. She waited, watched . . . still could not move.

She could now clearly hear the steady, rumbling rhythm of the enemy's siege engines. Fear and adrenalin surging through her body, she pulled her horn from its sheath and let out two harsh, urgent blasts that screamed a warning – the invaders had arrived.

Kitty crouched behind a merlon, both hands gripping her iron-tipped spear. Slowly, she lifted her head.

Rob shifted from side to side, pointing his arrow with deadly accuracy at every movement.

Tom stepped sideways out of the shelter of the merlon, and let his arrow fly.

Hauling back the cords, Kitty and Tom loaded a quarrel into the groove, leaned over the parapet, and with a ripple of noise, they fired as one, shooting into the mass of men gathered below – a hail of quarrels slicing down onto their heads. They reloaded again and again, not giving their opponents any time to seek cover.

Together, they lifted the huge boulder out over the edge, and then pushed as hard as they could, sending the massive stone straight onto the heads of the attackers.

Rob raced from building to building, hammering on doors, gathering as many people as he could to form a line to pour hot tar into buckets.

Every muscle in her body was screaming in agony, as Kitty leaned down the stairs to take yet another bucket of hot tar from Rob.

With a groan, she swung round and passed the bucket up to Trish, who was waiting at the top of the battlements.

With his arm outstretched, Andrew signalled with his hands to those crouched around the buckets of hot tar.

With a massive heave, they tilted the cauldrons of boiling pitch on their sides. They ducked back behind the stone wall as the scalding liquid cascaded down onto the soldiers working at the base of the castle.

Steeling himself, Rob stepped towards the wall. Keeping his head down, he threw the flaming torch onto the bubbling pitch.

Kitty staggered backwards, arms flailing, and threw herself flat as an orange column of flames roared up the walls and engulfed the invaders below in an inferno.

Crouching on all fours, Kitty manoeuvred around the top of the bastion and peered out. She watched and waited, eyes probing for any movement, any sound; a warning that the sappers were burrowing into the walls.

They waited motionless in the barbican, listening nervously to the deafening boom of the battering ram pounding the portcullis. Their senses were on high alert, their bows nocked and ready to fire the moment the first defences were breached.

Katie strained her neck to look down through the murder hole in the floor. Beside her, the others were clustered around the buckets of boiling water, ready to drop them through the holes the moment she gave the signal.

Knowing that time was running out, Andrew sprinted for the stairs, bounded up the steps, faster and faster, taking them three at a time, and raced along the ramparts to the cannon.

Hauling the dead man away from the touch hole, he placed the slow match on the hole, and sprang back as the cannon bucked and exploded.

Opening her tinder box, Kitty set light to the tube at the end of her spear and hurled it at the catapult. She glanced nervously over the wall. She waited, but for what seemed an eternity, nothing happened. Then, she ducked beneath the ramparts as a column of flames lit the sky.

Ann clutched the flaming torch, as she and John waited nervously beside the straw. When the assault engines were close enough, John heaved the roll of straw onto the wall, set it alight and, together, they pushed the flaming missile down onto the attackers.

Once the straw rolls had been launched over the wall, John pumped furiously at the handle, spraying petrol out of the nozzle onto the burning straw and the enemy machines.

As Tom rose up to peer over the wall, Katie gestured madly for him to get down. She pointed at the massive boulder that was being loaded into the trebuchet below them.

The floor shook beneath her, and she clutched frantically at the battlements.

Rob ducked as a boulder smashed into the ramparts.

He ran in a low crouch, his shield over his head, dodging crumbling masonry.

Rob launched himself at the ladder, and sent it tumbling from the walls. There was a crash behind him, and he whirled round to stare at the unfolding horror. More and more ladders were rising up on the walls behind him.

Her heart sank as the enemy drums renewed their beat and a chant rose among the soldiers massed at the gates. Kitty twisted to look over her shoulder, just in time to see that the invaders had breached the wall.

They knelt and began to crank their crossbows, as all around them planks crashed down onto the battlements and hundreds of metal-clad invaders spilled onto the wall, charging across the battlements towards them, slashing with their swords.

Dragged along blindly by the desperate throng of people rushing to lock themselves behind doors, Katie was suddenly pitched forward. She didn't even have time to break her fall but went down hard, twisting her ankle, and slamming her chin into the ground.

Tom looked over his shoulder as he weaved in and out of the crowd. It was becoming more and more difficult to pick out Kitty amongst the sea of terrified faces filling the courtyard. Silently, he prayed that she had made it to the keep.

He was surrounded by devastation and chaos, but Rob gripped his sword and stood silently waiting for the gate to burst open and the breach to be flooded.

All around them, their loyal servants had gathered to fight the enemy, standing silently in the inner courtyard, staring at the gates, wincing with every pounding crash, clasping their weapons – pitchforks, axes, hammers and spears.

As the gates burst open, Kitty raised her sword above her head and, as one, they ran to meet the intruders and drive them back.

Katie knelt, cranked her crossbow, ready to unleash a hail of arrows. Even when a dagger clashed into the stone wall above her head, she merely gripped her bow tighter, keeping her eyes fixed on the gates.

16

Damage and destruction

SECTION 1 – SETTING

WORDS	

Nouns

Chaos, disarray, confusion, mayhem, bedlam, pandemonium

Destruction, demolition, obliteration

Sky, air, haze

City, streets, castle, tower, battlements, courtyard

Houses, buildings, walls, gate, doors, roof, window, floor, ground, base, foundations

Cannon, gunpowder, blast, explosion

Swords, cudgels, baton, mace

Battering ram, blow, thud

Gates, bar, hinges

Missiles, boulders, stones, rocks, wood, sticks, arrows, bolts

Shower, hail, billows, sheets, chunks

Fragments, splinters, shrapnel

Fire, Greek fire, flares, flames, inferno, light, heat, smoke, embers, ash, steam

Debris, rubble

Hole, gap, crack, breach

Silence, peel, chime, clang, ring, rumble, thump, thud, crash, boom, crackle

Cry, moans, groans, screams, shrieks

Similes/ Metaphors	**Huge, black arrows, each larger than a man**; a blazing bedlam; balls of flames like fiery comets; rampaging, swirling tongues of fire; blown like shrapnel; a wave of fire; rocked like the deck of a ship in a storm; hung like a stilled breath on everything it touched; echoed like gunshots
Adjectives	**Wounded**, injured, dying
	Inward, outward
	Still, silent, quiet, eerie
	Large, huge, enormous, massive
	Few, couple, several
	First, next, final
	Wood, iron, metal
	Black, grey, dark
	Fiery, flaming, blazing, smouldering
	Swirling, whirling, churning, rampaging, uncontrollable
	Non-existent, missing, damaged, crushed
	Hollow, muffled
	Booming, roaring, ear-splitting
	Ominous, menacing, foreboding
	Horrifying, frightening, terrifying
Verbs	**Flew**, shot, slung, tossed, burst, ripped, hurled, hurtled, launched, propelled, blasted, exploded
	Rolled, bounced, landed, thumped
	Poured, hailed, rained, sprayed, showered, plunged, plummeted
	Hit, smashed, crashed, slammed, punched, battered, pounded
	Cracked, splintered, crumbled, shattered, crushed, flattened, wrecked
	Shook, shivered, shuddered, juddered, rocked, swayed, toppled, collapsed
	Bent, tore, hung, dangled
	Gathered, collected, massed, piled
	Swept, slithered, dispersed, expanded
	Began, started, ended, finished

Rose, curled, wrapped, blew, billowed, surged, raged

Grew, spread, flared, erupted, blazed, flashed

Covered, lost, screened, masked, draped, enveloped, swathed, cloaked, choked, suffocated

Remained, left, survived

Held up, propped

Charred, blistered, scorched, seared, singed

Echoed, rang, resounded, resonated, reverberated

PHRASES – NOUNS AND ADJECTIVES

* Every day
* Day after day
* Night after night
* Hour after hour
* Relentlessly, night after night
* *For the first few days*
* Over the next few days
* After days of . . .
* More than a week went by before . . .
* *On the fifth morning*
* That evening
* Later that day
* *As the light started to fade*
* Almost dusk when . . .
* Still dark when . . .
* *Almost at once*
* At that very moment
* All of a sudden
* *In the distance*
* From somewhere below her
* Throughout the castle
* All around him
* *Whole building*
* Floor under their feet
* Wall over the gate
* *Several boulders*
* Small chunks of wood and stone
* Stone missiles
* A hail of sticks, stone and arrows
* Iron bolts

- ✴ Huge, black arrows, each larger than a man
- ✴ Fire arrows
- ✴ A flaming arrow
- ✴ Battering ram with its huge, iron beak
- ✴ *First few boulders*
- ✴ Next couple of boulders
- ✴ Final boulders
- ✴ *The smell of gunpowder*
- ✴ Black smoke
- ✴ A streak of orange flame
- ✴ A column of fire
- ✴ In an enormous flash of light
- ✴ A wave of fire
- ✴ A blazing bedlam
- ✴ Balls of flames like fiery comets
- ✴ Rampaging, swirling tongues of fire
- ✴ *Flakes of smouldering embers*
- ✴ A blizzard of ash
- ✴ Wisps of steam
- ✴ *A hail of shattered fragments*
- ✴ Shards of stone and splinters of wood
- ✴ With a blast of splinters
- ✴ A pile of rubble and beams
- ✴ Objects only a short distance away
- ✴ *Quiet and unnaturally still*
- ✴ Clanking chains
- ✴ Eerie, booming thud
- ✴ Enormous clang
- ✴ Hollow boom
- ✴ A horrifying rumble and crash
- ✴ Ring of swords and thump of cudgels
- ✴ Crackle of flames
- ✴ A cacophony of peeling, chiming, clanging
- ✴ *A muffled cry*
- ✴ Cries of fear and pain
- ✴ Moans and screams from the wounded and dying

PHRASES – VERBS

- ✴ Just below where he was standing
- ✴ *It was only a matter of time before . . .*
- ✴ *Flew through the air*
- ✴ Ripped through the air

- ✶ Filled the air
- ✶ Blasted towards the castle
- ✶ *Landed short*
- ✶ Bounced against the wall
- ✶ Hurtled high over the wall
- ✶ Rained down on the castle
- ✶ Smashed into the wall
- ✶ Crashed into the walls
- ✶ Slammed into the doors
- ✶ Pounded the battlements
- ✶ Punched hole after hole into the stones
- ✶ *Cracked and exploded*
- ✶ Cracked the stones
- ✶ Sent a shower of stone splinters into the air
- ✶ Blown like shrapnel
- ✶ Sprayed in every direction
- ✶ Shook with every explosion from the huge cannon
- ✶ *Standing beside them were . . .*
- ✶ Thrown into the streets below
- ✶ *Breached the walls*
- ✶ Shuddered and began to crumble inward
- ✶ Crumbled and flattened buildings and houses
- ✶ Rocked like the deck of a ship in a storm
- ✶ As part of the wall collapsed on its own foundations
- ✶ Gathered at the base of the castle
- ✶ *Like the city was holding its breath*
- ✶ Shattered the silence
- ✶ Ended as abruptly as it began
- ✶ *Shot out of the darkness*
- ✶ Hurled over the walls
- ✶ Plunged down towards them in a blazing arc
- ✶ Plummeted to the ground
- ✶ Crashed through the window
- ✶ Crashed onto the rain-sodden courtyard
- ✶ Spread like glue over the ground
- ✶ Slithered across the streets
- ✶ Boiled with flames from the Greek fire
- ✶ Blasted into the air
- ✶ Seemed to explode around them
- ✶ Lit up the sky
- ✶ Poured into the sky
- ✶ Rained down on them in billows and sheets
- ✶ Spurted in all directions
- ✶ *Was in flames in many quarters*

* Raged through the castle
* Blew across the courtyard
* Rose from within the walls
* Poured through cracks in the doors
* Wrapped around the buildings
* Curled up the walls
* Surged rapidly up and along the roof
* Billowed out of many of the buildings
* *Choked the air*
* Turned the air grey
* Lost in the haze
* Hung like a stilled breath on everything it touched
* *All that remained of the . . .*
* Held up a non-existent roof
* Had already been charred by the heat from the explosion
* Curled from the ground around the debris
* Had grown to an inferno
* Flared to life in all directions
* *As the battering ram was dragged back and forth*
* Battered the gates
* Shivered and shuddered with every blow
* Grated slowly open
* Shattered the wooden bar that secured the gates
* Exploded inwards
* Bent and cracked the gates
* Tore through the gates
* Hung off their hinges
* *Had gone ominously quiet*
* Did not last long
* Echoed like gunshots
* Echoed throughout the city
* Rang out from every corner
* Resounded through the city
* Added to the sense of chaos and destruction
* Raged throughout the streets

SENTENCES

Several boulders sailed through the air.

They were showered with small chunks of wood and stone that poured from the sky.

A hail of sticks, stones and arrows rained down on the castle.

Iron bolts flew through the air to smash into the wall just below where he was standing.

The stones cracked and exploded. A hail of fragments, blown like shrapnel, sprayed in every direction.

The first few boulders landed short and bounced against the wall; the next couple hurtled high over the wall to crumble and flatten buildings and houses.

The final boulders crashed into the walls and pounded the battlements – cracking the stones and sending a shower of stone splinters into the air.

A horrifying crash ripped through the air, as several boulders slammed into the wall, filling the air with shards of stone and splinters of wood.

The whole building shuddered. The floor under their feet rocked like the deck of a ship in a storm and many of the archers standing beside them were thrown into the streets below.

It was only a matter of time before the walls were breached.

There was a rumble and crash as part of the wall collapsed.

The wall over the gate shuddered and began to crumble inward.

The stone missiles punched hole after hole into the stones, until one of the towers collapsed on its own foundations, its shattered fragments gathered at the base like a felled tree of monstrous stone.

The walls shook with every explosion from the huge cannon.

The city was quiet, like it was holding its breath. It was unnaturally still.

A muffled cry from somewhere below her shattered the silence, and in the distance there was a scream that ended as abruptly as it began.

Fire arrows shot out of the darkness and plunged down towards them in a blazing arc.

As the Greek fire crashed onto the rain-sodden courtyard, it spread like glue over the ground.

A streak of orange flame slithered across the streets.

All around him the ground boiled with flames from the Greek fire that had been hurled over the walls.

The city was in flames in many quarters.

Fire lit up the sky. Flames billowed out of many of the buildings. Smoke spurted in all directions as the fire raged through the castle.

The smell of gunpowder choked the air.

Everything seemed to explode around them in an enormous flash of light.

Black smoke rose from within the walls and poured into the sky.

Flakes of smouldering embers rained from the sky.

Smoke poured through cracks in the doors. A blizzard of ash blew across the courtyard.

Fire and smoke curled up the walls. The air turned grey, hanging like a stilled breath on everything it touched. Objects only a short distance away were lost in the haze.

All that remained of the kitchen were walls holding up a non-existent roof, a pile of rubble and beams that had already been charred by the heat from the explosion. Wisps of steam curled from the ground around the debris.

Apart from the crackle of flames and the moans and screams from the wounded and dying, everything had gone ominously quiet. It did not last long.

A wave of fire surged rapidly up and along the roof.

The city was a blazing bedlam with rampaging, swirling tongues of fire that flared to life in all directions.

Raining down on them in billows and sheets, the balls of flames were like fiery comets that plummeted to the ground and wrapped themselves around the buildings.

The clanking of chains filled the air as the battering ram was dragged back and forth to batter the gates.

The gatehouse shivered and shuddered with every blow; its eerie, booming thud echoing like gunshots throughout the castle.

Finally, with a hollow boom, the gates parted and grated slowly open.

The wooden bar that secured the gates shattered, and exploded inwards with a blast of splinters.

With an enormous clang that echoed throughout the city, the battering ram with its huge, iron beak, bent and cracked the gates until, finally, it tore through and the gates hung off their hinges.

The bells rang out from every corner – a cacophony of peeling, chiming, clanging that added to the sense of chaos and destruction.

The battle raged throughout the streets.

The ring of swords and thump of cudgels resounded through the city.

SECTION 2 – INTERACTION

WORDS

Nouns

Alarm, warning

Fury, anger, horror, shock, despair

Range, direction, danger, battle

Time, seconds, minutes, moments

Head, hair, scalp, face, shoulder, arm, hand, palms, fingers, knuckles, knees, feet, side

Wall, ditch, shield, ground, floor, building

Courtyard, alleys, stairs, ledge, ridge

Missile, boulder, stones, wood, debris, rubble

Crossbow, bolt, arrows

Whistle, hiss, creak, crash

Heat, blast, explosion

Fire, flames, smoke

Crack, gap, edge

Shout, cry, scream, yell, howl

Similes/ Metaphors

Speed and power of a cornered animal; like an uncoiled spring

Adjectives

Mere, just, only

Distinctive, characteristic

Deadly, fatal, lethal

Rigid, stiff, still, motionless

Searing, burning, blazing

Large, fist-sized

Low, flat

Verbs

Alerted, warned, responded, reacted

Terrified, petrified, scared, horrified

Looked, stared, peered, peeked, strained, watched, spotted

Smashed, burst, exploded

Landed, embedded, lodged

Sent, scattered, showered, pelted, peppered, strafed, bombarded

Drifted, wafted, filled, pervaded

Burned, seared, sucked, suffocated

Forced, made, dictated

Missed, evaded, avoided, dodged

Raised, lifted, held up, wrapped

Covered, shielded, protected

Flailed, thrashed, writhed, floundered

Gripped, dug, crushed

Buried, rubbed, twisted, tugged

Braced, steadied, secured, balanced

Stopped, halted, paused, waited

Paced, strode, marched

Backed up, whirled, spun, turned, staggered, scrambled, rolled, crawled

Dropped, crouched, ducked, dived, lowered, threw

Rose, lurched

Made for, headed towards

Leaped, jumped, lunged, caught

Scrabbled, groped, flung out, clawed, strained, hauled, pulled

Ran, sprinted, dashed, darted, bolted, fled, plunged, clattered, bounded, hurtled, barrelled, slammed, banged, thudded, shot past

Slipped, stumbled, staggered, slithered

Knocked, thrown, pitched, fell, sprawled, toppled

Draped, supported, helped, dragged, tugged, towed

Adverbs   **Narrowly**, barely, scarcely, hardly

Quickly, wildly, madly, instinctively, frantically, desperately

PHRASES – NOUNS AND ADJECTIVES

* ✶ With a shout of alarm
* ✶ *Within seconds*
* ✶ For a fraction of a second
* ✶ Not long afterwards
* ✶ Not a moment too soon
* ✶ Just in time
* ✶ Mere seconds before
* ✶ *Out of range*
* ✶ Just as a crossbow bolt . . .
* ✶ Distinctive, deadly whistle of an arrow
* ✶ *A blast of searing heat*
* ✶ The force of the blast
* ✶ *Face down*
* ✶ With an arm over their heads
* ✶ *With the speed and power of a cornered animal*

PHRASES – VERBS

* ✶ As a boulder smashed into the . . .
* ✶ Sent fist-sized stones in every direction
* ✶ Exploded in front of him
* ✶ Embedded itself in the wood
* ✶ *When she was sure it was safe*
* ✶ Not sure what had alerted her to the danger
* ✶ Reacted instinctively
* ✶ *Narrowly missed the missile*
* ✶ Landed where his head had been mere seconds before
* ✶ *Raised his shield to cover his head*
* ✶ Wrapped his arms around his head
* ✶ Held up her hands to shield her face from the heat
* ✶ Protected themselves from the falling debris
* ✶ *Pelted their heads and the backs of their legs*
* ✶ Never saw the thing that smashed into her shoulder
* ✶ *Drifted towards her*
* ✶ As the sound of . . . filled the air
* ✶ Filled with the crackle of burning flames
* ✶ *Burned through her fingers*
* ✶ Sucked all the air out of her lungs
* ✶ Forced back by the fire
* ✶ *Gripped her knuckles until they turned white*
* ✶ Dug his nails deep into the skin of his palms

- ✦ Crushed her nails into her palms
- ✦ *Buried her head in her hands*
- ✦ Rubbed his fingers into his scalp
- ✦ Twisted and tugged at her hair
- ✦ *Was rigid with fury*
- ✦ Braced his feet
- ✦ *Stopped dead in her tracks*
- ✦ Was afraid to move
- ✦ Waited a few minutes longer
- ✦ *Paced backwards and forwards*
- ✦ Not sure which way to go
- ✦ Was certain that she could no longer stay where she was
- ✦ *Terrified of raising his head*
- ✦ Looked up
- ✦ Stared upwards
- ✦ Raised her head cautiously
- ✦ Peered over the top at . . .
- ✦ Peered through the gap at the . . .
- ✦ Peeked over the muddy lip
- ✦ Raised his eyes above the wall
- ✦ Looked over the top of her shield
- ✦ Strained her neck upwards to peer through . . .
- ✦ Could watch without being spotted
- ✦ Spun back to stare at the unfolding horror
- ✦ *Backed up against the wall*
- ✦ Whirled round
- ✦ Staggered back with a yell
- ✦ Backed up so fast she almost tripped
- ✦ Scrambled madly backwards out of range
- ✦ Rolled onto her side quickly
- ✦ Rolled to the side
- ✦ Rolled quickly to his left
- ✦ Had to crawl on all fours, back the way she had come
- ✦ *Dropped to her knees behind . . .*
- ✦ Crouched low to the ground
- ✦ Ducked under the smoke
- ✦ Lowered herself to the ground inside the ditch
- ✦ Threw herself down behind . . .
- ✦ Threw himself flat
- ✦ Dived headlong onto the ground
- ✦ *Lurched to his feet*
- ✦ Rose to his feet
- ✦ Staggered to her feet
- ✦ Scrambled to her feet

- ⋆ Staggered upright, hugging his side
- ⋆ *Made for the stairs*
- ⋆ Made her way to the . . .
- ⋆ Staggered across the courtyard
- ⋆ *Leaped across*
- ⋆ Just managed to catch hold of the far side
- ⋆ Scrabbled with his feet
- ⋆ Strained his arms
- ⋆ Hauled himself up and over the ledge
- ⋆ *Began to run*
- ⋆ Ran at a low crouch
- ⋆ Sprinted to the wall
- ⋆ Darted forward
- ⋆ Turned and ran – backwards towards the . . .
- ⋆ Bolted at high speed through the alleys
- ⋆ Fled from the sounds of the battle nearby
- ⋆ Spun and dashed back to the stairs
- ⋆ Plunged down three steps at a time
- ⋆ Weaved in and out of the arrows
- ⋆ Clattered down the stairs
- ⋆ Bounded like an uncoiled spring
- ⋆ Hurtled headlong
- ⋆ Barrelled forward
- ⋆ Slammed into . . .
- ⋆ Barged through . . .
- ⋆ Thudded into . . .
- ⋆ Shot past . . .
- ⋆ Fought his way through . . .
- ⋆ Hurtled full pelt towards . . .
- ⋆ *Slipped, stumbled and staggered over the rubble*
- ⋆ With his arms flailing
- ⋆ Tried to keep his balance
- ⋆ Couldn't stay upright
- ⋆ Flung her hand out in front of her
- ⋆ Groped for something to break her fall
- ⋆ Threw himself forward
- ⋆ Managed to catch hold of her wrist
- ⋆ *Before she could steady herself*
- ⋆ Fell forward
- ⋆ Thrown violently backwards
- ⋆ Knocked backwards by the force of the blast
- ⋆ Crashed to the ground
- ⋆ Pitched forward into the wall
- ⋆ Sprawled face-down on the floor

* *Had opened up in front of him*
* Began to slither towards the edge
* Clawed desperately at the ground
* Stopped himself toppling into the massive crack
* *Dragged Rob by his arm*
* Draped his arm around Kitty
* Took Katie's full weight
* *Urged him to move faster*
* Groaned as she tried to put weight on her leg

SENTENCES

Trish stopped dead in her tracks, staring upwards, as the sound of the battering ram thudding at the gates filled the air.

Crouched on the ground, he was afraid to move. Terrified of raising his head.

Raising her head cautiously, she peered over the wall.

He raised his eyes above the wall and peeked over the top at the huge catapult.

Gail backed up against the wall and when she was sure it was safe, looked over the top of her shield.

Quickly rolling onto her side, Katie strained her neck upwards to peer through the gap.

Dropping to her knees, she squinted through the breach in the wall.

Lowering herself to the ground inside the ditch, she waited a few minutes longer and then peered over the muddy lip.

Kitty threw herself down behind the boulder so that she could watch without being spotted.

With a shout of alarm, Katie staggered back with a yell.

Rob scrambled madly backwards out of range, and lurched to his feet.

Not knowing exactly why, or what had alerted her to the danger, Kitty reacted instinctively and dived headlong onto the ground, rolled onto her side and looked up.

Tom rolled quickly to his left, just in time, narrowly missing the missile which landed where his head had been, mere seconds before.

Kitty backed up so fast she almost tripped. Suddenly, the distinctive, deadly whistle of an arrow drifted towards her.

He threw himself flat, and rolled to the side just as a crossbow bolt exploded in front of him, embedding itself in the wood.

As a boulder smashed into the battlements, sending fist-sized stones in every direction, Andrew ducked and raised his shield to cover his head.

He crouched low to the ground to duck under the smoke.

She held up her hands to shield her face from the heat, but it was no good, a blast of searing heat burned through her fingers and sucked all the air out of her lungs.

Staggering to her feet, she made her way to the great hall, but it was filled with the crackle of burning flames. Forced back by the fire, she had to crawl on all fours back the way she had come.

Katie scrambled to her feet and began to move, not sure which way to go, only certain that she could no longer stay where she was.

Running at a low crouch, they made for the stairs.

He rose to his feet and sprinted to the wall, dropping to his knees behind it.

He darted forward with the speed and power of a cornered animal, weaving in and out of the arrows.

They ran, each with an arm held high to protect themselves from the falling debris that pelted their heads and the backs of their legs.

He wrapped his arms around his head, his face down, and then he ran.

Kitty spun back to stare at the unfolding horror, then turned and ran towards the keep.

They bolted at high speed through the alleys, fleeing from the sounds of the battle nearby.

Tom began to run – dragging Rob by his arm – urging him to move faster.

Gail spun, dashed back to the stairs, and plunged down three steps at a time.

Tom leaped across, only just managing to catch hold of the far side. Scrabbling with his feet, straining his arms, he hauled himself up and over the ledge.

Katie darted forward. She slipped, stumbled and staggered over the rubble.

Arms flailing, he tried to keep his balance, and as he did so, the torch sailed from his hands and crashed to the ground.

Trish flung her hand out in front of her, groping for something to break her fall, but before she could steady herself, she fell forward to sprawl face-down on the floor.

Gail whirled round, but never saw the thing that smashed into her shoulder.

The force of the blast pitched Rob forward into the wall. Stunned, he staggered upright, hugging his side.

Rob threw himself forward, just managing to catch hold of Kitty's wrist as she began to slither towards the edge.

Desperately, he clawed at the ground to stop himself toppling into the massive crack that had opened up in front of him.

Tom draped his arm around Kitty, who groaned as she tried to put weight on her leg.

There was no turning back now. Taking Katie's full weight, Rob staggered across the courtyard.

17
Battles

SECTION 1 – SETTING

WORDS

Nouns

News, report, account

Approach, advance, arrival, appearance

Distance, horizon, skyline

Attack, assault, charge, ambush

Ridge, hill, slope, valley, forest, trees, river, stream

Figures, shadows, silhouettes

Army, force, enemy, men, troops, soldiers, warriors, vanguard, scouts, pickets

Horsemen, cavalry, archers, pike-men, drummers

Banners, flag, standard

Beasts, horses, head, hooves, reins, stirrups

Weapons, swords, scabbards, shields, bows, arrows, pikes, staves, spears, blades

Armour, chain mail, helmets, boots

Shield, cover, defence, protection, barricade, barrier, line, ditch, trench

Stones, rocks, boulders, saplings, logs

Chaos, commotion, confusion, maelstrom

Noise, sounds, racket, cacophony

Horn, trumpet, note, blast

Clash, clatter, clang, twang, whistle, hiss

Groans, moans, yells, screams, shouts, shrieks

Similes/ Metaphors	**A single armoured river**; like a pack of shuffling beasts; a forest of bristling staves
Adjectives	**Impending**, imminent, approaching, advancing
	Whole, entire, total
	Regular, frequent
	Black, dark, shadowy
	Single, couple, handful, small, large, hundreds, thousands
	Still, frozen, motionless
	Menacing, threatening, ominous, murderous
	Deadly, lethal, fatal
	Armoured, steel-clad
	Metal, iron, steel, steely
	Low, high, chest-high
	Thorny, sharp, barbed, spiky, pointed
	Glinting, flashing, flickering, shimmering
	Whistling, hissing, rumbling, thudding, thundering
	Triumphant, jubilant, victorious, exultant
	Well-drilled, practised
	Firm, tight
	Seething, chaotic, turbulent
	Flaring, snorting, squealing, shrieking
	Shrill, high, piercing, ear-splitting
Verbs	**Knew**, informed, expected, anticipated
	Felt, sensed, detected
	Saw, glimpsed, spotted, revealed, watched
	Rose, appeared, emerged, wound, climbed, vaulted
	Marched, trooped
	Arrived, reached, approached, advanced, headed
	Gathered, assembled, marshalled
	Protected, surrounded, encircled
	Instructed, ordered, commanded
	Waited, stood, halted

Stationed, positioned

Formed, organised

Led, walked, trotted, ran, cantered, galloped

Ambushed, surprised, trapped, ensnared

Narrowed, closed up, shrunk, contracted

Filled, grew, swelled, bulged, expanded

Disappeared, vanished

Flashed, glinted, glimmered, flickered, shimmered

Blew, swung, fluttered, flapped, billowed

Sounded, blared, echoed

Heard, thundered, thudded, rumbled, exploded

Banged, beat, thumped, rapped

Shattered, pierced, filled, pervaded

Shook, shuddered, juddered

Cleared, removed, hauled

Hammered, pounded, embedded

Covered, hid

Dropped, left, deposited

Muffled, wrapped, enfolded, swathed

Strapped, fastened, secured, lashed

Reached, grabbed, unsheathed, slithered, strung, nocked, planted

Held, gripped, clutched

Overlapped, jammed, rammed

Waved, brandished, flourished, lowered

Thrust, pushed, shoved, poked, jabbed, stabbed

Aimed, pointed, levelled

Challenged, tested

Reined in, wrenched, skidded, halted

Turned, whirled, wheeled away

Darted, raced, rushed, sprinted

Burst, erupted, exploded

Rolled, spun, careered

Bounced, rebounded, ricocheted

Arced, curled, curved

Plunged, plummeted, descended

Met, engaged, fought, struck, hacked, slashed, cut

Thrown, pitched, tossed, propelled

Fell, slumped, crumbled

PHRASES – NOUNS AND ADJECTIVES

* ⭑ News of the impending arrival
* ⭑ *Whole ridge*
* ⭑ In the distance
* ⭑ On the horizon
* ⭑ At regular intervals
* ⭑ *All around him*
* ⭑ In front of them
* ⭑ From ahead of him
* ⭑ *A man to his left*
* ⭑ Another man in front of him
* ⭑ Behind the spear-men
* ⭑ *Towards the oncoming army*
* ⭑ Into the shadows at the bottom of the slope
* ⭑ *For a moment*
* ⭑ At the last moment
* ⭑ *Within metres of their line*
* ⭑ Just out of pike range
* ⭑ *Ground on either side of the trees*
* ⭑ Men behind the temporary barricade
* ⭑ *A patch of shadow*
* ⭑ A cloud of dust
* ⭑ A handful of shadowy figures on horseback
* ⭑ *Black with horsemen*
* ⭑ A single armoured river
* ⭑ Motionless, menacing silhouettes in the gathering dusk
* ⭑ Small group of cavalrymen
* ⭑ Like a pack of shuffling beasts
* ⭑ A wide, glinting line of armoured soldiers
* ⭑ An ominously large force of men
* ⭑ Tens of thousands of men and beasts
* ⭑ *Rest of the men*
* ⭑ One of the cavalry

- ★ A line of archers
- ★ *Glinting armour in the distance*
- ★ Occasional glint of metal
- ★ Tell-tale glint of pike tips on the horizon
- ★ Metal armour and helmets
- ★ A bristling forest of staves
- ★ *A string of rocks*
- ★ A thorny barrier of sharpened saplings
- ★ A chest-high barrier
- ★ Shield to shield
- ★ A bristling wall of leaf-shaped blades
- ★ *Many horses*
- ★ Clouds of steam
- ★ Rumbling of hooves
- ★ Thunder of hooves
- ★ Neighing and terrified squealing of horses
- ★ *A distant blast of a horn*
- ★ A deep-throated war horn
- ★ A deep, mournful note
- ★ *Sounds of chain mail and weaponry*
- ★ Thunder of drums
- ★ Terrifying sound of thudding boots and hooves
- ★ *Steely clash of swords*
- ★ Clash of steel, clatter of metal on metal
- ★ A seething mass of flashing steel
- ★ *A ripple of twangs and hisses*
- ★ With a twang of bowstrings
- ★ Hiss of arrows
- ★ As the first wave of whistling arrows . . .
- ★ In a black menacing cloud
- ★ In a hail of deadly steel
- ★ *A cacophony of noise*
- ★ Shouts, groans, triumphant yells
- ★ Shrill screams
- ★ Moans of the wounded or dying

PHRASES – VERBS

- ★ Knew who they were
- ★ Had expected them long before they appeared
- ★ Had long since reached the city
- ★ *As he looked up*
- ★ Alerted him to the approach of . . .

* ★ Caught a glimpse of . . .
* ★ Could just make out one of the columns
* ★ Saw the horses first
* ★ Steadily revealed
* ★ Quickly followed by . . .
* ★ Caught sight of the king
* ★ *Rose on the horizon*
* ★ Approached from the east
* ★ Approached from behind
* ★ Marshalled south of the river
* ★ Marched slowly over the hills
* ★ Wound slowly down the ridge to . . .
* ★ Wound towards the city
* ★ Vaulted suddenly over the hill and into view
* ★ Rose up over the forest
* ★ *Flashed in the sunlight*
* ★ Glinted threateningly in the sunlight
* ★ *Became a shimmering black line*
* ★ Contracted like a huge python coiling inwards
* ★ Filled the spaces between the trees
* ★ Swelled as it came nearer and nearer
* ★ Disappeared briefly
* ★ *Stood in row after row*
* ★ Pike-men bearing pole-arms
* ★ Made up the column's vanguard
* ★ Marched behind
* ★ Stood in the centre
* ★ Surrounded by hundreds of mounted troops
* ★ Banners thudded and fluttered in the wind
* ★ Warned that pickets had been stationed
* ★ Watched, waited for their next move
* ★ *Had cleared the ground*
* ★ Hauled into place to create cover for the archers
* ★ Hammered into the ground
* ★ *Ordered to stay out of sight*
* ★ Fires had been banked
* ★ Could not reveal their position
* ★ Hid a large number of archers
* ★ Hidden from sight by a trench
* ★ *So that nothing would rattle and betray their position*
* ★ Dropped all their kit behind the wall
* ★ Muffled their boots with rags
* ★ Muffled the scabbards with cloth
* ★ Led away the horses

- Strapped their shields to their backs
- *Positioned either side of the road*
- Were ready to ambush any scouts
- *Banged rhythmically on shields*
- Gave the order to advance
- Sounded in the distance
- As a cry went up
- Shattered the silence
- Filled the air
- *Rose in his stirrups*
- Waved his sword high in the air
- Led his men into battle
- *Started to move forward*
- Moved towards them
- Walked at first and then . . .
- Trotted until they were in a headlong run
- As the charge gathered pace
- Sprang forwards into a gallop
- Lowered their armoured heads
- Swung their heads like mallets
- Heard the thundering of hooves
- Thundered out of the trees
- Thudded across the grass
- Shook the ground with its rumbling echo
- Galloped towards them
- Thundered towards them
- Came as one, from every side
- *Closed up in combat formation*
- *Everyone stood still*
- Frozen as they took in the message of the blast from the horn
- *Everyone started to move*
- Exploded in a maelstrom of noise
- Ran to their horses
- *Reached for their weapons*
- Slithered from their scabbards
- Strung their bows
- Planted a series of arrows into the turf in front of them
- *Formed a well-drilled line*
- Stood shoulder to shoulder
- Overlapped their shields
- *Jammed their pikes into the instep of their right foot*
- Thrust the pikes forwards
- Held firmly in line with a horse's chest or face
- *Challenged the enemy riders to rein in or to be impaled*

* Wrenched on his reins
* Stopped suddenly
* Brought his horse to a skidding halt
* Came within a few paces of their line
* Took aim with his crossbow
* Wheeled away
* Headed back down the slope
* *Could feel the horse's snorting breath on his face*
* Billowed from its flaring nostrils
* *Darted to the heavy logs*
* Began rolling them down the road
* Bounced and careered wildly down the hill
* *Erupted with archers*
* Arced up into the sky
* Filled with arrows
* Formed a black smudge in the sky above them
* Plunged towards them
* Plummeted like a thousand lethal thunderbolts
* *As the two sides engaged*
* As the men fought
* Hacked, slashed and cut in frantic fury
* *Pitched backwards*
* Slumped to his knees
* Crumbled beneath the murderous fire

SENTENCES

The whole ridge was black with horsemen – motionless, menacing silhouettes in the gathering dusk.

As news of the impending arrival had long since reached the city, he knew who they were, had expected them long before they appeared.

A handful of shadowy figures on horseback suddenly came over the hill and into view.

The rumbling of hooves alerted him to the approach of many horses. As he looked up, he caught a glimpse of the tell-tale glint of pike tips on the horizon.

A patch of shadow started to move, thudding across the grass, swelling as it came nearer and nearer, a single armoured river winding towards the city.

A cloud of dust rose on the horizon, which gradually became a shimmering black line approaching from the east.

He saw the horses first; the small group of cavalrymen that made up the column's vanguard.

An ominously large force of men marched over the hills slowly, like a pack of shuffling beasts, threatening and menacing.

They could just make out one of the columns moving towards them; it contracted like a huge python coiling inwards, filling the spaces between the trees, winding slowly down the ridge to disappear briefly into the shadows at the bottom of the slope.

The dawn steadily revealed glinting armour in the distance.

The occasional glint of metal warned that pickets had been stationed at regular intervals – watching, waiting for their next move.

Tens of thousands of men and beasts had marshalled south of the river, standing in row after row, their metal armour and helmets glinting threateningly in the sunlight.

Pike-men bearing pole-arms marched behind – a bristling forest of staves that flashed in the sunlight.

He caught sight of the king standing in the centre, surrounded by hundreds of mounted troops. All around him, banners thudded and fluttered in the wind. The king rose in his stirrups, waved his sword high in the air and led his men into battle.

A wide, glinting line of armoured soldiers stood tall in their stirrups; the sounds of chain mail and weaponry were only too distinctive.

The ground had been cleared and a string of rocks had been hauled into place to create a chest-high barrier capable of hiding a large number of archers.

In front of them, a thorny barrier of sharpened saplings had been hammered into the ground.

They had been ordered to stay out of sight; fires had been banked so that smoke could not reveal their position.

They dropped all their kit behind the wall, so that nothing would rattle and betray their position, muffled their boots with rags, then strapped their shields to their backs.

The horses had been led away, the scabbards muffled with cloth, and the rest of the men positioned either side of the road, ready to ambush any scouts.

Then he heard the thundering of hooves approaching from behind.

A distant blast of a horn rose up over the forest. For a moment, everyone stood still, frozen as they took in the message that the blast signalled.

A deep-throated war horn sounded in the distance, a deep, mournful note to chill the soul and send a wave of terror through them. The steely clash of swords banging rhythmically on shields quickly followed, and finally, the terrifying thudding of boots and hooves.

The drummers gave the order to advance and a cry went up. The thunder of hooves shattered the silence, filling the air as the charge gathered pace, shaking the ground with its rumbling echo.

The troops began moving forward, walking at first and then trotting until they were in a headlong run.

The horses lowered their armoured heads, which swung like mallets as they sprang forwards into a gallop.

They came thundering out of the trees. Suddenly, they closed up in combat formation, shield to shield.

One of the soldiers stopped suddenly and took aim with his crossbow.

The world exploded in a maelstrom of noise as suddenly everyone was moving, reaching for weapons, running to their horses.

Quickly, they formed a well-drilled line, standing shoulder to shoulder, shields overlapping. They jammed the end of their long pikes into the instep of their right foot – a bristling wall of leaf-shaped blades thrust forwards, held firmly in line with a horse's chest or face, challenging the enemy riders to rein in or to be impaled.

Behind the spear-men, a line of archers waited, their bows strung, arrows planted into the turf in front of them.

Darting to the heavy logs, they began rolling them down the road, towards the oncoming army, their embedded short spikes causing them to bounce and career down the hill.

One of the cavalry galloped towards them, then at the last moment, he wrenched on his reins, and brought his horse to a skidding halt within metres of their line. It was so close Tom could feel the horse's snorting breath on his face as clouds of steam billowed from its flaring nostrils.

The attackers came within a few paces of their line, just out of pike range, and then wheeled away, and headed back down the slope.

With a twang of bowstrings, the ground on either side of the trees seemed to erupt with archers who had been hidden from sight by a trench.

A ripple of twangs and hisses filled the air, forming a black smudge in the sky above them, as the first wave of whistling arrows thundered towards them, plummeting like a thousand lethal thunderbolts.

Arrows arced up into the sky in a black menacing cloud, and then plunged towards them in a hail of deadly steel.

The air filled with arrows and the men behind the temporary barricade collapsed beneath the murderous fire.

They came as one, from every side. Shrieks filled the air, while swords slithered from their scabbards.

All around him, men were locked in mortal combat.

As the two sides engaged, hacking, slashing and cutting in frantic fury, all around him became a seething mass of flashing steel.

From ahead of him, there was a cacophony of noise – the clash of steel, clatter of metal on metal; the hiss of arrows; neighing and terrified squealing of horses; the thunder of drums; shouts, groans, triumphant yells and shrill screams as the men fought.

A man to his left pitched backwards. Another in front of him slumped to his knees.

SECTION 2 – INTERACTION

WORDS

Nouns	**Army**, soldiers, troops, warriors, archers, pike-men, horsemen, cavalry
	Attacker, foe, opponent, assailant, adversary
	Defence, retreat, withdrawal, flight, escape
	Forest, trees, clearing, ridge, hill, rise, valley, ground
	Weapon, spear, lance, javelin, pike, quarterstaff, mace, spikes, axe, hammer, club, bludgeon, scythe, arrows, sling, stone, gravel
	Sword, broadsword, rapier, sabre, blade, hilt, guard, flat, shield
	Grasp, grip, hold, clasp
	Force, blow, whack, smack, stab, thrust, strike, swing, slash, jerk, impact, jolt
	Block, parry, riposte, reaction
	Movement, motion, manoeuvre
	Speed, pace, tempo
	Accuracy, precision
	Instinct, senses
	Moment, seconds, flash
	Body, shoulder, chest, legs, thigh, knees, feet, arm, hand, wrist
	Head, helmet, face, cheek, throat, jaw, mouth, teeth
	Pain, agony, suffering, torture
	Grimace, wince

Desperation, despair, distress

Shriek, clang, yell, cry, scream, moan, clang, clash, thud, thunder

Similes/Metaphors	**Swung it like a club**; fought like a demon; cut the air into a thousand slices
Adjectives	**Front**, back, side

Downward, upward, vertical, horizontal, sideways, back-handed

Whip-like, whipping, flicking, swishing

Sliding, gliding, snapping

Quick, swift, rapid

Light, deft, nimble, agile

Vast, huge, tremendous, enormous, massive, gigantic

Searing, scorching, blistering

Thrashing, thudding, charging, crushing wrist-numbing

Vicious, savage, fierce, ferocious, menacing, venomous

Deadly, lethal, fatal, mortal

Frantic, wild, desperate

Verbs **Appeared**, emerged

Marched, moved, advanced, swept, charged, surged, swarmed, attacked

Watched, spotted, fixed, glued, stared

Felt, touched

Warned, alerted

Started, recoiled, reeled, lurched, faltered

Braced, steadied, steeled

Moved, stepped, strode, sprang, danced

Darted, lunged, raced

Turned, spun, whirled

Ducked, dodged, dived, side-stepped, dropped, crouched, huddled

Jumped, hurdled, vaulted, somersaulted

Cleared, landed, alighted

Avoided, missed, evaded

Set, placed, positioned

Aimed, pointed, directed, levelled

Pushed, forced, heaved, shoved, shunted

Drew, unsheathed, slid, gripped, raised, tossed, flipped, flicked, twisted, wielded, swung, swiped, thrust, brandished, flourished

Lashed, whipped, swished, slashed, thrashed, jabbed, hammered

Seized, wrenched, yanked, knocked, struck, slammed, smashed

Anticipated, guessed, predicted, intercepted

Buried, planted, embedded

Cut, slit, pierced, nicked, grazed, lacerated, wounded, injured

Fitted, nocked, loaded, released

Picked, grabbed, flung, threw, sent, hurled

Blocked, countered, parried

Weakened, jarred, jolted, jerked, shook, vibrated

Crashed, stumbled, toppled, fell, slumped, plunged, pitched, plummeted

Clattered, clashed, clanged, thudded, thundered

PHRASES – NOUNS AND ADJECTIVES

- ✳ *Swords and spears*
- ✳ Vicious, red blade
- ✳ Long pike
- ✳ Blade of his spear
- ✳ Sound of sliding steel
- ✳ *To his right*
- ✳ Behind him
- ✳ Ahead of them
- ✳ *Across the ground away from . . .*
- ✳ Away from the thrashing hooves
- ✳ Beyond the range of the axe
- ✳ *In quick succession*
- ✳ In a flash
- ✳ For a fraction of a second
- ✳ Mere seconds before
- ✳ Just seconds before
- ✳ Almost at once
- ✳ In a matter of a few seconds

* At the same time
* At the very last moment
* *With such force*
* In a ferocious blow
* Equal to the move
* Each ferocious stab
* In a wrist-numbing clang
* With the weight of the blow
* With a tremendous thud
* In a massive sideways blow
* *In a vast arc*
* In a snapping parry
* Whip-like across his chest
* In a series of quick strikes
* With a deft flick of her wrist
* *In desperation*
* In a nimble move
* Quickly on his feet again
* In an impressive turn of speed
* With deadly accuracy
* *With a grimace*
* With a high-pitched shriek
* *A searing pain*

PHRASES – VERBS

* As they emerged in the clearing
* As they charged
* *Attacked again*
* Swarmed towards him
* Lunged directly at him
* *Watched as . . .*
* Spun round to see a gigantic warrior
* Turned to see one of the enemy soldiers had dismounted
* Spotted the shadow of an attacker to her left
* With his eyes fixed on the charging soldier
* Without taking her eyes from the horseman
* *Made Kitty start*
* Every instinct warned him that . . .
* Felt a rush of air by her shoulder
* *Moved first*
* Stepped forward
* Took a quick step forward

- ✦ Lunged forward
- ✦ Darted forward
- ✦ Sprang forwards
- ✦ Raced forward
- ✦ Tried to move forward
- ✦ *Whirled around*
- ✦ Turned at the last moment
- ✦ Danced to the side
- ✦ Darted from side to side
- ✦ Buzzed around like a wasp
- ✦ Launched himself off the ground
- ✦ Somersaulted over a line of shields
- ✦ *Dived to the side*
- ✦ Dodged at the last moment
- ✦ Leapt sideways
- ✦ Sprang aside
- ✦ Let her body sway out of reach
- ✦ Rolled sideways
- ✦ Rolled frantically over the ground
- ✦ Tumbled forward
- ✦ *Driven back*
- ✦ Staggered back
- ✦ Forced to retreat
- ✦ Jammed up against the wall
- ✦ *Dropped to his knees*
- ✦ Ducked beneath the blow
- ✦ Ducked under a sword blow
- ✦ Crouched behind his shield
- ✦ *Landed in front of his enemy*
- ✦ Emerged metres away
- ✦ Kept on moving towards the trees
- ✦ Cleared a way forward
- ✦ *Swung her shield from her shoulder*
- ✦ Gripped his shield and crouched
- ✦ Set his shoulder against his shield
- ✦ Pushed with all his might
- ✦ Lashed out with his shield
- ✦ Levelled her spear at the charging beast
- ✦ *Seized her ankle and yanked*
- ✦ Wrenched her foot away
- ✦ Slammed both feet into his face as hard as she could
- ✦ *Gripped the shaft of his spear*
- ✦ Swung the length of wood like a club
- ✦ Swiped furiously with his axe

- ⋆ Studded along the length of the club
- ⋆ Thrust with his spear
- ⋆ Swiped the air with her scythe
- ⋆ *Seized an arrow*
- ⋆ Fitted an arrow and let it fly
- ⋆ Let loose another arrow, and another
- ⋆ *Picked up a handful of gravel*
- ⋆ Picked up a stone from the ground
- ⋆ Flung it into his eyes
- ⋆ Released the stone
- ⋆ Swung the sling rapidly in circles around her head
- ⋆ *Drew his sword*
- ⋆ Wielded a huge sword
- ⋆ Raised his weapon high
- ⋆ Thrust his sword out in front of him
- ⋆ Swung his sword
- ⋆ Brandished her sword in his face
- ⋆ Slashed forward with his sword
- ⋆ Slashed and thrashed
- ⋆ Stabbed with his sword
- ⋆ Fought like a demon
- ⋆ Flipped his sword backwards
- ⋆ Let her blade slide until their guards met
- ⋆ Lunged upwards with her sword
- ⋆ Swept his blade down in a ferocious blow
- ⋆ Slashed his sword in a vicious arc
- ⋆ Flicked his blade lightly
- ⋆ Sword was a blinding blur
- ⋆ Cut the air into a thousand slices
- ⋆ *Clubbed any opponents close enough*
- ⋆ Clubbed a soldier with the hilt of his sword
- ⋆ Smashed another with the flat of his blade
- ⋆ Slashed and clubbed any enemy who came too close
- ⋆ *Slashed at his legs*
- ⋆ Slashed at his head
- ⋆ Delivered a series of crushing blows
- ⋆ Swept her sword sideways at the man's head
- ⋆ Jabbed the sword's point at Rob's throat
- ⋆ Smashed his jaw with her shield
- ⋆ Lashed out with a venomous back-handed stroke
- ⋆ Brought the enormous weapon crashing down
- ⋆ Smashed into his head
- ⋆ Took the brunt of the blow on his helmet
- ⋆ Hammered him in the chin

- ✶ Slammed the butt of her sword into the nearest helmet
- ✶ Buried her boot in his chest
- ✶ *Braced himself to parry the blow*
- ✶ Braced himself for the impact
- ✶ Each time the warrior swung
- ✶ Anticipated his attacker's move
- ✶ Instantly countered with light, flicking slashes
- ✶ Blocked the blade
- ✶ Parried the strike easily with his shield
- ✶ Parried another clumsy swing
- ✶ Parried half a dozen blows
- ✶ Sidestepped and parried the blow
- ✶ Blocked a low thrust
- ✶ Blocked a downward swing from his left
- ✶ *Forced the sword away*
- ✶ Shunted the blade to the side
- ✶ Pushed the weapon aside with ease
- ✶ *Flicked his wrist in a savage jerk*
- ✶ Twisted the hilt from his opponent's grasp
- ✶ Sent the weapon clattering across the ground
- ✶ Brought his sword across in a horizontal riposte
- ✶ *Narrowly avoided the spikes*
- ✶ Just where Rob's head had been
- ✶ Struck where his head had been
- ✶ Evaded the menacing mace
- ✶ Lunged and then darted out of reach
- ✶ Crashed down either side of his head
- ✶ Fought desperately to keep the sword from . . .
- ✶ Only just managed to right herself
- ✶ Might have cleaved Katie in half if she had not . . .
- ✶ Would skewer him before he got close enough
- ✶ *Jarred his arm painfully as he struck her sword*
- ✶ Jabbed into his shield
- ✶ Took the full force of the incoming blade
- ✶ Weakened his grip
- ✶ Let his guard down
- ✶ *Had his enemy stumbling back rapidly*
- ✶ Hurled him onto his back
- ✶ Sent him crashing to the ground
- ✶ Plunged deep into the warrior's thigh

They swarmed towards him, swords and spears slashing and thrashing as they charged.

The sound of sliding steel made Kitty start and she turned to see one of the enemy soldiers had dismounted and was drawing his sword.

Feeling a rush of air by her shoulder, Kitty turned to see a gigantic warrior wielding a huge sword, its red blade glinting menacingly.

An enemy darted forward from Tom's right, jabbing the point of his sword at Rob's throat.

Swinging the length of wood like a club, he screamed and lunged at Tom's head.

He delivered a series of crushing blows to Kitty's side.

With a grimace, he brought the enormous weapon crashing down in a ferocious blow that might have cleaved Katie in half if she had not dodged at the last moment.

With a high-pitched shriek, she swiped the air with her scythe just where Rob's head had been mere seconds before.

Kitty leapt sideways, narrowly avoiding the spikes studded along the length of the club.

He dived to the side to evade the menacing mace that slashed at his legs.

Rob watched as she lunged directly at him, and sprang aside at the very last moment.

Tom rolled frantically across the ground, away from the furious swipes of the axe that crashed down either side of his head.

Forced to retreat, jammed up against the wall, he crouched behind his shield. He fought desperately to keep the spear from slashing at his head, but each stab jarred his arm painfully, and was weakening his grip.

The spear jabbed into his shield with such force he staggered back.

He launched himself off the ground and was quickly on his feet again. Almost at once, a sword struck where his head had been just seconds before.

Kitty tumbled forward with the weight of the blow and only just managed to right herself as he attacked again.

He danced to the side in an impressive turn of speed.

With his eyes fixed on the charging soldier, he gripped his shield and crouched, his sword thrust out in front of him.

She darted from side to side, brandishing her sword in his face.

Like a wasp, he buzzed around, never letting his opponent get too close.

For a fraction of a second, his attacker had let his guard down and, in a flash, Andrew dropped to his knees and rolled sideways, to land in front of his enemy.

Tom ducked beneath the blow, rolled over the ground, and emerged metres away.

He ducked under a sword blow and kept on moving towards the trees.

Instinctively, she let her body sway beyond the range of the axe, just evading the weapon.

Every instinct warned him that the long pike would skewer him before he got close enough.

Tom braced himself to parry the blow.

Kitty sidestepped and parried the blow.

Deftly, Katie parried another clumsy swing.

Trish lunged and then darted out of reach.

Tom must have parried half a dozen blows in a matter of a few seconds.

Bracing himself for the impact, Tom's sword took the full force of the incoming blade.

With a grimace, Rob gritted his teeth, set his shoulder against his shield and pushed with all his might.

Swinging his sword, John parried the blow with his shield.

Each time the warrior swung, Tom easily parried and instantly countered with light, flicking slashes.

Rob had anticipated his attacker's move and easily blocked his low thrust.

The enemy moved first, lunging forward, but Tom was equal to the move, blocked the blade in a snapping parry and shunted it to the side.

Tom flicked his wrist in a savage jerk that twisted the hilt from his opponent's grasp and sent the weapon clattering across the ground.

Quickly, Rob brought his sword across in a horizontal riposte.

Whirling around, Rob raised his weapon high and blocked a downward swing from his left.

With a deft flick of her wrist, Katie pushed the weapon aside with ease.

Tom lashed out with a venomous back-handed stroke.

Springing forwards, he gripped the shaft of his spear and levelled it at the charging beast.

As they emerged in the clearing, she seized an arrow, fitted it and let it fly.

She let loose another arrow, and another, with deadly accuracy.

The soldier lunged towards her, seized her ankle and yanked. Wrenching her foot away, Katie leaned back and slammed both feet into his face as hard as she could.

Kitty buried her boot in his chest, and hurled him onto his back.

A searing pain jarred his arm as he struck her sword. In desperation, he flipped his sword backwards and hammered her in the chin with the hilt.

Kitty somersaulted over a line of shields and slammed the butt of her sword into the nearest helmet.

Tom smashed the soldier's jaw with his shield, and at the same time stabbed with his sword.

He clubbed any opponents close enough with the hilt until he had cleared a way forward.

Ann spotted the shadow of an attacker to her left, swung her shield from her shoulder and lunged upwards with her sword.

Darting forward, he slashed his sword in a vicious arc.

His sword was a blinding blur as Rob cut the air into a thousand slices.

Taking a quick step forward, John thrust with his spear.

Kitty swept her sword sideways at the man's head, but he turned at the last moment, so that his helmet took the brunt of the blow.

Lashing out with his shield, Rob tried to move forward and away from the thrashing hooves.

Katie lunged forward, swinging the long sword in a vast arc.

He struck at the soldier in a series of quick strikes that had his enemy stepping back, parrying furiously.

Stepping forward, he swung his blade in a massive sideways blow.

Rob clubbed one soldier with the hilt of his sword and smashed another with the flat of his blade.

Flicking his blade lightly, whip-like across his chest, he slashed the warrior across the cheek.

The blade of his spear plunged deep into the warrior's thigh.

He fought like a demon, slashing and clubbing any enemy who came too close.

Without taking her eyes from the horseman, she picked up a stone from the ground. She swung the sling rapidly in circles around her head, and then with a deft flick of her wrist, released it. She watched, holding her breath, until, with a tremendous thud, it smashed into his head and sent him crashing to the ground.

She picked up a handful of gravel, flung it into his eyes and smashed his jaw with her shield.

18

Reaction to fighting

Nouns

Soldiers, invaders, attackers, assailants, archers

Trebuchets, catapult, siege engines, battering ram, ladders, tower, walls

Crossbows, arrows, missiles, rocks, boulders, stones, tar, oil, pitch

Weapons, spear, sword, dagger

Blast, explosion, fire, flames, smoke

Thud, crash, boom, groan, creak

Images, scene, sights, events, details

Terrors, horrors, devastation, destruction, chaos

Escape, retreat

Anger, rage, fury

Hope, optimism, bravery, courage, determination, tenacity

Disbelief, horror, fear, dread, doom, foreboding, panic

Adrenalin, nerves, senses, muscles

Sweat, perspiration

Look, glance, stare, gaze

Mind, thoughts

Head, face, brow, forehead, nose, cheeks, eyes, mouth, jaw, lips, teeth, throat

Heart, pulse, veins, chest, ribs, stomach

Body, shoulder, hands, fists

Sound, noise, word, prayer

Breath, gasp, grimace, hiss, growl, cry, yell, shout, snarl, scream, shriek, screech, howl

Similes/ Metaphors	**Like a hard lump at the back of her throat**; fog of rage; anger like the embers of a fire; hit her like a flash flood; as if her brain was flooding with boiling blood; exploded like a volcano; like a tidal wave; flared like an angry bull; tidal wave of fear; like ice-cold water; icy claws of fear; like chips of ice; like he was preparing for a blow; as if a great iron fist had slammed into him; eyes like blazing beacons; burned like furnaces; fell over her face like a veil

Adjectives

Hundreds, thousands

Angry, furious, enraged

Frightened, terrified, panicked

Red, fiery, simmering, burning, blazing, menacing

Tingling, prickling

Cold, icy, chilly, frozen, bitter

White, pale, deathly, unhealthy

Small, thin, weak

Sudden, unforeseen, impending, imminent

Desperate, despairing, hopeless

Sheer, utter

Silent, low, muffled

Gleaming, glinting, flashing

Breathless, sweating, perspiring

Verbs

Emerged, rose, rolled, neared, loomed, roared

Rained, hailed, pelted, bombarded, battered

Cracked, broke, collapsed, breached

Urged, impelled, alerted, warned

Stunned, shocked, reeled, jolted, rocked, jerked

Prayed, hoped

Prepared, braced, steeled

Fuelled, flashed, burned, shot, exploded, erupted, poured, swept, surged, flooded, engulfed, overwhelmed

Raced, hammered, pounded

Shook, trembled, shuddered, writhed

Bubbled, sprouted, sent, collected, dripped, trickled

Fell open, clenched, tightened

Blew, sucked, choked back, escaped, blew out, breathed, gasped

Saw, glimpsed, spotted, witnessed

Looked, stared, squinted, kept, fixed, gazed

Glanced, flickered, exchanged

Glared, narrowed, darkened, glinted, burned, blazed

Turned, twisted, spun, whirled

Gripped, clutched, waved, brandished, hurled

Spoke, said, hissed, cried, shouted, yelled, barked, growled, roared, ranted, boomed, screamed, howled, shrieked, snarled, bellowed, stormed, thundered

PHRASES – NOUNS AND ADJECTIVES

- Sight of thousands of mounted soldiers
- More and more ladders
- Hail of arrows
- Column of flames
- Series of images
- *Thud and crash*
- With a resounding thud
- Screech in the distance
- *Fog of rage*
- Red mist
- Simmering fury
- A burst of fury
- Anger like the embers of a fire
- Hard lump at the back of her throat
- *Surge of adrenalin*
- Every nerve in his body
- A tingling sixth sense
- *Cold foreboding*
- Icy claws of fear
- A fog of sheer panic
- Sense of impending doom
- A thousand terrors
- *A sudden chink of hope*
- A desperate hope that . . .
- *A silent scream*
- A low moan of despair

* Eyes like blazing beacons
* Eyes wide with disbelief
* *Deathly pale*
* Look of sheer terror on her face
* Gleaming bubbles of perspiration

PHRASES – VERBS

* *As the battering ram rolled closer and closer*
* Loomed in front of the city
* Rained down from the sky
* Eventually breached the walls
* Caught a glimpse of two figures
* *Made him look up*
* As he turned his head
* When he caught sight of . . .
* *Rose up on the walls*
* Rose in front of her
* Roared up the wall
* Emerged from the base of the tower
* *As she fitted an arrow to her bow . . .*
* Looked at the scene of devastation
* Every detail burned into her mind
* *Hammered in his head*
* Trembled with rage
* Writhed with anger
* Fuelled his anger
* Swept through him like a tidal wave
* Wrath exploded like a volcano
* As if her brain was flooding with boiling blood
* Shot through him
* Surged through his veins
* Erupted inside his head
* *Made his heart race*
* Made his heart pound in his chest
* Hammered against his ribs
* Gripped his chest
* Bubbled beneath the surface
* Felt his stomach clench
* Like he was preparing for a blow
* As if a great iron fist had slammed into him
* *With rising dread*
* Stunned disbelief

* Reeled in horror at what she had witnessed
* Prayed that if he kept his eyes closed . . .
* Could almost feel the crossbows aimed at his head
* Shuddered at having his worst fears confirmed
* Overwhelmed by a tidal wave of fear
* Fear of what would happen when . . .
* Panic engulfed Kitty like ice-cold water
* Hit her like a flash flood
* Flashed through his mind
* *Steeled himself*
* Was on high alert
* Was conscious of every creak, thud and explosion
* Urged him to move
* As much as he could do not to . . .
* *Sweating and burning with rage*
* Sprouted on his brow
* Sent a shiver down his spine
* Dripped down his spine like chips of ice
* Collected on his forehead
* Trickled down the side of his nose into his eyes
* *Twisted with rage*
* Pressed his lips tightly together
* Nostrils flared like an angry bull
* Veins pulsed furiously in her neck
* *Fell over her face like a veil*
* Engraved with horror
* *Burned in his eyes*
* Blazed like beacons
* Eyes ablaze, fists clenched
* Burned like furnaces
* Glittered menacingly
* *Flitted quickly upwards*
* Glanced up quickly
* Kept her narrowed eyes fixed to . . .
* Stared at the scene before her
* Watched their every move
* Moved constantly
* Took in everything, every detail
* Blinked rapidly
* Darted to and fro
* Risked a quick glance over his shoulder
* Looked desperately round for a means of retreat
* *Afraid to look*
* Did not look at him

- Stared off to the left
- Squeezed her eyes shut
- *Snapped open in panic*
- Swept over the scene of devastation in front of him
- Jerked at every noise
- *Caught his eye*
- Flickered briefly to Robert's face
- Exchanged a terrified look
- Exchanged panicked glances
- Looked at one another
- *None of them spoke*
- No words came out
- No one said a word
- Moved her lips silently in prayer
- Before he could make a sound . . .
- Opened his mouth to scream a warning
- Gave a small cry of terror
- *Mouth fell open*
- Jaw tightened
- Clenched his jaw
- Left him breathless
- Sucked in his breath
- Choked his breath
- Choked back a gasp
- Escaped her lips
- Blew out her cheeks
- Sucked air through his teeth
- Sucked in a breath as shivers racked her body
- Hissed through her clenched teeth
- Snaked around his windpipe
- Wrenched its way out of her chest
- *Gripped his iron-tipped spear*
- Waved her spear wildly in the air
- Shrieked and hurled the spear at the . . .
- Clutched the rail until his knuckles went white

SENTENCES

She looked at the scene of devastation through narrowed eyes and a fog of rage.

The anger was like a hard lump at the back of her throat.

He was sweating and burning with rage.

Eyes ablaze, fists clenched, he gripped his iron-tipped spear.

She waved her spear wildly in the air, shrieked and hurled it at the catapult.

A burst of fury surged through his veins and he clutched the rail until his knuckles went white.

As the next boulder slammed into the wall beneath him, his jaw tightened; his breath hissed through his clenched teeth. He watched with horror as another group of archers were sent plummeting to the ground in a pile of dust and masonry.

Eyes narrowed and teeth clenched, she stared at the scene before with an expression of utter disbelief and horror.

Like blazing beacons, Kitty's eyes glittered menacingly as she fitted an arrow to her bow.

He prayed that if he kept his eyes closed, they would go away.

The sight of thousands of mounted soldiers charging towards him made his heart pound in his chest.

The siege engine sent a shiver down his spine. It was enormous, menacing, as if it were a predator looming in front of the city, searching for its next prey.

As a surge of adrenalin shot through him, every nerve in his body was on high alert.

He could almost feel the crossbows aimed at his head.

A tingling sixth sense made him look up. As he turned his head, he froze.

Cold foreboding dripped down his spine like chips of ice.

Her heart hammered against her ribs as the battering ram rolled closer and closer.

His heart thudded in his chest as the hooves thundered nearer and nearer.

Icy claws of fear gripped his chest.

Gleaming bubbles of perspiration sprouted on his brow.

Panic gripped him, snaking around his windpipe and choking his breath.

Katie was overwhelmed by a tidal wave of fear; fear of what would happen when they eventually breached the walls.

As a hail of arrows rained down from the sky, a silent scream erupted inside his head, urging him to move.

None of them spoke, and she was conscious of every creak, every screech in the distance, every thud and crash.

It was as much as he could do not to run and hide. The panic was bubbling beneath the surface.

As the battering ram hammered once more against the gates, it was as if a great iron fist had slammed into his chest. He knew that it would not be long before the invaders broke through.

Rob shuddered at having his worst fears confirmed.

Such horror rose in front of her that panic engulfed Kitty like ice-cold water.

A series of images flashed through his mind.

Stunned disbelief fell over her face like a veil.

The horror of what she was witnessing hit her like a flash flood – every detail burned into her mind

She was white, deathly pale. Her face engraved with horror.

There was a look of sheer terror on her face. She sucked in a breath as shivers racked her body.

Their eyes flitted quickly upwards.

A movement caught his eyes, and he glanced up quickly.

His eyes moved constantly, taking in everything, every detail.

Early that morning, she had caught a brief glimpse of two figures emerging from the base of the tower. For some time, she had kept her narrowed eyes fixed on the doors, probing for any movement, any sign that they had returned.

Sweat had collected on his forehead and was trickling down the side of his nose into his eyes. He squeezed them shut and blinked rapidly.

As the enemy swarmed towards them, Rob looked round frantically for a means of retreat.

She squeezed her eyes shut, afraid to look.

Her eyes darted to and fro, sweeping over the scene in front of her. A low moan of despair escaped her lips as she saw the trebuchets moving forwards.

His eyes swept over the scene of devastation in front of him.

Kitty's eyes flickered briefly to Robert's face and they exchanged a terrified look.

They looked at one another, exchanging panicked glances, but no one said a word – no one moved.

She wasn't looking at him, she was staring off to the left, her eyes wide with disbelief.

His mouth fell open but no words came out.

Clasping her hands in her lap, Kitty moved her lips silently in prayer.

Rob opened his mouth to scream a warning, but before he could make a sound a warrior lunged towards him, swiping the air with an enormous axe.

He spun round and gave a small cry of terror at the sight of more and more ladders rising up on the walls.

19

Reaction to wounds, injury and pain

WORDS	
Nouns	**Movement**, motion, action
	Pain, throb, ache, stab, spasm, blow
	Agony, anguish, trauma, torture
	Veil, shroud, cloak, blanket
	Thoughts, vision, consciousness
	Width, breadth, length
	Wounds, injury, cut, gash, graze, scratch, bruise, tear, laceration, gouge
	Head, neck, forehead, cheek, jaw, mouth, lips, teeth, tongue, nose, nostrils, ears, eyes, sockets
	Body, back, chest, side, stomach, shoulder, leg, thigh, knee, foot, ankle, arms, wrist, fists
	Skin, flesh, bones, nerves, muscles, tendons, blood, pus
	Whimper, groan, moan, wail, yell, sob, cry, scream
Similes/ Metaphors	**Like a clenched fist**; with a claw-like grip; like hot wire had been pressed into a nerve; as if it had been sliced all over with needles; like thousands of fiery needles
Adjectives	**Numerous**, many, countless, scores
	Breathless, sick, nauseous, queasy, bilious
	Huge, large, massive

Jagged, uneven, barbed

Ugly, hideous, gruesome, repulsive, grotesque, ghastly

Septic, putrid, festering, weeping, oozing, putrefying

Black, white, green, creamy

Red, scarlet, crimson, brown

Warm, hot

Metallic, coppery

Thick, sticky, viscous, syrupy

Sudden, unexpected

Sharp, painful, savage, acute, stabbing, intense, violent, raging, agonising, searing, blistering, throbbing, blinding, piercing, shooting, excruciating, unbearable, crushing, ferocious

Small, thin, weak, muffled

Loud, ragged, shrill, high-pitched

Verbs **Wounded**, hurt, injured, bruised, winded, bleeding

Shot, surged, tore, jerked, raced, pumped, swept, coursed

Throbbed, burned, sliced, stabbed, pierced

Seeped, bubbled, drizzled, dripped, poured, flowed, streamed, spattered

Put, covered, wrapped, clenched, clutched, gripped, flailed

Flared, spread, broadened

Creased, wrinkled, furrowed

Gulped, gasped, choked, let out, cried, uttered, emitted

Shut, squeezed, scrunched, screwed, rolled

Dropped open, lolled

Heard, rang, echoed

Drained, exhausted, sapped

Spun, swum, turned, whirled

Doubled over, writhed, rocked, rolled

Staggered, stumbled, lurched

Buckled, gave way, crumpled, sprawled, slumped

Collapsed, swooned, blacked out, passed out

Fell, hit, struck, slammed, crashed

PHRASES – NOUNS AND ADJECTIVES

* Every second
* Every movement
* *Crushing blow*
* Ferocity of the blow
* *Deathly pale*
* Pallor of a corpse
* *Numerous cuts on his head*
* An ugly looking wound on his head
* A massive, jagged wound
* Mangled flesh
* Festering, green wound
* Creamy pus
* Mass of seared skin
* *A trickle of warm blood*
* Red streaks
* Thick, sticky droplets of blood
* Dried patch of congealing blood
* A gruesome mask of blood
* *A bolt of pain*
* Searing pain
* Blistering pain
* An agony of daggers
* Blinding pain
* Like thousands of fiery needles
* A piercing pain
* Excruciating agony
* *In his shoulders*
* Through his knee
* In his chest
* Pain in his leg
* Left shoulder
* Right side
* At the back of his neck
* The width of his jaw
* At his temple

PHRASES – VERBS

* When he breathed
* As the next wave of pain surged through him
* As a wave of searing agony shot up her arm

* As the pain tore through his stomach
* *Put her hands to her head*
* Wrapped her arms around her . . .
* Clenched his fists
* Clutched the wound
* *Filled with the taste of metallic blood*
* Bleeding profusely
* Winded, bruised, and bleeding
* Could taste blood on her tongue
* Felt the warmth of blood
* *Spattered her face*
* Drizzled down her back
* Seeped from the wounds
* Poured from a gash in his leg
* Flowed in pulsing waves
* Streamed from his arm
* Dripped down from his forehead and into his mouth
* Bubbled at the corner of his mouth
* *Felt a sudden, sharp pain*
* With every movement she made
* Gripped him
* Throbbed unbearably
* Tore deep into her wrist
* Sent a shockwave of pain
* Shot up her leg
* Jerked with a claw-like grip
* Left him feeling breathless and sick
* Spread across his chest
* Burnt with an excruciating pain
* Gripped his head like a clenched fist
* Coursed up and down his legs
* Felt as if it had been sliced all over with needles
* Set fire to every nerve in his body
* Stabbed into her skin
* Like hot wire being pressed into a nerve
* Shot through his shoulder
* Throbbed savagely
* *Nostrils flared with the wave of agony that shot up her . . .*
* Creased the bridge of his nose
* *Gritted her teeth*
* Tried to speak
* As he opened his jaw
* Let out a small whimper
* Cried out in pain

- Made him scream in pain
- Let out a loud, ragged wail
- Uttered a high-pitched scream
- *Breath became laboured*
- Gulped frantically for air
- Choked as he tried to breathe
- Words came in painful gasps
- *All thought drained out of him*
- All he could hear was . . .
- Ringing in his ears
- The world was starting to spin
- Started to black out
- *Jerked to a halt*
- Could barely stumble to his feet
- Slumped in the corner
- As her head hit the ground
- Left him bent double
- Writhed in agony
- Got to his feet
- Rocked backwards and forwards
- *Buckled under her*
- Legs gave way
- Forced him to sink to one knee
- Dropped to the ground
- *Made him crumple in a heap*
- Went sprawling onto her side
- Crashed to the floor
- Staggered, lurched and crumpled to the floor
- *Uttered a final gasp*
- Mouth dropped open
- Tongue lolled out
- *Scrunched his eyes tight*
- Blinded by smoke
- Rolled back in his head
- Rolled in their sockets until only the whites were showing
- *Fell over her vision*
- Lost consciousness
- Everything went black

SENTENCES

The ferocity of the blow forced Rob to sink to one knee.

Katie's mouth filled with the taste of metallic blood.

He was bleeding profusely from numerous cuts on his head.

Winded, bruised, and bleeding from numerous cuts, he could barely stumble to his feet.

Kitty could taste blood on her tongue.

He had an ugly looking wound on his head.

Blood poured from a gash in his leg.

A trickle of warm blood dripped down from his forehead and into his mouth.

A trickle of blood bubbled at the corner of his mouth.

He dropped to the ground, feeling the warmth of blood at his temple.

His face was now a gruesome mask of blood.

He felt a sudden, sharp pain in his shoulders.

With every movement she made, Katie's hip throbbed unbearably.

Every second the pain was getting worse.

Every movement sent a shockwave of pain through his knee.

The pain in his leg jerked with a claw-like grip and left him feeling breathless and sick.

White pain spread across his chest.

His left shoulder burnt with an excruciating pain.

The pain gripped his head like a clenched fist.

The pain coursed up and down his legs.

Breathing was an agony of daggers in his chest.

Kitty's left side was in excruciating pain.

His head felt as if it had been sliced all over with needles.

The wound at the back of his neck throbbed and the blinding pain set fire to every nerve in his body.

It felt like thousands of fiery needles were stabbing into her skin.

Rob twisted in agony, as a piercing pain like hot wire being pressed into a nerve shot through his shoulder.

Wincing, Kitty put her hands to her head.

He tried to speak, but pain gripped him as he opened his jaw.

As the next wave of pain surged through him, Tom gasped.

With her arms wrapped around her, she slumped in the corner, and let out a small whimper.

Frantically gulping for air, her words came in painful gasps.

Writhing in agony, he clutched the wound in his stomach and groaned.

As a wave of searing agony shot up her arm, she uttered a high-pitched scream.

The crushing blow tore deep into Kitty's wrist, making her scream in pain.

Scrunching his eyes tight and clenching his fists, he rocked backwards and forwards.

The wound had been torn open again and was throbbing savagely. Nostrils flared and deep lines creasing the bridge of his nose, he gritted his teeth and got to his feet.

All thought drained out of him, as the pain tore through his stomach and left him bent double and writhing in agony.

He was blinded by smoke, choking as he tried to breathe.

Her breath became laboured and her throat choked.

The blistering pain made him crumple in a heap.

The world was starting to spin.

A stinging wave of fire made his head throb and turned his vision to a dazzling blanket of white.

All he could hear was the ringing in his ears as he started to black out.

Her mouth dropped open and her tongue lolled out. With one final gasp, her legs buckled under her and she crashed to the floor.

A black shroud fell over her vision and she lost consciousness.

Kitty's legs gave way; she went sprawling onto her side and as her head hit the ground, her eyes rolled in their sockets until only the whites were showing.

He staggered, lurched and crumpled to the floor. As he hit the ground with a resounding thud his eyes rolled back in his head, and everything went black.

Appendix

Planning a fantasy

1. The hero is in his ordinary world

The hero is in his own world that is considered to be ordinary and uneventful. The hero may possess some ability or characteristic that makes him feel that he doesn't entirely belong to that world – his abilities set him apart from his family, friends and neighbours.

★ Why is the hero different?

2. The hero is called away from his home by some sort of herald

The challenge or adventure is revealed to the hero. Quests don't happen in everyday life. Heroes may have to leave their ordinary world to travel to the fantasy world where they will embark on their quest, and they may switch between worlds as the story develops. But whatever the setting, the hero will have to leave their ordinary life and home, family and friends. He crosses from security to danger.

He may at first be reluctant to accept the quest, but agrees eventually, perhaps as a result of the discovery of a mystical object, a magical power on attaining a certain age, a prophecy or that his world is in danger.

He finds out about the new setting where the story is to take place.

★ Describe the event that gets the hero involved in the adventure.

3. Hero travels to the location

Describe the journey. If he is passing into another fantasy world, how does he get there?

★ Does he meet someone who may go on the journey, give advice or give him something to complete the quest – for example, an object with magical powers, a piece of valuable wisdom as to how to defeat the villain?

★ Does he find useful clues?

4. The adventure begins

The hero gets to the new setting, where the main adventure will take place. The new setting is either in a faraway land or very different to the original setting – for example, an underground kingdom, a secret forest, ruined city, castle or desert island. The setting could be full of dangers and threats, including knights, warriors, wizards, witches, sorcerers, talking animals or fantasy races, such as dwarfs, gnomes, goblins, giants or trolls.

As the hero has never been there before, you need to think about:

★ What does he see, hear, smell?
★ Are there any dangers/obstacles?
★ How does the new setting make him feel?

The hero will:

★ learn something about the villain that reveals the extent of the danger he faces.

5. A problem occurs in the setting/the hero meets the villain's allies

Dream up scenes and events where the hero is tested:

★ Storms
★ Losing his talisman
★ Caught up in a siege

The hero's experiences:

★ test his strength, bravery and determination.

The hero:

- ★ does not come face-to-face with the villain yet.
- ★ learns more about the villain or the location of the object(s), person.

Don't just tell the reader what is happening. Describe the hero's feelings (reaction) and his interaction (movements/actions) with the setting and/or the enemy.

6. Hero is in great danger (the 'black moment')

The hero has successfully survived a series of tests and obstacles and has arrived at the final, supreme challenge that he has journeyed to overcome. He comes face-to-face with the villain.

Imagine how and where the hero and villain meet.

- ★ Either the villain finds the hero, or, the hero has found the enemy's location.
- ★ Describe the route the hero takes through the setting.
- ★ Include lots of action.
- ★ Describe the hero's fear/nervousness.
- ★ Build the suspense and atmosphere before they meet by including sounds and shadows.
- ★ Ask the reader questions so that they are drawn into the story.

7. Climax – final struggle/the problem is solved

- ★ Devise a plan or find something that will help the hero to face the ultimate danger.
- ★ Where do they meet? Describe any barriers to entering the setting, any advantages that the setting provides for the villain.
- ★ How does the hero defeat the villain?
- ★ Does the hero have any help, for example, the special object, a protective figure?
- ★ How is he feeling?
- ★ Is he injured?
- ★ What happens to the villain?

8. Resolution – the journey home

★ The hero returns home victorious. What was the result of his completing the task?

★ How has the experience changed the hero?

Plot planning sheet

Where does the hero live? What ability or characteristic sets him apart from the rest of the people where he lives?	
What happens to get the hero involved in the adventure? Does he discover a hidden talent, magical power, message, prophecy? Does he discover a mystical object or that his world is in danger?	
What does the challenge involve?	
Describe the journey and route.	

Describe the fantasy world. Is there one or many different kingdoms? *Draw a map.* What fantasy creatures inhabit the fantasy world? Will they be allies or foes? Does the hero learn anything about the villain? Does he meet the villain's allies?	
How does the hero meet the villain? Where? What happens?	
CLIMAX The hero defeats the villain. How? Does he have help? How does his special object/ power help him? *What happens to the villain?*	

RESOLUTION

The hero returns home.

What is his reward?

How has he changed?

Additional notes

Hero planning sheet

Name Age	
Physical description Height/shape, face, eyes, mouth, ears, voice, clothes, armour, weapons Distinctive features	
What is the hero most afraid of? What is his weakness?	
Does the hero have any secrets, skills or unusual traits? Does he have a special object that enhances his powers and skills?	
What are the hero's main interests?	

Who are the members of his family? Are they his *real* family? What do they do? Do any of them have a secret? Are they keeping a secret from the hero?	
Who are his close friends? Will any of them help/hinder the hero? Does he have an older protective figure? Do they have any special skills or secrets?	
What has the hero got to gain by achieving the task, overcoming the challenge? What has the hero got to lose if he fails? How does the hero change? What is his reward?	
Additional notes	

Villain planning sheet

Name Age	
Physical description Eyes, voice, clothing, movement Distinctive features, e.g. scars	
Occupation Does he have any special skills, talents, objects, creatures?	
Who are his allies?	
What does he want and why?	

Where does he live? *Describe the location.* Is it scary, isolated, protected by hideous creatures? Are there many barriers, problems to getting into the location?	
Why is the hero a threat to him?	
What does he do to people who cross him?	
Additional information	

Creature planning sheet

Name Type Habitat	
Parts, size, shape Body Size Shape Colour Covering	
Head Eyes	
Arms and legs	

Wings and tails	
Smell Sound	
Movement	
Weapons/attack	
Defeat/destruction	
Additional information	

Fantasy character planning sheet

Name Type (elf, dwarf, faerie, goblin, giant, troll, sprite, gnome, etc.)	
Physical description Height/shape	
Head, face	
Eyes	
Mouth, teeth, ears	
Hair, facial hair	

Hands and fingers	
Voice	
Clothes, armour, weapons	
Does the fantasy character have any skills or unusual traits? Does he have a special object that enhances his powers and skills?	
Will he help or hinder the hero? How?	

Object planning sheet

Object	
Description	
How did the object come to be in the hero's possession?	
How does the hero discover what the object can do?	
For what purpose could the object be used? *(Guidance, protection, escape, weapon?)*	
How and when does the hero use the object?	
Additional information	

The setting

SETTING/CHARACTER	INTERACTION	REACTION

Magic

SETTING/CHARACTER	INTERACTION/OUTCOME	REACTION

Attacking/defending a castle or city

SETTING/CHARACTER	INTERACTION	REACTION

Battle

SETTING/CHARACTER	INTERACTION	REACTION

Printed in Great Britain
by Amazon

57187362R00169